JOURNAL FOR THE STUDY OF THE OLD TESTAMENT SUPPLEMENT SERIES

85

Editors
David J A Clines
Philip R Davies

BIBLE AND LITERATURE SERIES

19

General Editor
David M. Gunn

Assistant General Editor
Danna Nolan Fewell

Consultant Editors
Elizabeth Struthers Malbon
James G. Williams

Almond Press
Sheffield

19.61

FROM CARMEL TO HOREB

Elijah in Crisis

Alan J. Hauser
& Russell Gregory

Edited by Alan J. Hauser

The Almond  Press · 1990

Bible and Literature Series, 19

General Editor: David M. Gunn
(Columbia Theological Seminary, Decatur, Georgia)
Assistant General Editor: Danna Nolan Fewell
(Perkins School of Theology, Dallas, Texas)
Consultant Editors: Elizabeth Struthers Malbon
(Virginia Polytechnic Institute & State University, Blacksburg, Virginia)
James G. Williams
(Syracuse University, Syracuse, New York)

Published by Almond Press

Editorial direction: David M. Gunn
Columbia Theological Seminary
P.O. Box 520, Decatur
GA 30031, U.S.A.

Almond Press is an imprint of
Sheffield Academic Press Ltd
The University of Sheffield
343 Fulwood Road
Sheffield S10 3BP
England

Typeset by Sheffield Academic Press and
Printed in Great Britain
by Billing & Sons Ltd
Worcester

British Library Cataloguing in Publication Data

Hauser, Alan J.
  From Carmel to Horeb.
  1. Bible. O.T. Kings, 1st —Critical Studies
  I. Title   II. Gregory, Russell   III. Series
  222.5306

  ISSN 0260-4493
  ISSN 0309-0787
  ISBN 1-85075-128-5

#21081139

CONTENTS

PREFACE

Any attempt to interpret good literature involves the reader in a dialogue with the text that will result in a unique event. While a close examination of the text, indeed, a living with the text, will set basic bounds within which this event takes place, the text itself can never define and focus all the potential that is called forth in the dialogue between reader and text. One might say that good literature will give birth to a variety of experiences, to a creative spectrum of nuances, aspects of which lay beyond the writer's consciousness when the text was written. Such plurality ought not to be feared or questioned, but rather embraced.

Interpretation is a delicate process which must hover between a subjectivism which leaves the text behind and uses it only as a point of departure for journeys into worlds alien to the text, and an objectification which attempts to embrace in one study all that the text is or can be expected to be. If one grants the need to pursue an interpretive focus carefully poised between these two extremes, it becomes apparent that one can expect to find different interpretations of the same text, each of which can stand as a legitimate experience of what the text "means". Each interpretation can call the others into question in productive, edifying ways without undermining their legitimacy. Plurality is thus a sign of enrichment rather than of error.

The narrative unit in 1 Kings 17–19 presents the reader with a rich texture of images, themes, and characterizations. To suggest that any one interpretation could exhaust the richness of this texture would be to confine the text in a way which would obscure its wealth and stifle the reader's ability to engage in dialogue with the text. Thus, the two studies in this volume are not advanced as competing interpretations, nor are they presented as a two-pronged analysis which exhausts the text's meaning. Rather, they are offered as complimentary and hopefully stimulating interpretations that will evoke in the reader a desire to explore even further the richness of 1 Kings 17–19.

Alan J. Hauser

Russell Gregory

ABBREVIATIONS

Bib	*Biblica*
BJRL	*Bulletin of the John Rylands Library*
BZAW	Beihefte zur Zeitschrift für die Alttestamentliche Wissenschaft
CBQ	*Catholic Biblical Quarterly*
ET	*Expository Times*
HUCA	*Hebrew Union College Annual*
Int	*Interpretation*
JBL	*Journal of Biblical Literature*
JNES	*Journal of Near Eastern Studies*
JSOT	*Journal for the Study of the Old Testament*
Jud	*Judaism*
LB	*Linguistica Biblica*
Sem	*Semitics*
SR	*Sewannee Review*
VT	*Vetus Testamentum*
ZAW	*Zeitschrift für die Alttestamentliche Wissenschaft*

YAHWEH VERSUS DEATH—
THE REAL STRUGGLE IN 1 KINGS 17-19

Alan J. Hauser

That the stories in 1 Kings 17-19 are anti-Baalistic is self-evident. This may be seen in the dramatic confrontation of Elijah with the prophets of Baal during the famous contest on Mt. Carmel (1 Kgs 18.17-40), in the numerous references to Jezebel's Baalism and her persecution of the prophets of Yahweh (1 Kgs 16.31-33; 18.4, 13; 19.2), in Elijah's statements about Israel's tendency to worship the Baals (1 Kgs 18.18-19, 21-22, 37; 19.10, 14), and even in the sub-plot concerning Obadiah (1 Kgs 18.3-4, 12-14). However, a key element in this three chapter unit,[1] the motif of Yahweh's struggle with death, has not been discussed in detail. This study will examine that motif as a major component in the structure of 1 Kings 17-19.

It is not surprising that the motif of Yahweh's struggle with death would play so important a role in 1 Kings 17-19. The cycle of Baal's periodic submission to Mot (death) and the consequent presence of drought and sterility throughout the land, which was followed by Anat's defeat of Mot, the resuscitation of Baal, and the return of fertility to the land,[2] was a crucial element in Canaanite religion. The Canaanites' equating of fertility with the presence of a live and vibrant Baal, who as the storm god sent the life-preserving rains onto the land, and their equating of drought and famine with the periodic death of Baal, set the stage for the stories in 1 Kings 17-19. However, in these chapters Baal is not portrayed as a god who periodically must submit to death, only to rise again and restore life to the earth. Rather, Baal is shown to have no power at all in the realm that is supposed to be his, the sending of the annual rains. He is, in fact, quite dead (1 Kgs 18.26-29). Drought is pictured as coming at the will of Yahweh, not as a result of his or Baal's submission to death. If, according to Canaanite mythology, Baal has to struggle periodically with death and lose, in 1 Kings 17-19 Yahweh confronts death, and wins. Yahweh is thus portrayed as the God of life who has ultimate control over death.

The writer asserts this point repeatedly throughout chapters 17-19. However, in order to make this three chapter unit an effective and convincing piece of drama, the writer allows death to pose numerous challenges to Yahweh's power, almost as if death were a personified force, like the Canaanite god of death, Mot. Death has to have the ability to act independently and powerfully if the story line is to build to a climax.[3] Yahweh's overcoming these numerous challenges is the writer's means of showing not only that Yahweh has control over death (unlike the repeatedly dying Baal), but also that Yahweh, and not Baal, is the true God of life. It could therefore be said that in 1 Kings 17-19 Yahweh asserts his unchallengeable power in the realm of two Canaanite gods—Baal and Mot.

The Setting for the Conflict: 1 Kings 16.29-33[4]

While structurally not part of the tightly-knit three chapter unit, 1 Kgs 16.29-33 lays the groundwork for chapters 17-19 by tersely listing Ahab's sins. Ahab is described as being worse than his predecessors, who walked 'in the sins of Jeroboam the son of Nebat', since he went beyond them by marrying Jezebel, a Baal-worshipping princess of the Sidonians, and engaging in the worship of Baal. The altar to Baal built by Ahab, and the temple to Baal in Samaria are listed. At this point there is no description of the degree to which Baalism had come to be practiced in Israel, nor is there any indication of the extent to which Jezebel will vigorously promote her God. Also omitted is the challenge of death to Yahweh's power. These elements will be added at the appropriate time in chapters 17-19, helping to augment the dramatic unfolding of the contest. Only enough information is given to focus the reader's attention on the serious threat posed by Baalism and on Ahab's promotion of the cause of Baal.

I. The Structure of 1 Kings 17[5]

The structure of chapter 17 is carefully designed to present Yahweh as the God whose power enables him to feed or not to feed, to send water or drought, to grant life or cause death, as he wills. The writer presumes that the reader knows the periodic cycle of death Baal undergoes, during which time he is unable to send the life-giving rains. Building on that knowledge, the writer presents a contrasting picture of Yahweh as the living god who selectively sustains life in the midst of the drought he himself has sent. In presenting this picture, however, the writer allows death to present a series of challenges to Yahweh, as noted earlier. These challenges build in intensity as we progress through the three basic scenes of the chapter. In the first scene (vv. 2-7), Elijah faces death through thirst and starvation, but Yahweh sustains the prophet through the forces of nature. In the second scene (vv. 8-16), the drought and famine become severe, and the lives of Elijah, the widow, and her son are preserved through the rations sent by Yahweh in the never-failing jar of meal and cruse of oil. In the final scene (vv. 17-24), Yahweh dramatically asserts his power over death by restoring life to the widow's son, whom death had suddenly claimed.

A. *The Stage is Set and the Challenge Posed—1 Kings 17.1*

As chapter 17 opens, the polemic against Baal is undertaken immediately, but not in an explicit and detailed way. When Elijah appears before Ahab, he simply announces that there will be neither dew nor rain except by his word. He does not mention Baal by name and inform the king that the drought is sent either as a punishment for Ahab's worship of Baal or as a direct challenge to Baal's authority as a storm god. In fact, Baal is not once mentioned by name in all of chapter 17. Yet, the challenge to Baal is there, and is more powerful precisely because it is indirect and implicit, forcing the reader to focus the polemic against Baal in his own mind. It is reasonable to assume that any Israelite living during Elijah's time or during subsequent years would have been aware of Baal's status as the storm god in Canaanite religion. Thus, the statement by the prophet (whose very name sounds like a partisan campaign button, אליהו, 'My God is Yahweh')[6] that the rains would not return until he says so, constitutes a direct but unelaborated challenge to Baal's authority over the rains. Furthermore, the prophet's very first words חי יהוה אלהי ישראל, '(As) Yahweh lives, the God of Israel', constitute not only a claim that Yahweh, and not Baal, is the true God of Israel, but also emphasize Yahweh's status as the god who *lives*. While חי is often used in oaths, as here, where the speaker swears by the life of Yahweh, it also is used repeatedly in the OT to describe something as being animated and alive.[7] Given the common knowledge about Baal's periodic submission to his enemy Mot (death), the very oath that Elijah takes before Ahab asserts that Yahweh, unlike Baal, is the God who lives.

Elijah's assertion that Yahweh is alive and has the power to stop the rains will assume, however, an ironic dimension. The prophet will have to face the possibility of his own death due to the drought he has called upon the land. There is also the possibility of Ahab and Jezebel's anger against Elijah. Will they try to slay him? For now the reader is left to wonder. The only hint that Elijah may suffer at their hands is Yahweh's command in verse 3 that Elijah hide himself

(ונסתרת) by the Brook Cherith. The royal response to Elijah's challenge will be developed later (as in 18.17; 19.2). In chapter 17 Elijah has the more immediate problem of how he will survive the drought. Thus, the rest of chapter 17 will focus on the preservation of Elijah's life and the life of the widow and boy with whom he eventually comes to live. Intriguingly, throughout all of chapter 17 after verse 1, there is not a single word about Ahab, Jezebel, and Israel or how they fared during the drought. We learn of the severity of the drought through Elijah's journeys in search of food and through the desperate situation in which Elijah finds the widow and her son.

B. *Scene 2: By the Brook Cherith—1 Kings 17.2-7*

In verses 2-7 Elijah is alone by the Brook Cherith, and no one except the prophet knows of the life-giving power of Yahweh. Elijah receives life from sources that have nothing to do with the agricultural cycle of civilized society, with which Baal was commonly associated.

The scene opens with the word of Yahweh coming to Elijah (v. 2). Yahweh takes the initiative to save the prophet from death, commanding him to take life-sustaining action through the imperative לך מזה, 'Depart from here!' and the strong imperfect[8] נסתרת, 'Hide yourself!' In verse 4 Yahweh's role in preserving Elijah's life is stressed again by the words ואת הערבים צויתי לכלכלך שם, 'I have commanded the ravens to sustain you there'. Yahweh is described as one who not only controls the rains (v. 1), but also creatures within the natural order. The use of the more inclusive verb כול, 'to sustain',[9] rather than אכל, 'to feed' (in Hiphil) also helps emphasize Yahweh's power. Yahweh does not just feed: he sustains life. Furthermore, since Baal's power is so closely associated with water, it is noteworthy that verses 3-6 repeatedly stress the presence of water. God and Elijah may have sent a drought which will eventually cripple the land, but the fourfold mentioning of the Wadi Cherith (vv. 3, 4, 5, 6) emphasizes the abundance of water for the one Yahweh chooses to sustain. This is further emphasized by the twofold use of the verb שתה, 'to drink' in verses 4 & 6. If the dead Baal is powerless to send water during a drought, Yahweh can provide water even in the midst of a drought.

The repetition of words and phrases throughout this scene heightens the stress on Yahweh's control over events. He gives his word (v. 2, דבר יהוה), and it is done according to his word (v. 5,

כדבר יהוה). Elijah is commanded to go (לך), to hide himself by the Brook Cherith which is east of the Jordan (ונסתרת בנחל כרית אשר על־פני הירדן), and to drink from the wadi (מהנחל תשתה), vv. 3 & 4; he goes (וילך), he dwells by the Brook Cherith which is east of the Jordan (וישב בנחל כרית אשר על־פני הירדן), and he drinks from the brook (ומן הנחל ישתה), vv. 5 & 6. God commands the ravens to sustain Elijah (ואת־הערבים צויתי לכלכלך שם), v. 4, and they bring him bread and flesh in the morning and bread and flesh in the evening (הערבים מביאים לו לחם ובשר בבקר ולחם ובשר בערב), v. 6. Thus, the picture of Yahweh up to this point is of a god who can send water or withhold rain, provide life-giving support or withhold such support, as he wills, and of a god whose words convey power and must be obeyed.

However, there is a sudden reversal at the end of the scene. The wadi dries up! The threat to Elijah's life is thereby intensified, and Yahweh's power as the giver of life seems suddenly to be called into question. The reader is led to ask whether Yahweh really controls the rains and the seasons, providing life where he will, or whether Yahweh, like Baal, has no power to stop the return of drought and death to the land. The statement at the end of verse 7, כי לא היה גשם בארץ, 'Because there was not any rain in the land' points back to Elijah's bold claim in verse 1 about the stopping of the rains, but no word is provided giving reassurance that this is indeed a drought sent at Yahweh's will. Why could not the god who commanded the ravens to supply Elijah with bread and meat also command the wadi to keep flowing? The reader is left to wonder whether death will indeed be victorious over Yahweh.

C. Scene 3: A Morsel of Bread—1 Kings 17.8-16

Elijah must relocate due to the drying up of the wadi. He goes to the Phoenician city of Zarephath, where we are introduced to the widow and her son. Yahweh will now sustain the life of three people, not just one. However, his power as the God of life is not reasserted through anything as dramatic as the sending of rain or the replenishing of the wadi; the water/rain motif will be delayed until the climactic contest on Mt. Carmel. Rather, even though Yahweh's power is reaffirmed at times through the repetition of key words and phrases from the previous scene, verses 10-12 pose another serious challenge to his power, the challenge being overcome only in a limited manner in verses 13-16.

The scene opens with the word of Yahweh coming to Elijah once again, and exactly the same words are used as in verse 2, ויהי דבר יהוה אליו לאמר, 'And the word of Yahweh came unto him, saying. . .' As in the previous scene, God is taking the initiative to keep Elijah alive, and he addresses the prophet with imperatives (קום, 'Arise!' and לך, 'Go!'; cf. לך and נסתרת in verse 3). Just as Yahweh had commanded (צויתי) the ravens to care for Elijah (v. 4), so now he commands (צויתי) a widow to care for the prophet (v. 9). The same verb לכלכלך, 'to sustain you' is used as in verse 4. Thus, after the threat posed by the drying up of the wadi (v. 7), we again have the image of a God who is in control, who has anticipated and prepared for all eventualities, and who can make things happen at his discretion.

However, even as Yahweh's life-giving power is reaffirmed, it is done in the face of a growing famine. Elijah had previously been fed bread and meat by the ravens twice daily, and had drunk from the flowing water of the wadi. Now, he approaches the widow and says (v. 10) קחי נא לי מעט-מים בכלי ואשתה, 'Please bring me a little water in a vessel, that I may drink'. The repetition of שתה, 'to drink' from verses 4 and 6 helps underline the contrast between the ample water he once had from the wadi and the small amount he now requests from the widow. Elijah goes on to ask the widow for (v. 11) פת לחם בידך, 'a morsel of bread in your hand'. The prophet who had been amply fed twice a day by the ravens and had drunk his fill from the wadi now is reduced to begging minimal rations from a widow. If Yahweh has commanded the widow to sustain Elijah (v. 9: כול), it is clear that this sustenance will be more meager than that provided by the ravens.

Furthermore, the scene takes an unexpected turn in verse 12. The widow, who had been commanded by Yahweh to sustain Elijah, and who was willing to provide him with water, balks at Elijah's request for a morsel of bread, since she herself is near starvation. Her words at the end of verse 12 describing her lack of food are especially powerful: ועשיתיהו לי ולבני ואכלנהו ומתנו, 'I will prepare it for me and for my son, and we will eat it, and we will die.' Both the word אכל, 'to eat', and the word מות, 'to die', are used here for the first time in chapter 17, and their appearance highlights the progression of matters thus far in the chapter: God commands the ravens to sustain (כול) Elijah, and he is well fed (vv. 2-6). God commands the widow to sustain (כול) Elijah, but she is only able to provide him water. In fact, for the widow and her son it is not a matter of sustaining or being sustained: it is only a matter of eating what is left and dying. Thus, the combination of the verbs אכל (which clearly is used here with a strong ironic twist) and מות confirms the growing intensity of the drought and famine, as the reference to the drying up of the wadi had done earlier (v. 7).

This emphasis on the intensity of the famine is strengthened by the structure of verse 12, which moves dramatically toward a climax on the final word. The widow's opening words, חי יהוה אלהיך, '(As) Yahweh your God lives', initially suggest that the widow is affirming Yahweh's status as the God of life, especially since they echo Elijah's words in verse 1. The words, however, have a sarcastic twist, as becomes immediately obvious when the widow goes on to describe in vivid detail the meager rations she has left: אם יש לי מעוג כי אם־מלא כף קמח בכד ומעט־שמן בצפחת 'I do not have a cake, but only a small portion of flour in a jar and a little oil in a jug.' In fact, so meager is her supply that a couple of sticks (שנים עצים) will suffice to prepare it. The implication of the widow's words is that if Yahweh is a God of life, she certainly has not enjoyed the benefit of his provisions. Her final words show that she has no confidence at all in Yahweh's power to sustain life, since she anticipates that she and her son will die. Thus, the verse moves rapidly from a seeming assertion of Yahweh's power as the God of life, to words which seriously call that power into question, to the climactic and emphatic word ומתנו, 'and we will die'. This final, piercing word by the widow stresses the power of the threat death poses.

God's power to sustain life has thus been seriously challenged. His attempt to preserve Elijah's life by sending him to a new site and commanding the widow to sustain him seems feeble and ineffective. It appears as if Yahweh is powerless to overcome the growing onslaught of death, which is about to claim the widow and her son, and perhaps also Elijah.

The scene reaches its nadir at the end of verse 12. The remaining four verses provide assurance that Yahweh is capable of dealing with the threat to life. Elijah tells the widow 'Do not fear' (אל־תיראי), countering her anticipation of the nearness of death. He tells her to continue her routine of preparing the meal for herself and her son, but to bring him a small portion of food first. He then gives a word from Yahweh which provides the reason for the assurance: כד הקמח לא תכלה וצפחת השמן לא תחסר עד יום תתן יהוה גשם על־פני־האדמה, 'The jar of flour will not fail and the jug of oil will not run dry until the day when Yahweh sends rain upon the land'. Not only do these

words assert for the widow, for her son, and for Elijah the immediate
preservation of their lives: they also assert once again Yahweh's
control over the life-giving rain, which will return when he wills. The
widow, who earlier had balked at Elijah's command to bring him
bread, now obediently prepares the meal, having received assurance
of Yahweh's intention to sustain life.

Unlike the second scene, which concludes (v. 7) with the wadi
drying up and death therefore becoming a serious threat to Elijah,
the third scene concludes with Yahweh's words being carried out.
The first part of verse 16 repeats word for word the assurance the
widow was given in verse 14 that the flour and oil would not fail:

כד הקמח לא תכלה	(v. 14) the jar of flour will not fail,
וצפחת השמן לא תחסר	and the jug of oil will not run dry
כד הקמח לא כלתה	(v. 16) the jar of flour did not fail,
וצפחת השמן לא חסר	and the jug of oil did not run dry

We then have the concluding words כדבר יהוה אשר דבר ביד אליהו,
'According to the word of Yahweh which he spoke by the hand of
Elijah'. This completes a pattern regarding the word of Yahweh
which goes back to verse 8. There, the word of Yahweh had directed
Elijah to move in order to save his life. The widow, however, had
temporarily blocked Yahweh's word by refusing to feed the prophet.
It required a second word from Yahweh (v. 14) to get things back on
track and get the three people fed. Verse 16 then concludes by
reminding the reader that things have occurred as Yahweh had
directed through his word. Even though at this point only a handful
of people are being sustained, Yahweh still possesses his power to
maintain life in the face of death, the drying up of the wadi and the
widow's sparse supply of food notwithstanding.

Thus, in contrast to scene two, which closed with a strong threat
to Yahweh's power, scene three concludes with Yahweh in control.
Unlike the setting in verses 7 and 8, there is no need for a word from
Yahweh at the beginning of the next scene to counter a threat.
Instead, scene three concludes with a word from Yahweh that has
been fulfilled.

D. *Scene 4: Your Son Lives!—1 Kings 17.17-24*

There remains, however, the most dramatic and powerful challenge posed by death to Yahweh's power in chapter 17. Throughout the chapter the challenges by death have grown in intensity, though no one has yet died. Yahweh has responded to the challenges by sustaining life, as most recently in his efforts to save all three persons through the never-failing jars of flour and oil (vv. 14-16). Now, however, death no longer threatens: it acts preemptively, seizing the widow's son.

The power of death is accentuated through the detailed description of the boy's death: חלה בן האשה בעלת הבית ויהי חליו חזק מאד עד אשר לא נותרה בו נשמה, 'The son of the woman, the mistress of the house, became ill, and his sickness became very strong, so strong that there was not any breath left in him'. Since the presence or absence of breath in a person is one of the common ways used in the Tanak to express life or death,[10] the writer places before the reader the vivid picture of the gravely sick child who ceases breathing. By providing this detail and thereby also lengthening the time the reader's attention is focused on the child's death, the writer stresses the power and impact of the challenge death poses to Yahweh.

Once this dramatic challenge by death has been presented, however, the remainder of the scene proceeds in several ways to emphasize Yahweh's power over both death and life. When the widow confronts Elijah immediately after her son's death (v. 18), she does not assume that Yahweh's efforts to feed her and her son have been ineffective, nor does she assume that a force beyond Yahweh's control has killed her son. Rather, she assumes that her son has died because Yahweh is punishing her for her sins: באת אלי להזכיר את־עוני, ולהמית את בני, 'You have come to me to cause my sins to be remembered, and to cause the death of my son'. When Elijah prays to Yahweh, pleading for the lad's life, he presumes that Yahweh has caused the death of the boy: יהוה אלהי הגם על האלמנה אשר אני מתגורר עמה הרעות להמית את־בנה, 'O Yahweh, my God, have you also brought evil upon the woman with whom I am dwelling, by causing the death of her son?' Thus, both the widow and Elijah see death, like life, to come from Yahweh. Death is not seen as a separate force which can challenge Yahweh's power and perhaps even his life, as in the case of the Baal legend, but is rather a tool of Yahweh which he uses as he wills.

Verses 22-24 continue to emphasize this point. After Elijah pleads with Yahweh to return the lad's breath into his body (v. 21), we are told (v. 22): וישמע יהוה בקול אליהו ותשב נפש הילד על קרבו ויחי, 'And Yahweh hearkened to the voice of Elijah, and returned the life of the child into his body. And he lived.' Both Elijah's praying to Yahweh and Yahweh's granting of Elijah's request to restore the lad's life focus attention on Yahweh's powerful control over death. Likewise, the simple statement ויחי, 'and he lived' points back to the two earlier oaths (vv. 1 & 12), each of which stated, in part חי יהוה, 'Yahweh lives', or, in the context of the oath, 'As Yahweh lives'. This structural linkage through the verb חיה, 'to live, be alive', emphasizes for the reader the fact that the boy lives because Yahweh lives. The point is strengthened by the words in verse 23 חי בנך, 'Your son lives', which directly parallel חי יהוה. The words ויחי and חי בנך also point the reader back to the end of verse 12, where the widow had anticipated the imminent death of herself and her son due to the lack of food: ומתנו, 'and we will die'. The reader is thereby reminded that the God who restored life to the dead boy and returned him to his mother is the same God who earlier had provided the food necessary to save the widow and her son from death by starvation.

The widow's words in verse 24 provide an apt conclusion to the chapter: עתה זה ידעתי כי איש אלהים אתה ודבר יהוה בפיך אמת, 'Now I know that you are a man of God, and that the word of Yahweh in your mouth is truth'. In one way, these words seem a bit out of place, since presumably the widow would earlier have had a chance to see that Elijah spoke a true word from Yahweh when the jars of flour and oil kept being replenished. Nevertheless, the bringing of the widow's son back to life constitutes by far the most powerful expression in chapter 17 of Yahweh's control over death, and the widow's emphatic response is therefore quite appropriately placed here. This verse also forms a tidy inclusio with verse 1. There Elijah had spoken a word to Ahab as Yahweh's prophet, a word which heralded the coming of drought and the resultant famine. Yahweh is there a God who challenges Ahab's god Baal by sending the very drought and death so feared in the Canaanite religion. In verse 24 the Canaanite widow affirms that Elijah indeed speaks a true word from Yahweh, not through drought and death, as in verse 1, but through the giving of life and the overcoming of death. The chapter ends, as will chapter 18, with an affirmation of Yahweh's power as a God of life, thereby affirming not only his power over death, but also his desire to send life rather than death.

Summary: Structure of 1 Kings 17

Chapter 17 is intricately woven together in order to highlight Yahweh's powerful control over both life and death. Several elements bind this chapter together:

1. The words חי יהוה, 'Yahweh lives', or variants thereof, appear at the beginning, middle, and end of the chapter. These are the very first words Elijah speaks in verse 1 as he pointedly affirms Yahweh's power over life and death. These are also the first words which the widow speaks (albeit in sarcasm) as she is introduced near the middle of the chapter. The fact that these are the first words spoken by both Elijah and the widow gives them added emphasis. The writer again emphasizes Yahweh's power as a God of life near the end of the chapter, in verses 22 & 23, but here he varies the pattern. Rather than stating חי יהוה, 'Yahweh lives', he states (v. 22) concerning the widow's son, ויחי, 'and he lived', thereby affirming Yahweh's power to give life. This is followed almost immediately by the words, spoken when Elijah presents the living son to the widow, חי בנך, 'Your son lives'. These words directly echo the words of Elijah and the widow, חי יהוה, 'Yahweh lives'. If Elijah's and the widow's words received emphasis by being the first words placed on their lips, the words concerning the widow's son receive emphasis by being in one case the last word spoken in a sub-scene (v. 22) and in the other case essentially the only words spoken by Elijah to the widow as she receives her son back (v. 23).

2. The chapter contains numerous challenges posed by death, challenges which grow in intensity as the chapter proceeds. The first threat is that Elijah will starve during the drought he has helped to cause, which accompanies the hint of a possible danger to Elijah's life posed by Ahab's wrath (see נסתרת, 'Hide yourself', v. 3). The second threat to Elijah's life comes when the Wadi Cherith dries up. This is followed by the threat to the widow and her son when their supply of flour and oil is about to be exhausted. The final and most intense challenge posed by death comes when it suddenly seizes the widow's son, depriving him of life.

3. These four challenges by death are answered by four life-giving responses from Yahweh. In response to the upcoming drought and the possible wrath of Ahab, Yahweh directs Elijah to hide by the Brook Cherith and drink its water, and Yahweh commands the ravens to sustain him. In response to the drying up of the wadi, Yahweh commands a widow to sustain the prophet. When the widow

proves incapable of feeding Elijah, herself, and her son, Yahweh
ceases commanding others and instead acts himself, causing the
supply of flour and oil to be sustained. Finally, when the widow's son
is seized by death, Yahweh acts decisively to restore life to the child.
Thus, as the challenges by death grow in intensity, God himself
becomes more actively involved in the life-sustaining process, no
longer commanding others, but himself taking the initiative against
death and overcoming death's challenges.

II. *The Battleground Broadens—1 Kings 18.1-46*[11]

As we move into chapter 18, the scope of the conflict broadens
markedly. No longer do the prophet, the widow, and her son fill the
stage. Rather, we are shown a famine which has ravished the land
(v. 2), Jezebel's attempts to eradicate the prophets of Yahweh (vv. 4,
13), the dramatic contest between Yahweh and Baal before all Israel
on Mt. Carmel (vv. 20-40), Elijah's annihilation of the 450 prophets of
Baal (v. 40), and Elijah's restoring of the rains while he is in contact
with the king (vv. 41-46). The contest between Yahweh and Baal,
which constitutes the central scene in the chapter, is interwoven with
the conflict between Yahweh and death. Yet, despite the centrality of
the scene in which Baal is silent and ineffective while Yahweh
exceeds the requirements necessary to win the contest, Baal is not
mentioned in the first major section of the chapter (vv. 1-16), and the
concluding scene (vv. 41-46) also fails to refer to him directly. This is
partly due to the writer's implicit style, whereby he chooses to
express the struggle with Baal indirectly, but it is also due to the fact
that death is the foremost opponent of Yahweh in chapter 18, as it
was in chapter 17.

A. *The Stage is Set Once Again—1 Kings 18.1-2*

Just as chapter 17 opened with a very brief scene which set the stage
for the remainder of the chapter, so in chapter 18 the opening scene
sets the stage for subsequent events. The first words ויהי ימים רבים,
'After many days', or close variants thereof are frequently used in the
Tanak not only to indicate the passage of time, but also to denote a
substantial shift in the direction of a story.[12] The next phrase, 'and
the word of Yahweh came to Elijah', directly parallels 'And the
word of Yahweh came unto him, saying. . .' from vv. 2 and 8 in
chapter 17. In those verses the word of Yahweh initiated action by

Elijah to change the location and scope of his activity (לך, 'Go!' and נסתרת, 'Hide yourself!' v. 3; קום, 'Arise!' and לך, 'Go!' v. 9). The same is also true in 18.1 (לך, 'Go!' and הראה, 'Make yourself known'). The command to reveal himself to Ahab reverses the earlier command (17.3) to Elijah to hide himself, and signals the reader that the focus of the story is now likely to become broader and more confrontational. The last words in the verse also point to a major change in the story line, ואתנה מטר על־פני האדמה, 'And I will send rain upon the face of the land'. However, even though these words again affirm Yahweh's power as the God of life and death who can send the rains when he will, they leave unanswered the question of why the rains will return. There is no hint of the dramatic victory over Baal that is to follow, or of Elijah's ritual to renew the rains (18.41-46). These words, with their ambiguity about the reason for the return of the rains, balance nicely the ambiguous words in 17.1, אם יהוה השנים האלה טל ומטר כי אם לפי דברי, 'There will not be dew or rain these years except by my word'. Just as in 17.1, the sinfulness of Ahab and Israel in worshipping the Baals is not specified as the reason for the coming of the drought, so here the reader is not told that the victory of Yahweh over Baal which is soon to be achieved is the reason for the return of the rains. There is only a hint of things to come.

Verse 2 again shows Elijah to be the obedient prophet. וילך, 'And he went', and להראות אל אחאב, 'to reveal himself unto Ahab', directly parallel the commands given to him in verse 1, just as וילך, 'and he went', and ויעש, 'and he did' in 17.5 parallel the commands given in 17.3, and just as ויקם,'and he arose', and וילך, 'and he went' in 17.10 parallel the commands given in 17.9. It is important to note that this is the only time in chapter 18 that a word from God directly commands Elijah to act. Elijah's consistent obedience here and in the instances in chapter 17 will later provide a stark contrast to Elijah's flight in chapter 19 and his reluctance to serve any longer as a prophet.

The last words in 18.2 are terse but pointed: והרעב חזק בשמרון, 'And the famine was intense in Samaria'. Ever since the announcement by Elijah in 17.1 that the rains would cease, there has been no information about the fate of anyone other than Elijah, the widow, and her son. The reader must infer from the near starvation of the widow and her son (17.12) and the drying up of the Brook Cherith (17.7) that the drought must be causing severe hardships throughout the land. Now, however, the severity of the drought is made explicit, not only through the use for the first time in chapters 17-19 of רעב,

'famine' and through the modifying of רעב by the word חזק, 'strong, intense', but also by the sentence structure, which through its placement of the noun at the beginning of the clause lays added emphasis on רעב. Furthermore, even though the writer in 18.1 has reaffirmed Yahweh's power to send the rains when he wills, those rains do not come until the end of chapter 18, after several more scenes have been presented. Thus, as in chapter 17, the writer allows death to pose serious threats to Yahweh's power, and forces the reader to wonder whether the famine will continue to be intense, or whether Yahweh will be able to send the rains and overcome the famine. The writer is teasing the reader by leading the reader to ask whether Yahweh, who had overcome death by reviving the widow's son but nevertheless had not kept the wadi flowing (17.7) and had had to feed Elijah, the widow, and her son on meager rations (17.14-16), will be able to act on a larger scale, send the rains, and end the famine.

B. *Scene 2: 'He Will Slay Me'—1 Kings 18.3-15*

The last words in 18.2 lead directly into 18.3-15, the first major scene in chapter 18, where the intensity of the famine and the threat of death are the center of attention. It is the famine which leads Ahab to search throughout the land for water and grass, so that his horses, mules, and cattle will not die. Interwoven with this search are the threat of death to Yahweh's prophets, which is emphasized twice through the description of Obadiah's attempts to save some of the prophets, and the threat of death to Obadiah himself.

Several patterns and thematic chains are used to tie this scene together and to focus the reader's attention on the contest between Yahweh as the God of life, and death as the chief threat to Yahweh's power. The first of these revolves around Obadiah's name and his status as Ahab's servant. Obadiah is described in verse 3 as a faithful worshipper of Yahweh: ועבדיהו היה ירא את-יהוה מאד, 'And Obadiah feared (worshipped) Yahweh greatly' (see also v. 12). Obadiah's name, עבדיהו, means 'servant of Yahweh'. He is, however, by occupation a servant of Ahab, being in charge of Ahab's household. Given the description in 16.31-33 of Ahab's vigorous promotion of Baal, the reader has to conclude that there will be a difficult division of Obadiah's loyalties. Even though he is a dedicated worshipper of Yahweh, Obadiah also fears greatly any possibility that he will offend his master Ahab, as indicated by his intense and lengthy statement

(vv. 9-14) that Ahab will kill him for, as Ahab would perceive it, misleading Ahab into thinking that Elijah could be found at a certain place (v. 12). The statement in verse 12 about Obadiah's fear of Ahab regarding this specific issue leads the reader to ponder a point the writer does not develop: What will happen if Ahab discovers that Obadiah has been hiding 100 prophets of Yahweh in a cave? By not enunciating this obvious question, and instead leading the reader to see on his own the grave threat to Obadiah's life that his hiding the prophets of Yahweh poses, the writer heightens the reader's awareness of the powerful tension between Obadiah's desire to serve his king and remain in the king's favor (and thus alive), and Obadiah's desire to remain faithful to Yahweh. The writer underlines this tension by twice mentioning Obadiah's hiding of the prophets (vv. 4-5, 13).

The tension between Obadiah's desire to serve Yahweh and his desire to serve Ahab is emphasized in other ways, as in verse 3, wherein Obadiah's loyalty to Ahab and his loyalty to Yahweh are directly juxtaposed. This verse, which introduces Obadiah to the narrative, opens with the words, ויקרא אחאב אל־עבדיהו, 'And Ahab called Obadiah'. The writer does not tell immediately what Ahab said, but rather holds the reader in suspense regarding Ahab's purpose in calling Obadiah while an extensive description is given of Obadiah's zealous commitment to Yahweh and of his sustaining of Yahweh's prophets. Ahab is, in a sense, made to wait for Obadiah's services because Obadiah is also in the service of Yahweh. Only in verse 5 does Ahab finally give Obadiah his orders to search the land for water and grass. Ahab's need to wait because Obadiah is in the service of Yahweh is balanced by the scene in verses 8-15, wherein Elijah and Yahweh are made to wait because Obadiah is in the service of Ahab and fears to offend his powerful master.

Obadiah's torn loyalties are clearly in evidence in Elijah's command to Obadiah (v. 8) and in Obadiah's extensive protest (vv. 9-14). Just as Ahab had told Obadiah to go (לך, qal imperative) on a mission for Ahab (v. 5), so Elijah commands Obadiah to go (לך, qal imperative) on a mission for Elijah and Yahweh (v. 8). However, while in verse 6 we are told that Obadiah went (הלך) in obedience to Ahab's command, he balks at Elijah's command, his reluctance to go being emphasized by the threefold use of הלך, twice as he incredulously repeats Elijah's command that he go to Ahab and announce Elijah's presence (vv. 11, 14), and once (v. 12) as he anticipates the consequences for himself[13] of going to Ahab to make such an

announcement. Clearly, despite Obadiah's repeatedly emphasized
loyalty to Yahweh, he displays a great fear of death, thereby giving
expression once again to the serious challenge posed by death to
Yahweh's power in chapters 17–19. Obadiah does reaffirm his belief
that Yahweh is a God of life when, in taking an oath, he says (v. 10):
חי יהוה אלהיך, 'As Yahweh your God lives'. These are exactly the
words spoken by the widow in 17.12, and closely parallel the words
spoken by Elijah in 17.1. However, just as the widow, after stating
the life-giving power of Yahweh, had immediately succumbed to the
fear of death (17.12), so Obadiah, both before and after affirming
Yahweh's life-giving power, expresses his fear that death will seize
him.

The writer builds up Obadiah's fear of death as we proceed
through the response of Obadiah to Elijah.[14] He first asks Elijah
(v. 9): מה חטאתי כי־אתה נתן את־עברך ביד־אחאב להמיתני, 'What is my
sin, that you would give your servant into the hand of Ahab, to cause
my death?' In verse 12 Obadiah expresses the fear that when Ahab
does not find Elijah הרגני, 'He will slay me'. The writer has switched
to the verb הרג, 'to slay', which more clearly denotes a violent
death.[15] As if to emphasize his point, Obadiah refers (v. 13) to the act
of Ahab's wife Jezebel in slaying the prophets of Yahweh (הרג). In
verse 14 Obadiah again expresses his fear of death, claiming that
when he tells Ahab of Elijah's presence הרגני, 'He will slay me'. Thus,
the repeated and emphatic use of the verb הרג, 'to slay', in the last
three verses,[16] and the use of הרגני, 'He will slay me', as the
concluding word in Obadiah's protest to Elijah, focus the reader's
attention on Obadiah's intense fear of death and on the power of
death as a threat to Yahweh.

Even though the reason given by Obadiah for Ahab's trying to kill
him (v. 12) is Ahab's misperception that Obadiah was lying to him
about Elijah's whereabouts, there is a subtle and more basic reason
why Obadiah is unwilling to announce Elijah's presence. Elijah had
commanded Obadiah (v. 8) to say to Ahab הנה אליהו, 'Behold, Elijah',
and Obadiah twice repeated these two words (vv. 11, 14) as his
understanding of what Elijah had commanded him to say. While
these two words may initially seem innocuous, they carry a double
meaning, since הנה אליהו can also mean, 'Behold, my God is Yahweh'.
Understood in this way, the words Elijah asks Obadiah to speak to
Ahab would be a direct confession of Obadiah's allegiance to
Yahweh. Given the effort that Obadiah has apparently taken to
conceal his devotion to Yahweh, as evidenced by his great care in

hiding the prophets in a cave, it is understandable that he would be reluctant to confront Ahab directly with his Yahwism, lest he lose his life as a consequence. This makes his explanation in verse 12 about his unwillingness to announce Elijah's presence to Ahab appear to be an excuse to cover up the real reason for his fear, namely, that Ahab would discover Obadiah's devotion to Yahweh and punish him severely. Ironically, even though Obadiah fears to confess to Ahab his allegiance to Yahweh, his own name, עבדיהו, 'Servant of Yahweh', declares his devotion to Yahweh. The incompatibility of Obadiah's reluctance to confess 'Behold, my God is Yahweh' with the fact that his very name means 'Servant of Yahweh' is yet another technique used by the writer to underline the tension between Obadiah's two loyalties.

The tension between Obadiah's desire to remain in the king's favor and preserve his life, and his desire to remain faithful to Yahweh exemplifies, as his symbolic name 'servant of Yahweh' suggests, the personal struggle of those individuals in Israel who desired to remain faithful servants of Yahweh but did not have Elijah's courage and forcefulness of character to act decisively in the face of death.[17] Obadiah's extreme reluctance to offend Ahab is used by the writer to emphasize once again the challenge posed by death to Yahweh: it threatens to deny Yahweh loyal followers who are able to do his will and speak on his behalf.[18] Obadiah is at the same time courageous and fainthearted. Even though he winced at the request that he announce 'Behold, my God is Yahweh' to Ahab, he did have the courage to be a closet Yahwist and hide the prophets. Presumably, most people in Israel did not have even that much resistance to the threat posed by death.

Another device used to focus the reader's attention on the struggle between Yahweh and death is the twice-mentioned description of Obadiah's hiding the prophets of Yahweh (18.4, 13). We are told that he took 100 prophets and hid them by fifties in caves, sustaining them with bread and water. The need to hide them was brought about by Jezebel's efforts to cut off (כרת, v. 4) and slay (הרג, v. 13) the prophets of Yahweh. These two brief verses develop motifs introduced earlier in 17.3-7. In 17.3 Elijah was told by Yahweh to hide himself, these words providing only an oblique hint that perhaps Ahab would seek Elijah's life. Now, however, the challenge by the advocates of Baal is much more pointed: Jezebel seeks to cut off and kill not just Elijah, but all the prophets of Yahweh. Jezebel, who up to this point has been in the distant background, being mentioned only in the brief comment in 16.31, suddenly bursts into the narrative as a powerful, murderous force. The suddenness and violence of her introduction emphasizes the intensity of the challenge which death poses to Yahweh through her actions.[19] This challenge is also developed by means of the description in verse 10 of Ahab's efforts to find and extradite Elijah from the surrounding countries. While the writer does not specify what Ahab wants to do with Elijah, the reader is led to conclude, given the emphasis on death throughout Obadiah's long speech, that Ahab seeks vengeance against Elijah for the drought. If Ahab would kill Obadiah for 'lying' about Elijah's whereabouts, it would seem unlikely that he would hesitate to kill the prophet who had caused the drought. Thus, the challenge of death to Yahweh is emphasized through the efforts of both Ahab and Jezebel to eradicate the prophets of Yahweh. One should also note the ironic nature of the efforts by the advocates of Baal to use death to stamp out the worship of Yahweh. Death in Canaanite mythology is the foe who periodically conquers Baal, and Baal will be portrayed in 18.26-29 as one in whom there is no life.

Verses 4 and 13 also hark back to chapter 17 in their reference to the sustaining of the prophets by Obadiah with bread and water. Elijah had been sustained (כול, 17.4, 9) at Yahweh's command first by bread, meat, and water (17.3-7) and then with water, flour, and oil (17.8-16) at the widow's home. In 18.4 and 13 the same verb, כול, is used, and the minimal rations of bread and water are again mentioned, but the scope of those being kept alive is greatly expanded, with 100 prophets now being sustained. Furthermore, the scope of the threat is also expanded. In chapter 17 death challenged Yahweh's power by threatening to deprive Yahweh's prophet Elijah of food and thus of life. Now, in 18.4 and 13 all of Yahweh's prophets are in danger of death, and death threatens not only through the shortage of food, as in chapter 17, but also through the murderous intentions of Jezebel. The source of deliverance, however, has decreased. In chapter 17 Yahweh's commands and actions preserved Elijah and the widow's household. In chapter 18 the prophets' sustenance comes from Obadiah, a faint-hearted servant who fears to offend his master and to reveal his devotion to Yahweh. Death, which in chapter 17 had posed a serious threat to one prophet of Yahweh, now seems to be on the brink of seizing all of Yahweh's prophets. The writer does not specify how many prophets, beyond Obadiah's 100, have been killed by Jezebel, but the way the descriptions are worded in verses 4 and 13 suggests that the numbers were considerable:

בהכרית איזבל את־נביאי יהוה, 'In Jezebel's cutting off of the prophets of Yahweh'; בהרג איזבל את־נביאי יהוה, 'In Jezebel's slaying of the prophets of Yahweh'.

The brief scene in which Ahab instructs Obadiah to help him search the land for grass and water (18.5-6) also helps focus the reader's attention on the struggle between Yahweh and death. The reader has already learned that the famine is intense, not only through Elijah's movements in search of food, but also through the widow's desperation as she and her son are about to eat their last morsel of food (17.12), and through the terse but pointed statement in 18.2 that the famine was severe in the land. Ahab, however, who as king of Israel ought to have been seeking assistance for his hungry people, is instead concerned primarily about his own animals. Note that Obadiah, whom Ahab commands to search for grass for the animals, is in charge of Ahab's household (v. 3): עבריהו אשר על הבית, 'Obadiah, who was over the household'. Ahab thus is not even looking after the cattle of his people, which the people might eat in order to stay alive, but is looking after only his own herds. The use of the word בית, 'household', also reminds the reader of the household (17.15,[20] 17) of the starving widow and her son, further emphasizing the way in which Ahab's efforts to maintain his own flocks evidence a callous disregard for the numerous households facing death as a result of the famine. Furthermore, Ahab's use of the verb כרת (to cut off) when he expresses the hope to Obadiah that the cattle will not perish (18.5, ולוא נכרית מהבהמה, 'So that the cattle will not be cut off') reminds the reader of Jezebel, who is making every effort to cut off (כרת) the prophets of Yahweh (18.4). While the people starve, Jezebel works zealously to kill Yahweh's prophets, and Ahab works to save his cattle instead of trying to preserve the lives of his hungry people. Jezebel will subsequently (18.19) be presented as one who feeds 450 prophets of Asherah at her table even as she persecutes Yahweh's prophets. Thus, Ahab and Jezebel are agents not only of Baal but also of death.

As the reader leaves the Obadiah scene and moves on to the confrontation between Ahab and Elijah and the famous contest on Mt. Carmel, several threats by death are in the forefront: death threatens to destroy all the prophets of Yahweh; death threatens to consume many of the people with famine; and death threatens to frighten Obadiah so severely that he will cease to do Yahweh's bidding. However, just as in 17.13-16 and 19-24 there were reversals, with Yahweh asserting his power as the God of life in the face of the threats from death, so in 18.16-46 Yahweh will again win the victory, this time over both Baal and death. Death will become not only a description of Baal's permanent condition, and the tool used to rid Israel of the prophets of Baal, but also the foe who is dramatically vanquished when the rains are restored to the land. By the end of ch. 18 Yahweh will have asserted his total dominance over both Baal and death.

C. Scene 3: 'Gather all Israel to Me'—1 Kings 18.16-19

Verse 16 is transitional, both concluding the Obadiah scene and initiating the first contact between Elijah and Ahab in three years. This transition is effected not only through the movement from Obadiah to Ahab and then from Ahab to Elijah, but also through the abruptness of the sudden flurry of activity. For nine verses (7-15) there had been no movement at all as Obadiah doggedly and loquaciously resisted Elijah's command to go and speak to Ahab. During Obadiah's long protest the reader comes to wonder whether Obadiah will ever budge from the spot where he stands. When he does move, he is gone in an instant, and the reader is whisked into the next scene: וילך עבדיהו לקראת אחאב ויגד לו וילך אחאב לקראת אליהו, 'So Obadiah went to Ahab, and he told him. And Ahab went to Elijah'.

The questions unanswered by these words and by Obadiah's disappearance after v. 16 are many. What exactly was it that Obadiah declared to Ahab? The two words ויגד לו, 'and he told him' convey only the point that a message was delivered, a message which the last words in the verse tell us led Ahab to go immediately to Elijah. Given Obadiah's wordiness before Elijah, his virtual silence in v. 16 is striking, and draws the reader's attention. Did Obadiah convey the words which Elijah had commanded and which are spelled out three times in vv. 8, 11, and 14: הנה אליהו, 'Behold, Elijah', or 'Behold, my God is Yahweh!' Given the fact that the second possible meaning of these words would place Obadiah in a position of confessing to Ahab his allegiance to Yahweh, and act which could cause Obadiah to fear for his life, one is left wondering whether Obadiah did not modify the message in order to make it less offensive to Ahab. What was Ahab's response to Obadiah's words? Since a key motif in vv. 7-15 is Obadiah's fear of Ahab, and since the tension mounts concerning Obadiah's fate at the hands of Ahab as Obadiah continues to blubber out his fears,[21] the silence of Ahab after Obadiah delivers his message is both surprising and anti-climactic, and fails to resolve the tension.

All these questions are left unanswered, not because the writer was in a hurry to get on to the next scene, but rather due to the way in which the writer chose to develop the challenge by death in ch. 18. Unlike ch. 17, where the intensity of the challenge posed by death increased in each subsequent scene, culminating in death's seizure of the widow's son (17.17), in ch. 18 the challenge posed by death is strong in the opening scene and in Elijah's dialog with Obadiah, but after v 15 death quickly loses its power as a threat and does not achieve a victory over Yahweh and his people. This is not to say that Yahweh's power is not in evidence in 18.1-15. It clearly is, as in v. 1 where Yahweh tells Elijah that he will again send rain on the earth, or in vv. 10 and 15, where the words 'As Yahweh your God lives' and 'As Yahweh of Hosts lives' are used, and carry the full implication of Yahweh's being the living God. However, despite these usages, in vv. 1-15 the power of Yahweh is basically subdued and in the background in order that the writer might more fully develop the seriousness of the challenge death poses to Yahweh. The writer has developed the threat of death so extensively in order to make even more emphatic and decisive the victory Yahweh achieves in vv. 20-46.

Verses 16-19 therefore serve as a transition between death as a threat and the scenes wherein death is vanquished (18.20-46). Having allowed death to express (in 18.1-15) the full force of its threat against Yahweh, his prophets, and his servant Obadiah, the writer begins to reverse the flow of the chapter in vv. 16-19, and from this point on, as the threat of death recedes, the power of Yahweh and his servant Elijah quickly comes to the forefront. Beginning in v. 20, events move clearly and directly toward Yahweh's victory over Baal and over death. Even though the reader is at times reminded (as in vv. 19, 21, and 22) of the threat death can pose, the threat is not as serious as it was in 17.1-18.15, and in the larger context of Yahweh's victory in 18.21-46 these reminders are only an echo of the powerful challenge death had earlier presented to Yahweh's power.

Consequently, since death will not again pose a real threat until ch. 19, the writer simply drops the questions raised in the scene featuring Obadiah. They are no longer important to the development of the story line of the conflict between death and Yahweh. However, even though the writer discards the specific issues concerning Obadiah's relationship to Ahab, he does carry over some of the tension he has pictured in that relationship. Ahab's failure to give any response to Obadiah helps to focus the reader's attention on Ahab's caustic response to Elijah in v. 17. The regal anger that

Obadiah feared would be directed against him turns out in fact to be directed against Elijah. By leading the reader to anticipate Ahab's rage against Obadiah, and by then leaving that anticipation unfulfilled, the writer increases the force of Ahab's wrath when it is unleashed against Elijah in v. 17.

The final words in v. 16, וילך אחאב לקראת אליהו, 'And Ahab went to Elijah' point both forward and backward. Immediately after Elijah delivered to Ahab the message about the drought, Yahweh had commanded Elijah to hide by the Brook Cherith (17.3). The command to hide implied, as was shown above, that Elijah might have cause to fear for his safety, due to his words which brought about the drought and implicitly challenged Baal's power. Furthermore, by the time the reader reaches 18.16, Ahab and Elijah have not met for three years (18.1), and during that time Ahab has been searching everywhere for Elijah, forcing other kingdoms to take an oath that they have not seen the prophet (18.10). Given this background, the reader can only wonder what Ahab has in store for Elijah when the two meet. Even though Elijah initiated the contact between the two (18.8, 15), the reader must ask whether Ahab would have gone to all this trouble to find Elijah if he did not mean to do him some harm, to punish him for his words causing the drought.[22] If Obadiah was devoured by his fear of death at the hands of his master Ahab, perhaps it is Elijah who needs to be afraid.

Ahab's words to Elijah in v. 17 lend credence to the idea that Elijah has cause to fear Ahab: האתה זה עכר ישראל, 'Is it you, you troubler of Israel?' The question has been formulated in a parallel form to Obadiah's question in v. 7: האתה זה אדני אליהו, 'Is it you, my lord Elijah?' Obadiah's question was one of reverence, accompanied by his falling on his face before Elijah. This honor rendered Elijah in Obadiah's question helps highlight by contrast the antagonism in Ahab's, who sees Elijah as an outcast because he has troubled Israel.[23] Since Ahab makes it known that he views Elijah as the cause of the drought, the reader may well wonder whether a command to seize and/or harm Elijah will not follow these opening words. Given the flow of ch. 18 to this point, it would not be surprising for Elijah to suffer persecution and death just as many of the prophets of Yahweh had (vv. 4, 13). Ahab's angry question thus indicates that death can still pose a real threat.

This is, however, the last time in ch. 18 that the threat of death will be presented through Ahab. Having been allowed one brief moment of rage against Elijah, he will now recede and become a compliant figure in relationship to the dominant Elijah. In fact, Ahab will not speak again in this three chapter unit (17-19), except to follow Elijah's command to send for the people (18.20), and to tell Jezebel what Elijah has done (19.1). In both of these cases, Ahab's words are not even recorded in the text. He makes no attempt to stop Elijah from carrying out the contest, and when the contest has been won by Elijah and Yahweh he makes no attempt to stop Elijah from slaying the prophets of Baal (v. 40). He is portrayed as following Elijah's instructions to go up to eat and drink (vv. 41-42), and to prepare his chariot to go down from the mountain (vv. 44-46). Significantly, of the three individuals (the widow, Obadiah, and Ahab) who receive commands from Elijah in chs. 17 and 18 (17.10-12; 18.8-15; 18.19-20, 41-46), it is Ahab alone who is immediately compliant once the command from Elijah has been given. The widow (17.12) and especially Obadiah (18.9-14) had resisted Elijah's command.

The reversal which takes place in ch. 18, with death appearing early as a serious threat to Yahweh and his prophets, but then later being overcome by Yahweh and used to his purposes, is expressed to a considerable degree in this characterization of Ahab. Early in the chapter he and his wife Jezebel are presented as the primary agents of death. Jezebel cuts off the prophets of Yahweh (vv. 4, 13), and Ahab ignores his starving people while he seeks grass to save his own animals (vv. 5-7). Ahab is most especially presented as a figure who conveys death in the Obadiah scene, where Obadiah imagines him to be the one who will fly into a rage and impose death on Obadiah simply for appearing to misinform Ahab about Elijah's presence. Subsequently, Jezebel will appear at the beginning of ch. 19 as *the* conveyor of death against Yahweh and his prophet. Ahab, however, undergoes a considerable change, and the point in the narrative (v. 20) where there is a change in his portrayal is the same point where the threat posed by death declines markedly. Thus, while both Ahab and Jezebel are used in the first portion of ch. 18 to embody the threat and challenge posed by death, Ahab is allowed to express this threat only until the role of death is reversed in ch. 18, with Ahab appearing for the last time as the agent of death in v. 17. After 18.13, and during the victory by Yahweh over Baal and death, Jezebel is held in reserve[24] until, in 19.1-2, she reappears as the chief means whereby death reasserts itself.

Elijah, as Yahweh's prophet, becomes in v. 18 the dominant force for the remainder of ch. 18. If Ahab had seemed to challenge and threaten the prophet in v. 17 by calling him a 'troubler of Israel', Elijah in v. 18 throws the charge back against Ahab, asserting that Ahab and his father's house have troubled Israel by forsaking the commandments of Yahweh and going after the Baals. However, this verse not only asserts the dominance of Elijah over Ahab, who does not again challenge the prophet until 21.20; it also inaugurates Elijah's absolute dominance of the next several scenes. Obadiah had complied with Elijah's command only after he had strongly objected and the command had been repeated (18.9-15). Beginning with Ahab, however, all parties follow Elijah's commands immediately and without objection, including the people of Israel, who agree to Elijah's terms for the contest and apparently bring the bulls he requests (vv. 23-26), the prophets of Baal, who follow Elijah's directions to go first (vv. 25-26) and even his directions to cry aloud to their god (vv. 27-28), the unnamed persons who three times at Elijah's command fill four jars with water and pour it on the offering (vv. 33-34), the people of Israel once again, who obey Elijah's directive to slay the prophets of Baal (v. 40), Ahab once again, who obeys two more of Elijah's commands (vv. 41-42, 44-45), and Elijah's servant, who seven times goes to look out to the sea (vv. 43-44). As will be shown in the discussion of the remainder of ch. 18, Elijah's domination for the rest of the chapter is a key means used to assert Yahweh's power over both Baal and death. Just as Ahab's assertiveness was used in 18.1-15 as a means of emphasizing the power and threat of death, so in 18.16-46 the assertiveness of Elijah is used to express the power and victory of Yahweh.

Verses 18 and 19 serve as a transition to the contest between Yahweh and Baal. Even though there have been implications of Yahweh's conflict with Baal, as in 17.1, or in 17.10-12, where a Canaanite widow presumably under Baal's care is close to starvation, Baal is never mentioned by name in chs. 17 and 18 until 18.18, and death has dominated the stage as Yahweh's opponent. That will now change. Yahweh's contest with Baal will come to the forefront as Elijah wins his stunning victory. Nevertheless, Yahweh's ultimate power over death will also be expressed strongly, as death is used by Yahweh to overcome both Baal and his prophets, and is then itself overcome as Yahweh returns the life-giving rains. Thus, in the remainder of ch. 18 the conflicts of Yahweh with death and with Baal are interwoven.

Elijah's words to Ahab conclude in v. 19, which ends the brief scene of Elijah's confrontation with Ahab and also sets the tone for the contest with Baal. Elijah directs Ahab to gather כל־ישראל, 'all Israel', to Mt. Carmel, along with the 450 prophets of Baal and the 400 prophets of Asherah. In ch. 17 the scope of activity was very limited, with first only Elijah, and then Elijah, the widow, and her son filling the stage. At the beginning of ch. 18 the scope expanded considerably, with the reader's attention being focused on the severity of the famine (v. 2) and on the persecution by Jezebel of Yahweh's prophets, 100 of whom Obadiah hides (vv. 4, 13). Nevertheless, much of ch. 18 up to v. 19 focused on the two personal exchanges, between Elijah and Obadiah, and between Elijah and Ahab. Beginning with v. 19, however, events are painted on a grand scale, with all Israel as the audience and with Elijah facing directly his many Baalistic opponents. This expansion effectively heightens the intensity of the drama which is about to take place.

Verse 19 also provides another reminder of the threat death has posed in ch. 18. We are told that the 450 prophets of Baal and the 400 prophets of Asherah were אכלי שלחן איזבל, 'eating at the table of Jezebel'. In the midst of drought and famine, Jezebel's prophets eat! The widow of Zarephath and her son, who were close to starvation when Elijah came to them, come immediately to mind. There are also the words about the severity of the famine in Samaria (18.2). And, most recently, there is the image of the prophets of Yahweh who have been persecuted and slain by Jezebel (18.4, 13). The picture of the many Baalistic prophets who enjoy royal sanction and protection and no doubt eat quite elegantly at Jezebel's table provides a stark contrast to the prophets of Yahweh whom Obadiah tries to save. They have to be hidden in caves to preserve their lives from Jezebel's attacks, and they are fed a very sparse ration of bread and water. Furthermore, the fact that this description of the comfortable lifestyle of the prophets of Baal and Asherah is placed on Elijah's lips gives it a sarcastic twist. Although the reader does not know it yet, Elijah's insistence that all these prophets be called to Mt. Carmel will set the stage not only for their defeat in the contest, but also for their death (v. 40). Those who have enjoyed luxury through the favor of Jezebel while Yahweh's prophets went hungry and were killed will soon suffer the same fate intended by Jezebel for all of Yahweh's prophets. Thus, the reversal discussed earlier, wherein the power and threat of death (vv. 1-15) is replaced by the power and victory of Yahweh (vv. 20-46), is expressed not only through the change in the roles of Elijah and of Ahab, as discussed previously, but also through the change from a situation in which the prophets of Yahweh are under dire threat while the prophets of Baal prosper, to a situation in which the prophets of Baal are vanquished.

D. *Scene 4: The Contest is Joined—1 Kings 18.20-40*

As we have seen, vv. 16-19 are transitional, with both the threat posed by death and the beginnings of the sequence leading to Yahweh's victory being in clear view. As one moves into vv. 20-40, the references to the threat of death will briefly continue (vv. 21 and 22), but before the reader is too far into the scene they recede. Thereafter, death will express itself only against Baal and his prophets.

The scene is divided into two sub-scenes. The first, in vv. 20-29, depicts Elijah setting the terms for the contest and shows the frantic but ineffective attempts of the prophets of Baal to arouse their god to meet those terms. The second, in vv. 30-40, presents the decisive victory of Yahweh and Elijah. While there are substantial differences between the two sub-scenes, there are also parallels between them, as in the descriptions of the preparations for the contest. Both the differences and the parallels serve to emphasize the helplessness of Baal and the power of Yahweh.

1. *Sub-Scene A: 'Perhaps He is Asleep'—1 Kings 18.20-29*

As previously noted, the scope of the conflict is expanded greatly in this scene. Baal and his many prophets now come directly into the picture as opponents of Yahweh, and Elijah, who earlier had had to deal only with the elements of nature and with several individuals (the widow and her son, Obadiah, and Ahab), now confronts the many prophets of Baal and Asherah and all the people of Israel. Israel's presence in vv. 20-40 is highlighted through the phrases כל בני ישראל, 'all the sons of Israel' (v. 20), and כל העם, 'all the people' (vv. 21, 24, 30, 39), and through the term העם, 'the people' (vv. 21, 22, 37). This emphasis on Israel, when combined with the fact that Ahab disappears after v. 20 and does not reappear until v. 41,[25] transforms the contest from a battle between Ahab and Elijah into a struggle between Yahweh and Baal for the hearts of the people.

Israel is not openly hostile to Yahweh. The people give no evidence of the type of malicious intent toward Yahweh and his prophets demonstrated earlier by Jezebel. Rather, the problem they pose for

Elijah is that they are torn between conflicting options. Earlier in the chapter, Obadiah had wanted to be a faithful worshipper of Yahweh, but his courage wavered. He had difficulty deciding whether to follow Elijah's command and openly be faithful to Yahweh or to follow the voice of his own fear and avoid placing himself in a dangerous position. Like Obadiah, the people of Israel do not know what to do. Elijah's words in v. 21, עד־מתי אתם פסחים על־שתי הסעפים, 'How long will you limp[26] upon two crutches?'[27] provide a vivid picture of someone hobbling along ineffectively and indecisively, and directly challenge Israel to make up its mind. To reinforce his demand that they make a decision, Elijah spells out the options they have, and urges that they choose to worship one god or the other. אם יהוה האלהים לכו אחריו ואם הבעל לכו אחריו, 'If Yahweh is God, go after him; but if Baal, go after him'. His appeal for a decision is confronted, however, only with silence. ולא ענו העם אתו דבר, 'But the people did not answer him a word'.

Given the intensity of the drought and famine (17.7; 18.1-2, 5), which could lead even a devoted worshipper of Yahweh to wonder if Yahweh really is the god of life who controls the rains, the silence of the people is understandable. During this period of Israel's history Baal was seen by many inhabitants of Palestine to be the storm god, and it is therefore understandable that many Israelites, including those who felt a strong commitment to Yahweh, would be afraid to offend Baal by not paying him homage. Especially during a drought there would be a strong fear of offending any god who might possibly send rain. In this context, Elijah's demand that the people worship only one god would no doubt seem unreasonable unless there was clear-cut evidence as to which god possessed the power. The people's silence thus sets the stage for the contest in which a decisive answer will be provided to this crucial question.

The people will dramatically break their silence in v. 39, after Yahweh wins the contest. Both in words and in deed they will express their commitment to Yahweh. For now, however, their silence is filled with anxiety and uncertainty. Given the persecution of Yahweh's prophets by Jezebel (vv. 4, 13), which could easily lead any Israelite to fear that Jezebel might attack all worshippers of Yahweh, and given the perils to life posed by the drought and famine (17.7; 18.1-2, 5), the people's unwillingness to make a commitment indicates that what they fear most is death. Whether from Ahab and Jezebel, who may inflict it immediately and violently, or from the fickle and jealous gods, who can cause it slowly through hunger and

Reason why they couldn't speak to Elijah

starvation, death poses a powerful threat to the people. It clearly
denies to Yahweh a contingent of worshippers he can rely on as his
own, just as it had earlier temporarily denied to Yahweh the services
of Obadiah. Thus, even though the power of death is declining, as
indicated in the previous discussion of the reversal which begins in
vv. 16-19, the writer still keeps the threat of death before the reader
in order to emphasize the power and significance of the victory
Yahweh will achieve.

Verse 22 also points to the threat of death. Elijah tells the people
אני נותרתי נביא ליהוה לבדי ונביאי הבעל ארבע מאות וחמשים איש, 'I, I alone
am left as a prophet to Yahweh, but the prophets of Baal are 450
men'. The structure of the first clause places much emphasis on
Elijah's being the only prophet left to Yahweh. This is accomplished
through the reversal of the normal sentence structure, with the
pronoun אני, 'I', being the first word in the clause (thereby
receiving added emphasis), through the use of לבדי, 'I alone', at the
end of the clause, and through the use of the verb יתר, 'to be left,
remain', which emphasizes the smallness of Yahweh's following.
Elijah's claim that he alone is left as a faithful prophet of Yahweh will
be repeated in ch. 19 (vv. 10, 14), where it will be a key to the
development of that chapter. The claim's primary function in 18.22,
however, is to point again to the threat that death poses to Yahweh's
followers. Elijah's words remind the reader of Jezebel's slaying of the
prophets of Yahweh (vv. 4, 13), implying that she has been very
successful in her attempts to cut off and intimidate the prophets of
Yahweh, and also remind the reader of the reluctance of so faithful a
servant as Obadiah (recalling that Obadiah's name means 'servant of
Yahweh') to declare his commitment to Yahweh. Elijah's claim that
he alone is left as a prophet of Yahweh thus reminds the reader that
death has been a very real threat to Yahweh, whether directly,
through the slaying of his prophets, or indirectly, through the
intimidation of his servants.

Furthermore, the mentioning of the 450 prophets of Baal
immediately after Elijah's claim to be alone suggests that death has
not chosen to attack Baal's prophets, who are thriving. Not only does
the reference to the large number of the prophets of Baal help to
emphasize, by contrast, the power of the threat posed to Yahweh,
who has only one prophet left: it also prepares for vv. 26-29 and 40,
in which death will no longer pose a threat to Yahweh but will rather
seize both Baal and his prophets. Thus, while v. 22 states the
conditions at the beginning of the contest, with Yahweh and his

prophets being threatened and Baal's prophets being favored, it also sets the stage for the decisive reversal which is about to take place through Yahweh's victory in the contest.

As we move into the contest itself beginning in v. 23, the prose style changes from one in vv. 16-22 that has been essentially terse and rapid-paced, to one that is repetitive, detailed and, in vv. 26-29, quite sarcastic. The repetition serves as a device to heighten the drama of the contest, and to emphasize the inability of Baal and his prophets to perform as expected. By dwelling in detail on the contest and thereby placing it emphatically in the mind of the reader, the writer intensifies the failure of Baal's prophets to rouse their god, who is dead and powerless, as vv. 26-29 will emphasize.

The preparations for the contest receive considerable attention. After Elijah asks that two bulls be brought (v. 23), he describes what the prophets of Baal are to do: ויבחרו להם הפר האחד וינתחהו וישימו על העצים ואש לא ישימו. 'Let them choose for themselves one bull, and cut it in pieces, and set it upon the wood. But they will not set a fire.' Elijah then describes his own preparations in parallel terms: ואני אעשה את־הפר האחד ונתתי על־העצים ואש לא אשים, 'And I, I will prepare the other bull, and place it upon the wood. But I will not set a fire.' A number of these words and phrases will again be paralleled in v. 25, when Elijah commands the prophets of Baal to take these actions. In v. 23, however, there are a couple of key differences between the words describing the actions of the prophets of Baal and those describing Elijah's actions. Elijah gives Baal's prophets the opportunity to choose the bull they want, suggesting thereby that Elijah is even willing to let them choose the bull they consider to be the more desirable of the two and thus more likely to elicit the desired response from Baal. Also, Elijah begins the description of his own preparations with the pronoun אני, 'I'. The appearance of the pronoun as the first element in the clause, reversing the normal word order, places emphasis on the 'I' and therefore on Elijah. This again stresses Elijah's visibility as the only prophet of Yahweh, as was done with the words אני נותרתי, 'I, I alone am left' in verse 22.

Verse 24 presents the standard for determining victory: the god who answers with fire will be declared the true God. The writer adds emphasis to this criterion for victory by twice anticipating it in v. 23 through the words ואש לא ישימו, 'But they will not set a fire' and ואש לא אשים, 'But I will not set a fire'. By anticipating the standard of victory without actually stating it, the writer gives added emphasis to the statement in v. 24. This in turn helps highlight the pathetic attempts of the prophets of Baal to get their god to send down fire, and also helps highlight the power of Yahweh's victory, since he sends down fire (v. 38) immediately after Elijah requests him to do so.

It is especially noteworthy that fire is used as the means whereby Baal and Yahweh are to indicate their power as a god. In Canaanite mythology Baal, as part of his role as the god of rain and fertility, is said to control fire and lightning. This can be seen not only in some texts from Ugarit, but also in a stele from the second millennium BCE found at Ras Shamra. In his left hand Baal holds a stylized rod of lightning.[28] Thus, for Elijah to propose that Baal should answer with fire would have seemed quite fair to all, since all would expect him to possess great power over fire and lightning. This means, however, that his failure to answer in this manner is especially damning, undermining his claim to be a god.

The verb עָנָה, 'to answer' is used twice in v. 24. Elijah says הָאֱלֹהִים אֲשֶׁר יַעֲנֶה בָאֵשׁ הוּא הָאֱלֹהִים, 'The god who answers with fire, he is God', and, in response וַיַּעַן כָּל הָעָם וַיֹּאמְרוּ טוֹב הַדָּבָר, 'All the people answered, and said, "What you say is good"'. This verb will be used twice in v. 26 and once in v. 29, where the prophets of Baal will cry out to Baal for a response but none will be given. The crisp presentation of Elijah's proposal in v. 24 and the immediacy of the people's answer therefore stands in stark contrast to the long, protracted pleading of the prophets of Baal for an answer in vv. 26-29, when none is forthcoming. The verb עָנָה will also be used in v. 37, where Elijah will twice ask Yahweh for an answer and one will immediately be given.

The people's quick response 'What you say is good' again reveals their fear and ambivalence. This ambivalence was earlier presented (v. 21) as a means of showing the threat that both death and Ba'al pose to Yahweh. In v. 24 the people readily accept the terms of the contest because it provides a way of determining who really is the god they should worship.[29] For the duration of the contest, the people will take a passive stance, waiting to see what will happen. All they do is to draw near when Elijah calls them (v. 30), and to pour water on his sacrifice and altar (vv. 33-34), as requested. Once Yahweh answers with fire (v. 38), however, the people emphatically affirm his deity (v. 39) and become very aggressive advocates of his cause, slaying all the prophets of Baal (v. 40). Thus, the ambivalence of the people of Israel in vv. 20-24 serves to emphasize the seriousness and intensity of the struggle before the contest is joined, and their action in vv. 39-40 serves to emphasize the decisiveness of the victory Yahweh achieves.

Elijah has been addressing the people of Israel in vv. 21-24. In v. 25 he speaks for the first time directly to the prophets of Baal, and the attention of the story turns to them for the next five verses. The change of verb forms as Elijah speaks to the prophets of Baal is significant. In vv. 23-24, where Elijah spells out the terms of the contest to the people, the verbs are imperfect, some with jussive force: ויתנו, 'Let them be given', ויבחרו, 'Let them choose', וינתחהו, 'and they will cut it in pieces', וישימו, 'and they will set it', etc. In v. 25, however, Elijah speaks to the prophets of Baal almost entirely in imperatives: בחרו, 'Choose', ועשו, 'and prepare', וקראו, 'and call'. Only the last phrase ואש לא תשימו, 'But a fire you will not set' contains an imperfect. As noted earlier, Elijah's presence comes to dominate the scene in ch. 18 beginning in v. 18. That dominance is in clear view in v. 25. Even though this is a contest between Yahweh and Elijah, on the one hand, and Baal and his prophets, on the other, it really is no contest. Elijah can command the prophets of Baal, and they have no choice but to do his bidding. They had not even been asked about the contest: it was the people of Israel (v. 24) who agreed to the contest's terms. Even when Elijah vigorously mocks the prophets of Baal in v. 27, they do not respond to Elijah or retaliate, but simply intensify their pathetic efforts to arouse Baal.

The repetition of the details of the contest helps, as was noted earlier, to emphasize the ineffectiveness of the ritual conducted by the prophets of Baal as they attempt to rouse their god. In v. 23, when Elijah describes the terms of the contest, he says that the prophets of Baal will choose one of the two bulls, cut it in pieces, and lay it on the wood. In v. 25 he commands them to choose a bull and prepare it, and in v. 26 they obediently take the bull and prepare it. In v. 24 Elijah, speaking at that point to the people of Israel, says that they will call on the name of their god, meaning Baal. In v. 25 he commands the prophets of Baal to call on their god, and in v. 26 they call on the name of Baal. This attention to detail continues, and becomes bitingly sarcastic in v. 26, where we are told that the prophets of Baal ויקראו בשם הבעל מהבקר ועד-הצהרים לאמר הבעל עננו ואין קול ואין עשה אשר המזבח על ויפסחו ענה, 'called on the name of Baal from morning until noon, saying, "O Baal, answer us"'. But there was no voice, and no one answered. And they limped around the altar which they had made'.

The words 'from morning until noon' (v. 26) underline the obvious inability of Baal to answer, as does also the prophets' pathetic cry עננו, 'Answer us!' The use of עננו in this context is a key device used by the writer to mock the prophets of Baal and their god. In v. 24 Elijah had proposed that the god who answered (ענה) with fire be declared god, and the people had promptly answered (ענה), accepting those terms. Now, when the prophets of Baal plea for an answer from their god, no one answers. It is noteworthy that the word עננו (v. 26) is in the imperative. Elijah, prophet of the rival God Yahweh, had commanded the prophets of Baal to take certain actions, and they had obeyed. But when these same prophets try to command their god to answer them, there is no answer. Thus, the writer has structured both his description of the details of the contest and his use of verb forms and individual words so as to set up Baal and his prophets for some very biting sarcasm.

The writer's artistry can also be seen in the structuring of the words ואין קול ואין ענה, 'But there was no voice, and no one answered'. The twofold use of the negative אין at the beginning of each clause gives added emphasis to what is said and stresses Baal's inability to perform as expected, especially after all the attention to the details of the contest in vv. 23-26. The stress on the fact that there was no voice makes a strong impression on the reader after the frequent use of the verb קרא, to call, in vv. 24 (twice), 25, and earlier in v. 26.

If these four words emphasize the inability of Baal to respond, the final words in v. 26 mock the ineffective efforts of the prophets of Baal to get a response. In v. 21 Elijah had asked the people how long they would go limping (פסח) upon two crutches. Since he subsequently urged them to make a decision for Yahweh or for Baal, the main thrust of the limping image was to stress Israel's indecision and consequent ineffectiveness in the struggle between Yahweh and Baal. Since the writer uses the same verb (פסח) in v. 26, he thereby suggests that indecision and insecurity have also come upon the prophets of Baal. They cannot get an answer from Baal, and do not know what to do. They limp ineffectively around the altar because their god is totally ineffective.

This emphasis on Baal's ineffectiveness intensifies in v. 27. At noon, after they have had a chance to appeal to their god all morning, Elijah begins to mock (התל) the prophets of Baal. This verb, which most likely is derived from תלל,[30] can carry the implication of trifling and playing with someone who is at a disadvantage, as can be seen in the use of תלל in Gen. 31.7; Exod. 8.25 (Heb); and Judg. 16.10, 13, 15. The use of התל sets the stage for the rest of v. 27, in which Elijah toys with the ineffective prophets and their god.

Elijah's words to Baal's prophets are filled with sarcasm: קראו בקול־גדול כי־אלהים הוא כי שיח וכי שיג לו וכי־דרך לו אולי ישן הוא ויקץ, 'Cry out with a great voice! Surely he is a god! Surely he is musing, and is in the privy, and has turned aside![31] Perhaps he is asleep and must wake up!' It will be recalled that the verb קרא, 'to call, cry out', was used in v. 24 to describe the terms of the contest: each contestant was to cry out to his god to send fire from heaven. Thus, Elijah's commanding the prophets of Baal (note the use once again of the imperative form of קרא, as in v. 25) to cry out to their god is brutally sarcastic, since that is what they have been doing all morning to no avail. The sarcasm is intensified by the words בקול־גדול, 'with a great voice', which imply that they simply haven't been crying out loudly enough. These words are ironic, since the prophets of Baal have not been meekly imploring their god up to this point, but have been energetically crying out all morning to Baal to answer them. The words also raise in the reader's mind the question of why one should have to cry out with a great voice to be heard by a god.

Elijah's next words כי־אלהים הוא, 'Surely he is a god', underline the sarcasm of Elijah's suggestion that they cry with a loud voice, and also intensify the ironic nature of Elijah's comments. That Baal is a god is precisely what these prophets have been unable to demonstrate. The structure of the clause places emphasis on the word אלהים, 'god', the very word which at this point seems to be a most inappropriate designation for Baal. In v. 24 Elijah had proposed concerning the god who answered with fire that הוא האלהים, 'he is the god'. By reversing the order of these words in v. 27 to place the emphasis on אלהים, and thereby scornfully asserting Baal's deity in the face of Baal's clear inability to perform according to the terms of the contest, Elijah effectively undermines the claims of Baal's advocates.

All the remaining clauses in Elijah's words continue the ridicule of Baal. כי שיח, 'Surely he is musing', would normally indicate concern with or attention to a particular matter.[32] In this context, however, where it appears immediately adjacent to the similar-sounding וכי־שיג, 'and (surely he) is in the privy',[33] it takes on clearly scatological overtones. The third phrase וכי־דרך לו, 'and (surely he) has turned aside' is, in this context, most reasonably understood as referring to a trip to the privy.[34] Elijah is thus leveling a very crude and contemptuous criticism at Baal and his prophets, one which would elicit sneering guffaws from even the simplest farmer or child.[35] By using this crude assessment of Baal's reasons for not responding to the pleas of his prophets, Elijah suggests the degree of 'serious' consideration Baal deserves and effectively removes any trace of dignity from Baal's claim to be a living god.

In Elijah's last words, אולי ישן הוא ויקץ, 'Perhaps he is asleep, and will wake up', the writer presents a statement of a different type and magnitude. The previous four clauses had each begun with the particle כי, 'surely', which had linked together the sarcastic statements about Baal's being a deity and about his bathroom activities. Now, however, the clause begins with אולי, 'perhaps', the writer thereby alerting the reader that the next thing said will be in a different vein.

Elijah's last words to the prophets of Baal contain the most penetrating sarcasm and irony in the chapter, precisely because they tie in to the motif of life and death that has been pervasive since the beginning of ch. 17. As we have seen, death has repeatedly posed a threat to Yahweh and his prophets, and at times, as in the story of the death of the widow's son (17.17-24) it has seemed as if death were about to achieve the victory. Meanwhile, the forces supporting Baal, including Jezebel, Ahab, and the prophets of Baal, have appeared to be on the ascendancy. Now, however, all that is changed, and it is Baal who is held captive by death. The association of sleep with death is quite a universal phenomenon. Thus, when Elijah makes the ironic understatement that Baal is asleep, he underlines what has already become obvious to everyone through Baal's inability to answer with fire—Baal is dead. Elijah's mocking indulgence of the prophets by entertaining the possibility that Baal is merely asleep only serves to heighten in the reader's mind the grim reality of Baal's death.

The last word, ויקץ, 'and he will wake up', further intensifies the irony, since this is precisely what everyone now knows Baal cannot do.[36] It also sets the stage for vv. 28-29, in which the prophets of Baal try frantically to rouse their god. Furthermore, these sarcastic words at the end of v. 27 also bring to mind the other death already presented, that of the widow's son. When Elijah cried (קרא; 17.20, 21) to Yahweh to restore the child's life, we are told that Yahweh heard (שמע) the voice of Elijah, and the child lived (ויחי, 17.22). By contrast, Baal not only is not capable of answering the crying out (קרא) of his prophets: he cannot even hear them, because he himself is dead, in a sleep from which he will not awaken.

In v. 27 Elijah had sarcastically commanded Baal's prophets to
קראו בקול־גדול, 'Cry out with a great voice!' In v. 28 they obediently do
so, as is underlined by the writer's use of directly parallel words,
ויקראו בקול גדול 'And they cried out with a great voice'. This helps
amplify Elijah's dominance of the whole contest scene, as discussed
previously. Baal's prophets had already been crying out to their god (v.
26) before Elijah's sarcastic words, but now there is a marked
increase in the intensity of their efforts and in the writer's sarcastic
portrayal of the futility of their attempts. They cut themselves with the
swords and lances until their blood flows כמשפטם, 'as is their custom'.
One immediately wonders whether the prophets are trying to rouse Baal
to action by evoking his sympathy. But perhaps there is also the
sarcastic implication of the draining of life not only out of Baal, but
also out of his prophets and his supporters. Blood (דם) is commonly
used in the Old Testament to denote the life which a person or
animal possesses. When that blood is spilt, the person is dead.[37]
Thus, by cutting themselves and shedding their own blood the
prophets of Baal present an image suggesting the death of the
Baalistic movement and anticipating their own death at the hands of
Elijah and the people of Israel (v. 40).

In v. 29 we are told that 'They raved on' (ויתנבאו) [38] until the time
of the offering of the *minhah*. It is important to note the progression
from v. 26 to v. 29. The prophets of Baal first prepare the bull and
simply call on Baal from morning to noon to answer them (v. 26).
Then, at noon, after Elijah's mocking, they become desperate,
inflicting bodily wounds in hopes of getting Baal to respond (v. 28).
The last image we see of them (v. 29) is that they are in full prophetic
ecstasy, trying everything they can in a frantic attempt to get an
answer. The writer uses this progression to mock the prophets,
whose rapidly growing anxiety suggests their growing realization
that their god is not capable of answering.

The frantic gyrations of the prophets of Baal stand in stark
contrast to Baal's total lack of activity: ואין־קול ואין־ענה ואין קשב,
'There was no voice, and no answering, and no heeding'. Intense,
desperate activity is followed by stony silence. The writer has
skillfully balanced these two basic images in v. 29 in order to
underline once again the reality that Baal is dead. After the wild
prophesying at the beginning of the verse, the threefold use of ואין
strikes like hammer blows emphasizing Baal's lack of life and
incapability of doing anything. The writer underlines Baal's total
lack of activity by repeating ואין קול and ואין ענה from v. 26 and then

adding ואין קשב as a new element to intensify the stress on Baal's silence.

It is most noteworthy that nowhere in vv. 26-29 does the writer explicitly state that Baal is dead. Rather, the reader must reach that conclusion on his own, through the references to the lack of a voice and the lack of an answer, and through Elijah's mocking words in v. 27. Since the reader must formulate on his own the conclusion that Baal is dead, the scene ultimately has a more powerful effect than if there had been a direct statement to that effect.

Sub-scene A of the contest on Mt.Carmel thus ends with two vivid pictures in the reader's mind. One is of the frenetic activity of Baal's prophets pursuing the hopeless task of rousing their god. It is interesting that the writer does not describe their activities coming to a halt (at least not until v. 40). The writer leaves them suspended in their ranting and bleeding, still futilely trying to arouse Baal, while he switches his attention to Elijah and Yahweh's part of the contest.[39] The continuing, fruitless effort of Baal's advocates is made even more pathetic by the fact that there are so many of them. We see 450 prophets of Baal doing their utmost to arouse their god, and still there is no answer. The reader is left with the impression that, if Baal does not answer 450 frantic prophets, he is not likely ever to answer.

The second image left in the reader's mind is of the lifeless Baal. It will be recalled that throughout ch. 17 and the first half of ch. 18 death had posed an almost constant threat to Yahweh, his prophets, and the hungry people of Israel, but had never posed a direct threat to Baal. Now, in the contest with Baal, death becomes, in a sense, Yahweh's ally, indeed, Yahweh's tool, seizing the one whom Yahweh confronts in the contest for the allegiance of Israel. In earlier posing the terms of the contest (v. 24) Elijah had said that 'The god who answers with fire, he is god'. Not only does Baal fail to answer with fire: he fails to give any kind of response at all. Thus, death calls into question any status he might have as a god. Since it was an assumed part of Canaanite mythology that Baal would periodically succumb to death, the idea of his being dead for a time would not be all that unusual. Chapter 18, however, goes far beyond that, using the detailed description of his total silence in vv. 26-29 as one way of underlining the fact that he is permanently dead and has no power. This point will be amplified in vv. 41-46, where Yahweh sends the rains, a task the worshippers of Baal thought was the main function of their god. Indeed, one could say that the contest is not so much between Yahweh and Baal, but between Yahweh and Baal's followers. They are the ones who struggle with death, trying futilely to bring life to a 'god' who has no existence. As the writer goes to great effort to show, their struggle must meet with failure, not only as regards the lifeless Baal, but also as regards their own lives, since they will be put to death. Of the proponents of Baal active in ch. 18, only Ahab and Jezebel escape with their lives.

2. *Sub-Scene B: 'Yahweh, He is God'—1 Kings 18.30-40*

The writer alerts the reader to the new scene by having Elijah again speak to the people, as he did at the beginning of the previous scene (vv. 20-24), and by having him direct the people to draw near (נגש), just as he had drawn near to them in v. 21. He then focuses on Elijah's part of the contest, since Baal's prophets have failed. Elijah וירפא את־מזבח יהוה ההרום, 'repaired the altar of Yahweh that had been thrown down'. The verb הרס, 'to throw down, overthrow, ruin', indicates that it is not simply a matter of the altar's having fallen into disrepair through lack of use: it has rather been deliberately destroyed (cf. 19.10, 14). This brings to mind once again the threat death had posed to Yahweh through the efforts of Jezebel to cut off the prophets of Yahweh (18.4, 13) and through the fear that had been placed in the hearts of Yahweh's followers (18.9-14, 21). Reminding the reader of this threat to Yahweh enables the reader to appreciate more fully the significance of the victory that will be achieved.

These words also prepare the reader for the significance of the rebuilding of the altar, which is developed in vv. 31 and 32. The use of stones in the construction of an altar is quite common in the Old Testament, but in this context the use of 12 stones carries a particular significance. Exodus 24.4 presents a tradition in which Moses, when he reads the book of the covenant to the people and thereby consecrates them to the keeping of Yahweh's law, builds an altar and erects 12 stone pillars as part of the covenant ceremony. Likewise, in Joshua 4 there is described the carrying of 12 stones across the Jordan River into the promised land which Yahweh has given to his people, and the erection of twelve stones in the midst of the river. If these passages reflect traditions known to the writer of 1 Kgs 17-19, which would seem reasonable, it would appear that the writer would see Elijah to be reconstituting Israel through the act of rebuilding the altar בשם יהוה, 'in the name of Yahweh'. Just as Moses used 12 stones when the covenant was given, and just as Joshua used 12 stones when the promised land was given, so Elijah now uses 12 stones for what is seen as another major event in Israel's history, the reconsecration of Israel to the worship of her god Yahweh. The specific use of 12 stones would immediately convey to the reader the ideal Israel of the past, even if the political unity of the twelve tribes had long since disappeared following Solomon's death.[40] The ideal Israel is made even more explicit through the phrase כמספר שבטי בני־יעקב, 'according to the number of the tribes of the sons of Jacob', and through the reference to Jacob's other name, אשר היה דבר יהוה אליו לאמר ישראל יהוה שמך, 'to whom the word of Yahweh came, saying, "Israel will be your name"'. While the contest has not yet been won the writer has in vv. 31 and 32 laid the groundwork for Israel to again be the people of Yahweh, just as they were with Jacob, Moses, and Joshua. Given the people's indecision in v. 21, when they would not follow Elijah's directive and make a choice between Yahweh and Baal, Elijah's efforts in vv. 30-31 to reconstitute Israel set the stage for the people's dramatic response in v. 39. The ones who had abandoned Yahweh will come rushing back to express their loyalty.

A great deal of attention is paid to Elijah's preparations for the contest. After building the altar, he cuts the bull in pieces and places it on the wood, following the instructions given in v. 23. This basically parallels the instructions given to the prophets of Baal in v. 25 and their carrying out of the instructions in v. 26. A key difference, however, is the trench that is built around the altar and the four jars of water which are three times poured over the sacrifice and on the wood. The addition of this feature implies that not only will Yahweh be able to fulfill the terms of the contest, as Baal could not: he will even be able to exceed them by igniting a sacrifice saturated with water. Furthermore, by not merely mentioning that four jars of water were poured three times, but by listing each of the three instances of the pouring of the water and by having Elijah three times issue a command, the writer focuses the reader's attention on Elijah's deliberately making the contest more of a challenge for Yahweh. Verse 35 increases this emphasis by underlining the saturation of everything. The trench, which was dug large enough to hold two measures of seed (v. 32), was filled with water that ran off the sacrifice.

By dwelling in detail (vv. 25-26) on the preparations of the prophets of Baal for the contest, and thereby emphasizing their efforts, the writer made even more humiliating the defeat they suffered through their inability to rouse Baal. They tried hard, but failed. The even more detailed description of Elijah's preparations in vv. 32-36 sets the stage for Yahweh's powerful victory in v. 38. Thus, the format of vv. 30-40 enables the reader to savor Yahweh's victory, both because it devotes considerable space to the story, dwelling in great detail on the preparations for the moment of victory, and because it parallels the successful activities of Elijah to the completely unsuccessful activities of Baal's prophets.

At the beginning of v. 36 the words ויהי בעלות המנחה, 'And it came to pass, at the time when the oblation was offered up' point back to the same words, in slightly different form, in v. 29. There we were told that the prophets of Baal continued raving until the time of the offering of the oblation. The writer uses this link to strengthen the contrast between the prophets of Baal, who tried all day until the offering of the oblation, but failed, and Elijah, who had success as soon as he called on Yahweh.

The appeal of the prophets of Baal to their god entailed only two words, הבעל עננו, 'O Baal, answer us'. The description of their appeal focuses primarily on their actions: their calling on the name of Baal, and their limping about the altar (v. 26); their crying with a great voice, and their cutting themselves with swords and lances (v. 28); and their frantic prophesying (v. 29).

Elijah's appeal to Yahweh, however, involves no actions (once the sacrifice has been prepared), but rather a detailed verbal appeal to Yahweh for an answer. The contrast between the desperate and frenzied prophets of Baal and the prophet of Yahweh who calmly appeals for an answer is thus quite striking. This is not to say that Elijah's plea is lacking in urgency. His appeal is ardent, but its ardency is linked to a heritage which convinces Elijah his God will answer.

Elijah's opening words יהוה אלהי אברהם יצחק וישראל, 'O Yahweh, God of Abraham, Isaac, and Jacob' suggest once again, as in the reference to Israel (Jacob) in v. 31 and in the use of 12 stones to rebuild the altar, that Yahweh's victory in this contest will provide the opportunity for reconstituting Israel as she was in her formative years. This point is amplified by the plea היום יודע כי־אתה אלהים בישראל, 'Let it be known this day that you are God in Israel'. In the context of the threats posed by death to Yahweh's power and the threats posed by the proponents of Baal, this plea of Elijah calls on Yahweh to act decisively and thereby reclaim his wavering people (cf. v. 21). The word היום, 'This day', stresses the urgency of the situation: Yahweh must act before the few followers he has left (cf. vv. 4, 13, 22) are

overwhelmed. This plea for Yahweh to reclaim his people is repeated
in v. 37: וידעו העם הזה כי־אתה יהוה האלהים ואתה הסבת את־לבם אחרנית,
'In order that this people may know that you, O Yahweh, are God,
and that you have turned their hearts back to you'.

The language is intense and closely focused, since this is the
decisive scene in which Yahweh wins the victory. The implications of
Yahweh's victory are stressed twice through the clause כי־אתה אלהים,
'that you are God' (v. 36) and its close parallel, כי־אתה יהוה האלהים,
'that you, O Yahweh, are God' (v. 37). The emphasis in both clauses
is on אתה, 'you', so that the impact conveyed is 'that *you* are God', as
opposed to the other contestant, Baal. The clause in v. 36 is preceded
by the words היום יודע, 'Let it be known this day' and is immediately
followed by the word בישראל, 'in Israel'. This closely parallels v. 37,
where the clause is preceded by the words וידעו העם הזה, 'that this
people may know', referring to Israel, and is followed by a reference
to Yahweh's turning the hearts of the people back to him. These
references to Israel's need to know and to have her heart turned back
to Yahweh hark back to v. 21, where the people of Israel displayed
great ambivalence, being unwilling to commit themselves either to
Yahweh or to Baal. Thus, these words in vv. 36 and 37 help
emphasize Elijah's need for an answer from God *now*, so that the
people of Israel will be convinced to forsake their ambivalence and
return to Yahweh. The words add intensity to the scene as it builds
toward the climactic response in v. 38.

Other elements in vv. 36 and 37 are structured to emphasize the
importance of this scene. Since at this point in the three chapter unit
the contest is between Yahweh and Baal, with Yahweh needing to
assert that he is God, it is noteworthy that the divine name יהוה
(Yahweh) is used three times in vv. 36 and 37, where Elijah speaks
his plea to Yahweh, and is also used three times in vv. 38-40, where
Yahweh's response and the subsequent response of the people is
described. The writer has the name of the victorious God in the
foreground even as the victory is being won.

Likewise, we note that while Elijah's name has been used
repeatedly since 17.1, this is the first time (18.36) he has been called
הנביא, 'the prophet', by the narrator. The only other time the title
'prophet' is given to him is in v. 22, where he applies it to himself,
claiming he alone is left a prophet to Yahweh. The application of the
title 'prophet' to Elijah underscores the importance of the contest to
him, since all his work heretofore as a prophet of Yahweh will be
judged on the basis of whether or not he can elicit a response from

Yahweh. One could say that the writer has withheld applying the title 'prophet' to Elijah until the moment of his greatest victory.[41]

The importance of Yahweh's response to Elijah's plea is also underlined by the words at the end of v. 36: ואני עבדך ובדבריך עשיתי את כל־הדברים האלה, [Let it be known that. . .] 'I am your servant, and by your word I have done all these things'. The use of עבדך, 'your servant' immediately reminds the reader of Obadiah, 'servant of Yahweh', (vv. 3-16). Obadiah had been Yahweh's servant, but he was only willing to be such in private, and was unwilling to confront Ahab directly with his commitment to Yahweh. Elijah is also Yahweh's servant, but hardly in a private and timid way. He has directly confronted Baal, Baal's prophets, and the king. The question that immediately rings out is, 'Will Yahweh respond to Elijah's plea and show that he indeed is a servant of the true God?' Elijah's statement that by Yahweh's 'word I have done all these things' also focuses the reader's attention on what is at stake in the contest. Elijah's first act was to stop the rains (17.1), a step which constituted a direct challenge to Baal's power as the storm god. He has since challenged the forces of Baal to a contest and has mocked them for their inability to get Baal to respond. He has shown that Baal is dead, but all that he has done will be in vain unless he can also show that Yahweh lives. Else the people will conclude that Yahweh also is dead, like Baal, and all Elijah's efforts on behalf of Yahweh will have been in vain.

The writer also directs the reader's attention toward the climactic moment in v. 38 by means of Elijah's words (v. 37) ענני יהוה ענני, 'Answer me, O Yahweh, answer me!' The prophets of Baal (v. 26) had also used the verb ענה in their appeal to Baal. That Elijah uses ענה twice in his plea projects a sense of urgency, intensifying the reader's anticipation as Elijah awaits an answer from Yahweh.

The answer comes quickly in v. 38, without even a hint of the long period of agonizing silence and frustration that accompanied the plea of the prophets of Baal (vv. 26-39). Yahweh acts decisively and dramatically, sending the fire Elijah had requested. Any doubt the reader may have entertained due to the parallels between Elijah's preparations and plea and the futile preparations and pleas of the prophets of Baal only serves to intensify the impact upon the reader of Yahweh's decisive response. This contrast between Yahweh's answer and the total lack of an answer from Baal is vividly presented by the structure of v. 38. The terms of the contest had specified that the god who answered with fire would be declared god (v. 24). This has already been accomplished at the beginning of v. 38, as described by the words ותפל אש־יהוה, 'then the fire of Yahweh fell'. The rest of the verse is overkill, in which Yahweh's going far beyond the terms of the contest makes even more pronounced the difference between him and the dead Baal, who could do nothing in response to the pleas of his prophets. We are told that the fire of Yahweh consumed (אכל, literally, 'ate' or 'devoured') the burnt offering, the wood, the stones, and the dust, and licked up the water in the trench. The long list of what has been devoured by the fire intensifies with each added element the power and significance of Yahweh's victory. The sign of the definite object, את (not translated) is used before each item listed and, along with the definite article ה at the beginning of the single word following each את, serves to punctuate and thereby emphasize each item consumed by the fire of Yahweh.

The quick, powerful response by Yahweh in v. 38 is matched by the intense response of the people of Israel in v. 39. When they see what has happened, they fall on their faces before the god who has so convincingly demonstrated his power. The writer links the people's response in v. 39 to Yahweh's response in v. 38 through the verb נפל (to fall). When the fire of Yahweh fell (ותפל), the people in response immediately fell on their faces. The phrase כל־העם, 'all the people', also links back to several earlier verses in which the people appeared. In v. 20 Ahab, at Elijah's direction, had gathered all the sons of Israel (כל־בני ישראל) to Mt. Carmel, and in v. 21 Elijah had called on all the people (כל־העם) to choose Baal or Yahweh. They declined to commit themselves to either. In v. 22 Elijah bemoaned to the people (העם) the fact that he was the only prophet of Yahweh left, and in v. 24 got all the people (כל־העם) to agree to the terms of the contest. In v. 30 Elijah called all the people (כל־העם) to draw near to him, and they did, observing his rebuilding of the altar. Throughout all these appearances, the people have been neutral and non-commital, waiting to see what will happen. This makes their intense and dramatic confession in v. 39 that Yahweh is indeed God even more powerful.

The intensity of the people's confession יהוה הוא האלהים, 'Yahweh, he is God' is increased by its being repeated in exactly the same words. The impression conveyed is that the people, now that they have seen a demonstration of Yahweh's power, have instantly overcome their earlier doubt and hesitation and are now very eager to declare their zealous commitment to Yahweh. Stress in the clauses

falls on the middle word הוא, 'he', thereby placing emphasis on
Yahweh's being God, as opposed to Baal ('Yahweh, *he* is God').

The writer has carefully laid the groundwork for this declaration
in v. 39 that Yahweh is indeed God. In 18.24 Elijah had set the
standard for victory by saying והיה האלהים אשר יענה באש הוא האלהים,
'And the God who answers by fire, he is God'. In 18.27, when Elijah
had mocked the prophets of Baal for their inability to rouse Baal to
action, he had said with biting sarcasm קראו בקול־גדול כי־אלהים הוא,
'Shout with a loud voice: surely he is a god'. This underlined Baal's
impotence as a god, but the verdict was still out on Yahweh, as
Elijah's twofold plea in vv. 36 and 37 made plain. In v. 36 Elijah
called on Yahweh to let it be known כי־אתה אלהים, 'that you are God',
the emphasis falling on the word אתה, 'you'. Likewise, in v. 37 Elijah
called on Yahweh to answer him in order that the people would know
כי־אתה יהוה האלהים, 'that you, O Yahweh, are God'. The people's
decisive dual confession in v. 39 יהוה הוא האלהים יהוה הוא האלהים,
'Yahweh, he is God; Yahweh, he is God' thus points directly to these
earlier words and declares forcefully that the people see Yahweh to
have fulfilled the terms of the contest (v. 24), and that they see him,
rather than Baal (v. 27) to be the true God.

Sub-scene A of the contest had opened (vv. 20 and 21) with Ahab,
all Israel, the prophets of Baal, and Elijah all gathered on Mt. Carmel
for the contest. Ahab immediately dropped from the scene (to
reappear in v. 41) but the other three parties have been present
throughout the contest. Now that the contest has been won by
Yahweh, the moment of truth has come for the prophets of Baal.
Elijah tells the people to seize the prophets of Baal, and he then takes
them down to the Brook Kishon and slaughters (שחט) them there.
This verb is mainly used in the Old Testament to describe animal
sacrifices,[42] but is also used to refer to the slaying of human beings,
sometimes in a sacrificial context (e.g., Gen. 22.10, Isa. 57.5). Is
there perhaps a suggestion here of Elijah's offering the prophets of
Baal to the victorious Yahweh as a sacrifice? In any case, the slaying
of the prophets of Baal clearly balances the earlier references (vv. 4,
13) to Jezebel's attempts to cut off (כרת) and to slay (הרג) the
prophets of Yahweh. Now that Yahweh has won the victory, the
tables have been turned, and the prophets of Baal who had enjoyed
all the benefits of being the royal favorites (e.g., v. 19) will be favored
no more. The completeness of their defeat is stressed by the words
איש אל־ימלט מהם, 'You will not let a man of them escape'. Yahweh's

victory is to be total, with none of the prophets of Baal who opposed him being allowed to live.

The last 3 verses of sub-scene B are action-packed, moving quickly from one event to another in terse, pointed words. This style in vv. 38-40 is in sharp contrast to vv. 21-37, which consistently devotes considerable space to the events described. Elijah's challenging Israel to take a stand, and his subsequent setting of the terms of the contest takes 4 verses (21-24). The efforts of Baal's prophets are described in 5 verses (25-29), and their attempts to arouse the silent Baal are described in detail (vv. 26, 28-29). Elijah's preparations receive a very thorough description (vv. 30-35) and his plea to Yahweh, like the efforts of Baal's prophets, is presented in detail (vv. 36-37). All this time the audience has been held wondering, no answer having been given to the question of who will win the contest. When the answer is given, there is an avalanche of activity. In just three verses Yahweh sends his fiery response, the people's ambivalence is instantly removed and they profess allegiance to Yahweh, and Baal's prophets are seized and killed. By keeping the reader waiting for so long for the contest to be won, but then suddenly unleashing in staccato sequence the description of the victory and the victory's consequences, the writer adds emphasis to the power of Yahweh's victory.

As the contest ends, there has been a dramatic change in circumstances since the beginning of the contest. There, death had posed a very significant threat to Yahweh as Jezebel vigorously sought to kill Yahweh's prophets, as fear of death made Obadiah at best a timid servant of Yahweh, and as all the people of Israel wavered, unwilling to oppose the royal sanctioning of Baal. By the end of the contest, however, Yahweh has overcome the threat of death. Even though death has total control over Baal, who cannot even respond with a whimper, Yahweh shows that death has no power over him by responding immediately to Elijah's plea for fire. Death is even a tool used by Yahweh to rid him of his enemies, as Elijah slays all the prophets of Baal. Thus, by the end of v. 40 there is no doubt that Yahweh has been victorious over both Baal and death.

E. *Scene 5: 'There Was a Great Rain'—1 Kings 18.41-46*

In this scene, Yahweh's victory over both death and Baal becomes complete. Yahweh has just won the contest with Baal, showing he is very much alive while Baal is quite dead. There is therefore no longer any need to withhold the rains. Yahweh's servant Elijah, who had declared in 17.1 that there would be neither dew nor rain except by his word, now brings the rains back to Israel as the messenger of his victorious God. Yahweh, and not Baal, is shown to be the true storm God.

Yahweh's relationship to death is shown to be very different from Baal's. In Canaanite mythology, Baal's frequent conquest by death stopped the rains and led to periodic drought and famine. Yahweh, however, does not have to submit to death. Rather, as the true storm God he *chooses* to withhold the rains in order to demonstrate that he, and not Baal, is the God whom Israel should worship.

This victory by Yahweh over death had not always been a foregone conclusion. In ch. 17, after he flees from Ahab's presence and hides by the Brook Cherith, Elijah himself is threatened with death due to the drought (17.7). The reader is left to wonder whether death is not more powerful than Yahweh, having the ability to stop the rain, and using that ability to harass and threaten Yahweh's servant Elijah. Similarly, Yahweh's command to Elijah to go stay with the widow, which initially seems to address Elijah's need, turns out not to be very effective, for the widow herself is at the point of starvation and death. After death seizes the widow's son, Yahweh restores the lad to life, but even this victory over death is less than complete, as in the next chapter death seriously threatens Yahweh's prophets, intimidates Yahweh's faithful servant Obadiah, and leads the people of Israel to be silent when they are asked to choose which God they will serve. The reader must also wonder whether the drought and famine (18.2) were sent by Yahweh or are in fact the result of death's control over Yahweh.

The sending of the rains by Yahweh changes all that. Yahweh does not just send his prophet elsewhere for food, or feed a widow and her son, or restore a single person to life. He returns the most crucial source of life, water, to all the land. Everyone in Palestine will now benefit from his power as the God of life. It can hardly be doubted that in Canaanite mythology the most decisive expression of the power of Mot, death, came through the periodic droughts caused by Mot's ability to slay the storm god Baal. Yahweh's sending of the rains thus decisively demonstrates that in this key area of Mot's supposed power, Yahweh, not death, reigns supreme. Death cannot prevent Yahweh from sending rain.

Yahweh's power as the storm God is developed in detail in vv. 41-
46. However, before we examine these verses, we need to look at
three elements in vv. 30-40 which prepare for the expression of
Yahweh's power over the rains in vv. 41-46. In vv. 33-35 Elijah had
had a great deal of water poured on the bull and wood, filling the
large trenches. As noted above, this makes the consuming of the
offering more difficult, thereby adding emphasis to Yahweh's victory.
But it also ties in directly with Yahweh's power as the storm God.
The contest takes place during a drought, and for Elijah to expend
the precious water supply so lavishly during a devastating drought
(18.2-5) suggests that for Elijah water need be of no concern, since
his God can send or withhold water as he wills (17.1). Elijah's
pouring out of the water also provides a stark contrast to 17.3-16,
where Elijah, the widow, and her son had had a serious problem due
to the drought. If they had earlier suffered due to Yahweh's decision
to withhold water, now they and all the land will prosper due to
Yahweh's causing the rains to return.

In v. 38 the fire sent from Yahweh licks up the water in the trench.
The verb ותאכל, 'and it (the fire) devoured' had been applied to the
first four items consumed in v. 38. The use of a different verb, לחך (to
lick up) when the last item המים, 'the water' is mentioned highlights
and emphasizes the licking up of the water. This licking up of the
water serves to remind the reader of Yahweh's power to dry up the
waters of the land through a drought, a power Elijah had stressed in
the first words he spoke (17.1). Consequently, if in Canaanite
mythology it is claimed that Mot has the power to cause a drought by
slaying Baal, Yahweh's using fire to lick up the water in v. 38 is a
symbolic device used to assert that Yahweh, and not either Mot or
Baal, has the true power over the sending and withholding of
water.

When Elijah has the prophets of Baal slain, he takes them down to
the Brook Kishon, the main wadi flowing past Mt. Carmel. Since the
prime area of Baal's power was supposedly his ability to send rain, it
is appropriate that his prophets are slain by the wadi Kishon, one of
the many wadis affected by the drought. The reader is reminded that
Baal's prophets have been unable to arouse their deity and get him to
send the rains which would have filled the Brook Kishon and all
other wadis in the land.

These three incidents involving water in vv. 30-40 set the stage for
vv. 41-46 where Yahweh, who had earlier withheld the rains, and
who had sent down fire to lick up the water around the altar, now

acts as the true storm God who causes the rains to return. The climax of this scene comes in v. 45, where there is a torrential rain which breaks the prolonged drought and decisively demonstrates Yahweh's control over the rains. The writer employs several devices to lead up to that climax: he uses the verb עלה (to go up) to focus the reader's attention expectantly toward the skies; he delays the sending of the rain, holding the reader in suspense so that the coming of the rain may have more impact; he reintroduces Ahab, who has been absent since v. 20; and he once again uses the motif of eating and drinking. We will now examine each of these devices.

The verb עלה appears at the beginning of v. 41 and receives intensive use, being employed seven times in vv. 41-44. Elijah tells Ahab to go up (v. 41), and Ahab goes up (v. 42). Elijah then goes up to the top of Mt. Carmel (v. 42). Elijah commands his lad to go up and look toward the sea (v. 43), and he does. The lad eventually reports that a little cloud has gone up from the sea (v. 44), and Elijah immediately tells him to go up and speak to Ahab. In v. 40 Elijah had brought the prophets of Baal down (ירד) to the Brook Kishon in defeat, and his slaying them assured that they would not again challenge Yahweh. Their death brought to an end the claim that Baal was the storm god. With Baal thereby cleared away, the stage is set for the reader's attention to be directed heavenward toward the heavy rain which Yahweh will send. Mt. Carmel, which juts out into the Mediterranean and is the most commanding promontory in this part of Palestine, is also the scene where the contest has just been won. It is the obvious site for Ahab, Elijah, and the lad to ascend as the writer by that ascent has the reader looking to the heavens expectantly awaiting the rains. The lad's going up seven times to look out toward the sea (vv. 43-44) further directs the reader's attention toward the heavens, as does the tiny cloud which rises out of the sea (v. 44). The reader's attention will subsequently be directed downward, off the mountain and away from the skies, when the heavy rain falls (vv. 44-45).

As another means of building to the climax in v. 45, the writer reintroduces Ahab (v. 40), who has been absent since v. 20. The reader is led to wonder how the king who was presented as awe-inspiring and threatening in vv. 1-17 will respond to the defeat of Ba'al and the slaying of Baal's prophets. Obadiah's fear of Ahab (vv. 7-16) is still very much in the reader's mind. Ahab responds, however, very tamely, doing precisely what Elijah commands.[43] His deference toward Elijah, which began in v. 20 when he followed Elijah's

command and gathered all Israel to Mt. Carmel, will continue for the
duration of the story in chapters 17-19. The impression given is that
Ahab accepts the verdict of the contest, especially since the rains he
so desperately needed (18.3-6) are given. This regal submission
provides a striking contrast to Jezebel's response in 19.1-2.

The writer also builds the drama in vv. 41-44 by temporarily
postponing the rains and by having Elijah assume a relatively
inactive role until the rains come. Even though Elijah says in v.41
כי־קול המון הגשם, 'Because there is the sound of an approaching
rainstorm', until the end of v.44 there is nothing to suggest that the
rains are indeed approaching, and the reader may well wonder
whether Elijah's words are not overly optimistic. In vv.36-37 Elijah
had appealed fervently and directly to Yahweh to send fire from
heaven, and the fire had fallen immediately. In vv.41-44, however,
while Elijah does speak to Ahab and to the lad, he does not speak
even a word to Yahweh, and in fact assumes a physical posture (v.42)
connoting passivity while he waits for the rains.[44] Elijah seems
tentative and hesitant, and this leads the reader to wonder whether
the rains will really come. Furthermore, even though the lad's going
seven times to look out to the sea focuses the reader's attention on
the heavens, as noted earlier, it also focuses the reader's attention on
the absence of any sign of rain on all but the last of these trips. Even
the last trip produces only a little cloud, and one is left to wonder
momentarily if this pitiful cloud (עב קטנה ככף־איש, 'a small cloud like
a man's hand') is all there will be. Perhaps Yahweh, like Baal, is not
an effective storm god. Perhaps death has power over both of them,
power to prevent either from sending the rains.

Such suspicions with which the writer teases the reader disappear
as soon as Elijah's servant announces the small cloud. Upon hearing
these words Elijah abandons his passivity, announces the imminence
of a heavy rain, and orders[45] Ahab to go down (ירד) off the mountain
before the heavy rains stop him. Then, והשמים התקדרו עבים ורוח ויהי
גשם גדול, 'the heavens became dark with clouds and wind, and there
was a deluge' (v. 45). The writer's delaying the coming of the rains
since they were announced to Ahab in v. 41 heightens the dramatic
impact of the downpour when it arrives, as does also the stress on its
being a גשם גדול, 'a great rain'. Furthermore, the downpour in v. 45
also brings to an end a much longer wait for rain. In 18.1 Yahweh had
told Elijah ואתנה מטר על־פני האדמה, 'I will send rain upon the earth'.
While these words anticipate an end to the drought, the reader has to
wait a long time while the threat of death again expresses itself

powerfully in the first half of ch. 18, and while the contest is held that demonstrates that Yahweh is the living God. Only after all this has been completed is the time right for the rains to return. By using vv. 1 and 45 as a framework for all that happens in between, and by delaying until v. 45 the fulfillment of the promise given in v. 1, the writer skillfully builds the reader's sense of anticipation until the climactic moment of the sending of the deluge. If Yahweh's power as the storm God has been in question until that moment, it can be in question no more. Having won the contest with Baal through the sending of fire, he now sends rain to show that he, and not Baal, is the true storm God who is the source of life. The victory over both Baal and death is now complete, since Yahweh has shown that death cannot prevent him from sending the life-giving waters onto the land.

The coming of the deluge corroborates Elijah's words to Ahab in v. 41, where he had told him to עלה אכל ושתה, 'Go up, eat and drink'. Drought and the lack of food had been serious problems throughout chapters 17 and 18. Whether it was Elijah, the widow, and her son seeking food to sustain themselves (ch. 17), the prophets of Yahweh being kept alive with bread and water (18.4 and 13), or Ahab seeking pasturage for his own herd (18.3-6), food was very clearly in short supply (18.2). Only the prophets of Baal had a dependable source of food (18.19). Now, however, with them dead and their god shown to be powerless, it is fitting for the rains to return and to bring an abundant supply of food. Elijah's command to Ahab to eat and drink is thus a clear statement that the drought is over. Ahab henceforth need not show any concern regarding his eating or drinking, since there will soon be ample food.

The end of the scene (vv. 45 and 46) hints at the consequences that may follow from Yahweh's unquestioned victory. Ahab, in obedience to Elijah's command in v. 44, rides his chariot down to his summer residence at Jezreel, in the valley. Given Ahab's passivity before Elijah in vv. 41-44, one might easily conclude that Ahab will accept the verdict of the contest and henceforth worship Yahweh. He did not make any attempt to stop Elijah during the contest. He did not chastise him for mocking the prophets of Baal, he did not make fun of Elijah's preparations for the contest, and he made no effort to stop Elijah from slaying the prophets of Baal. Furthermore, he allows Elijah to run before his chariot all the way to Jezreel, thereby giving the appearance that Elijah now has royal sanction.

The writer is setting the stage for the dramatic reversal that will take place in ch. 19. Even though Yahweh and Elijah seemingly have won the day and have vanquished death, death will again assert itself strongly at the beginning of ch. 19 as Elijah crumbles before its threat. Just as death in the first part of ch. 18 had reasserted itself strongly after Yahweh had won a significant victory over it (17.17-24), so at the beginning of ch. 19 death will again pose a powerful threat to Yahweh. This time the threat will dramatically undercut the confidence of even Elijah, Yahweh's most faithful servant. In fact, one might say that Elijah's victorious run before Ahab to Jezreel could be seen as hubris in light of his subsequent wilting before the threat of death.

III. *The Victory Is Challenged—1 Kings 19*

Jezebel's sudden return to the story at the beginning of ch. 19 signals a dramatic change. Ahab's return to the story in 18.41 after an absence of 20 verses did not have much impact, with Ahab obediently following Elijah's orders. By contrast, Jezebel's return after her prolonged absence (since 18.13) resounds like a cannon shot in the narrative. Singlehandedly, she dramatically alters the course of events. Elijah, who had stood before the angry king of Israel (18.17) as an unrelenting and fearless supporter of Yahweh, and who had singlehandedly challenged and beaten 450 prophets of Baal, is transformed by Jezebel into a whimpering defeatist who desires that his own life be taken (19.4), seeing himself as the last prophet left who is faithful to Yahweh (19.10, 14).

In confronting Elijah so effectively, Jezebel serves once again, as she did in 18.4 and 13, as a powerful agent of death. Much of ch. 19 focuses on Elijah's fear of death, and Jezebel alone is the cause of that fear. Especially noteworthy is the way she changes Elijah, by her one brief message, into a figure who sounds very much like the fearful Obadiah Elijah had earlier ordered to go speak to Ahab (18.7-16). In contrast to Obadiah, who desperately tried to avoid speaking to Ahab, fearful that Ahab would put him to death, Elijah had stood as a pillar of strength. But now, after Jezebel's words, Elijah also is dominated by the fear of death. Just as the fear of death almost prevented Obadiah from being a faithful servant of Yahweh and doing Yahweh's will, so the fear of death causes Elijah in ch. 19 to lose sight of his mission as a prophet of Yahweh and to become consumed by self-pity and a powerful sense of defeat (19.4, 10, 14).

Yahweh's command to Elijah in 19.15 to be on his way and to do the business Yahweh requires of him sounds very much like Elijah's terse words to Obadiah in 18.15, which in effect tell Obadiah to quit blubbering and do what needs to be done. Thus, Jezebel's forceful words in 19.2 transform Elijah, the prophet who had been Yahweh's chief advocate in the struggle against death, into a victim of the fear of death who now appears to be incapable of doing what needs to be done on Yahweh's behalf.

A. *Scene 1: 'He Fled for His Life'—1 Kings 19.1-3*

There is a considerable contrast between the beginning of ch. 17 and the beginning of ch. 19. In ch. 17 Elijah confronted Ahab on behalf of Yahweh, directly challenging Baal and threatening the whole land by means of drought. His subsequent departure is more a hiding than a fleeing, and the food he receives both by the Brook Cherith and in the widow's house sustains the confident prophet until it is time to emerge for the contest in ch. 18. Elijah's courage is obvious, as in the words אל־תיראי, 'fear not' spoken to the widow in 17.13. In ch. 19, however, it is Jezebel the advocate of Baal who confronts Elijah, directly threatening his life and throwing him into a panic. His instant departure is definitely a flight and, as becomes obvious later in the chapter, his feeding by the angel (19.5-7) does not sustain him for future actions on Yahweh's behalf, but only gives him strength to utter his self-pitying complaints (19.10, 14). His lack of courage is frequently obvious, as in the word וירא, 'and he feared' (19.3).

There is also a significant contrast between the opening of ch. 18 and the beginning of ch. 19. In ch. 18 a word had come from Yahweh to Elijah, and Elijah was roused to decisive and victorious action against Ahab and the prophets of Baal. In ch. 19 the speech is from Jezebel to Elijah. Jezebel's threatening words do not, however, rouse Elijah to greater intensity in carrying out Yahweh's work (compare Ahab's ominous words in 18.17 which, if anything, seem to intensify the ardor of Elijah's devotion to Yahweh). Rather, her words to Elijah rouse him to flight. The message of death sent by Jezebel effectively immobilizes as a prophet of Yahweh the very one who had earlier been inspired by the word from Yahweh to show Yahweh's power over both Baal and death. That a message threatening death has so much power to affect Elijah is one means the writer has used to express again the power of death as a foe of Yahweh. Death, speaking through Jezebel, appears to have as much power to control Elijah as Yahweh did in 18.1-2.

In ch. 18 one means used to assert Yahweh's power over both Baal and death was Elijah's taking the defeated prophets of Baal down to the Brook Kishon, where he slew them. Death served as Yahweh's tool to subdue his foes. Jezebel's oath in 19.2, however, calls all that into question. Vowing by the gods, presumably including the very ones Yahweh has just confronted in ch. 18, Jezebel threatens אשים את־נפשך כנפש אחד מהם, 'I will make your life like the life of one of them'. For Elijah to be made like one of the dead prophets of Baal would mean that Yahweh does not have control over death, as ch. 18 seemed to indicate, but rather that Yahweh's prophets are as subject to the threat of death as Baal's. Elijah's instant flight from Jezebel after he is told her oath suggests that he is not at all sure that Yahweh has the power to deliver him from death. His bold confidence from ch. 18 has melted away.

The writer, who at times slowed the pace of his narrative considerably in order to make a point (as in 18.30-35), has in 19.1-3 accelerated the action to emphasize dramatically the challenge death again poses to Yahweh. In 18.46 Elijah the servant of Yahweh had been running in victory before Ahab's chariot as the king returned to Jezreel, apparently accepting the outcome of the contest. By 19.3, only three verses later, Elijah has already passed through Beer-sheba, which lies many miles south of the border of the Northern Kingdom, and is well on his way into the wilderness of Sinai. The writer stresses this sudden, overpowering change in Elijah's character by the quickness with which the writer moves from sub-scene to sub-scene within vv. 1-3, giving only very brief treatment to each unit. After Ahab describes the way in which Elijah had killed all the prophets with the sword (v. 1), Jezebel immediately sends a messenger to Elijah, vowing that she will have his life before another day passes (v. 2). Jezebel's quick and decisive reaction makes the threat she poses to Elijah seem even more powerful.

Elijah's response to the threat is also immediate, but hardly worthy of the prophet we have seen up to now. There are three consecutive verbs at the beginning of v. 3: וירא, 'And he feared', ויקם, 'And he arose', וילך, 'And he fled'. This rapid-fire sequence of three verbs depicts sudden, animated, terrified activity by Elijah in response to Jezebel's threat, fleeing without even a slight hesitation. The threefold use of ו, 'and', helps stress the rapidity and urgency of Elijah's flight, as does the fact that he is immediately seen passing

, through the fairly distant city of Beer-sheba. The urgency of his flight is also emphasized by the phrase אל־נפשו, 'for his life', which follows וילך and reminds the reader that Elijah is fleeing not only from Jezebel, but also from the threat death poses through her.

In three short verses the writer has totally changed the flow of the story. Victory seems to be transformed into defeat, the brave prophet into a cowering refugee, and the victory over death and Baal into an opportunity for death to reassert itself through Jezebel's oath to take Elijah's life. The next sections of ch. 19 (vv. 4-8, 9-18) flesh out the radical change that has come about in Elijah's character, and the efforts by Yahweh to restore Elijah to his role as a prophet.

B. *Scene 2: 'Arise and Eat'—1 Kings 19.4-8*

After the fast-moving action of vv. 1-3, and especially after Elijah's lightning retreat from Jezebel's threat, the pace slows considerably in vv. 4-8. Elijah journeys a day into the wilderness south of Beer-sheba, and sits down under a tree. The prophet who has struggled so valiantly against death in chapters 17 and 18 now wishes to surrender to death: רב עתה יהוה קח נפשי כי־לא־טוב אנכי מאבתי, 'It is enough, O Yahweh: take my life, for I am no better off than my fathers'. Elijah is clearly torn. On the one hand, he thinks enough of preserving his life to abandon his role as Yahweh's prophet before Ahab and launch a desperate flight for survival into the wilderness. On the other, he feels that all is lost. Just as his fathers are dead, so he too is as good as dead, and he asks Yahweh to proceed with the inevitable. Clearly these are the words of one who has abandoned hope, who seems to feel that his temporary escape from Jezebel is only a brief reprieve from her vow to bring about his death. His words also imply that all is lost for the cause of Yahweh, a point that will be developed in vv. 10 and 14.

Significantly, Yahweh's response is not powerful and dramatic, as it was in the two scenes which conclude ch. 18, but is rather low-key and simple throughout most of the chapter. It is as if Yahweh, having established his authority in ch. 18, chooses to avoid any additional display of his power (cf. vv. 11-12). Also, Elijah's words at the end of v. 4 appear to be baiting Yahweh, seeing if he will respond dramatically to Elijah's self-pity.[46] Yahweh does not take the bait, but responds to Elijah through very basic, non-miraculous means.

The stage on which ch. 19 is played out is intimate and restricted, unlike ch. 18, where all Israel observed and reacted to the spectacular

series of events. In this sense, ch. 19 resembles ch. 17, where the cast
of characters was also small and intimate. The strength of Yahweh's
power as the God of life who has overcome death is demonstrated, as
in ch. 17, in the lives of individuals.

His complaint and request in v. 4 having gone unheeded, Elijah
lies down under the tree and sleeps. As he sleeps, an angel (מלאך)
touches him and says קום אכול, 'Arise and eat'. This simple action by
the angel is pregnant with meaning, and ties in to a number of earlier
scenes. In v. 2 Jezebel had sent a messenger (מלאך) to Elijah with
words of death. The messenger (מלאך) in v. 5, however, is a
messenger of life, bringing Elijah the life-sustaining food he will need
in the wilderness. This comparison of the two messengers is
strengthened through the use of the verb קום, 'to rise, stand up'. In
v. 3, after Elijah had heard the words of Jezebel's messenger of death,
he arose (קום) to flee for his life. In v. 5 the messenger brings life,
urging Elijah to arise (קום) and eat. These words of the messenger to
Elijah in v. 5 also echo Elijah's words to Ahab in 18.41. There, Elijah
had used three imperatives (עלה, אכל, and שתה) to tell Ahab to rise up
to eat and drink. Yahweh's victory as the God of life had been won,
the rains were imminent, and Elijah had told Ahab to recognize the
lifting of the drought by eating and drinking. How things have
changed by 19.4! Now an angel from Yahweh must attempt to arouse
the despondent prophet who had earlier been so confident and
assertive. It is rather ironic that Elijah, who earlier as a messenger for
Yahweh had been so eloquent and effective in speaking and acting on
behalf of his God, asserting Yahweh's power as the God of life, is
himself now in need of a messenger to strengthen him and help him
believe that death has not won the final victory.

The messenger strengthens and encourages Elijah in the struggle
against death not by any bold pronouncement or decisive action,
such as Elijah had presented in ch. 18, but by the simple act of
feeding him. The scene is very domestic and intimate, as when a
member of the household touches (נגע) the sleeping person to arouse
him to a meal. Thus, the messenger asserts that Yahweh is the God
of life simply by performing an everyday task that is necessary if life
is to continue. If Elijah wishes to give in to death, the messenger, by
preparing food for Elijah, gently but firmly suggests that Elijah
should not succumb to death so readily.

Verse 6 is reminiscent of the scene in 17.8-16. There, in the face of
a severe threat from death posed through the drought, Yahweh had
sustained the widow, her son, and Elijah by means of the jar of meal

and the vessel of oil. When Elijah had first come to the widow, he had asked her for water and a morsel of bread, the minimum necessary to sustain life. This is precisely what the messenger now prepares for him in 19.6. In 17.8-16 the widow, her son, and Elijah had their lives preserved by Yahweh in a simple but vital way while the forces of death seemed powerful through the drought. Similarly, in 19.4-8 Elijah is being encouraged to see the hand of Yahweh giving life not only through dramatic events and demonstrations of power, as in ch. 18, but also by satisfying his people's daily needs even as the forces of death rage against them. Elijah is being encouraged to seek life, and not to give in to death, precisely because Yahweh will sustain him despite the threat that death has posed through Jezebel.

Elijah eats and drinks, and again lies down to sleep. This underlines once more Elijah's passivity, his unwillingness to carry any further the battle against Jezebel and death, even though Yahweh, through the angel, has given him a message of life by feeding him. There is a direct parallelism between the two verbs at the beginning of v. 5, וישכב, 'and he lay', ויישן, 'and he slept', and the two verbs at the end of v. 6, וישב, 'and he (re)turned', וישכב, 'and he slept'. This parallelism indicates that Elijah continues to be unresponsive even after Yahweh's attempt to encourage him through the giving of food and water. This unresponsiveness is strengthened by the use of the four verb cluster at the end of v. 6. There was a verb cluster earlier, in v. 3, after Jezebel had sent a messenger to Elijah indicating she would bring about his death. There we were told וירא ויקם וילך אל-נפשו, 'Then he feared and he arose and fled for his life'. Elijah's response to the message of death was instant, animated activity. He took the messenger of death very seriously. At the end of v. 6, however, he seems unaffected by the messenger who brings life: ויאכל וישת וישב וישכב, 'And he ate and drank, and turned and slept'. Elijah simply eats and drinks and resumes sleeping, which is what he had been doing (v. 5) after asking Yahweh to take his life. Thus, the use of the verb clusters at the beginning of v. 3 and the end of v. 6, in conjunction with the messenger of death (v. 2) and the messenger of life (vv. 5-6), serve to underline at this point in the narrative Elijah's capitulation to the threat of death. In fact, Elijah's repeated inclination to sleep indicates that death has gained control of him (cf. 18.27), and has turned him from an active, enthusiastic supporter of Yahweh into a passive, fearful defeatist.

It is necessary for the messenger of life to return. Again he comes (v. 7) and touches Elijah, commanding him to arise (קום) and eat

(אכל). The repetition of the two verbs קום and אכל, which appeared also in v. 5, strengthens the emphasis on Yahweh as the God of life who provides life-giving nourishment for his people. This time, however, the messenger gives added instructions: כי רב ממך הדרך, 'Else the journey will be too much for you'. This new element, the arduous journey for which Elijah will have to build up his strength by eating, raises a question in the reader's mind. Where will Elijah be journeying? He had earlier undertaken a hasty, frantic flight from Jezebel. Will he now be journeying back to Israel?

Verse 8 provides the answer, as Elijah journeys to הר האלהים חרב, 'the mountain of God, Horeb'. This verse begins with a cluster of four verbs: ויקם ויאכל וישתה וילך, 'And he arose and he ate and he drank and he went'. The first two verbs, which echo the words of the angel in vv. 5 and 7, indicate Elijah's compliance a second time with the imperatives spoken to him by the angel. This second obedience to the command that he arise and eat seems to imply that Elijah is moving away from the negative attitude expressed in v. 4, where he had asked that Yahweh take his life. That impression is strengthened by the last verb וילך, 'and he went', which indicates that Elijah has abandoned his self-pitying passivity and has undertaken the long journey to Horeb, the mountain of God, strengthened by the messenger's life-giving nourishment.

There is a direct parallelism between v. 8 and v. 3. In v. 3, after the message of death from Jezebel caused Elijah to fear, he arose (ויקם) and fled for his life (וילך אל-נפשו). In v. 8 the same verbs, קום and הלך are used, except now Elijah rises not in fear of Jezebel and death, but in order to eat and drink the food provided by Yahweh and to undertake his journey. At this point he no longer appears to be fleeing from death, but rather to be traveling to Horeb, the holy mountain where Yahweh, the God of life, made the covenant with his people Israel. Thus, the impression given in v. 8 is that for Elijah the tide has turned, and he is again willing to be fed and strengthened by God and to do God's will.

Verses 4-9 contain allusions to Israel's years of wandering after the exodus from Egypt. Elijah, like Israel, journeys into the wilderness (v. 4). Just as Israel was sustained in the wilderness with food sent from God, so is Elijah (vv. 5-8). Israel's wandering 40 years in the wilderness is paralleled by Elijah's 40 day journey to Mt. Horeb (v. 8), where Israel under Moses' leadership received Yahweh's covenant law. And, just as Yahweh appears to Israel at Mt. Horeb, so he appears to Elijah (v. 9). These parallels between Israel's years in the wilderness and Elijah's trip to Horeb could suggest that Elijah is going to Mt. Horeb to receive strength by visiting the site of Israel's first covenant with Yahweh, and perhaps to see how that covenant might be renewed in light of the victory of Yahweh in ch. 18.[47] These parallels also seem to reinforce the implication mentioned earlier that by the end of v. 8 Elijah has recovered from the threat of death posed by Jezebel, and is now ready to resume his role as a prophet.

C. Scene 3: 'I Only Am Left'—1 Kings 19.9-18

Verse 9 begins the next scene in a straightforward fashion, with no surprises. Elijah arrives at Mt. Horeb and lodges in a cave. The word of Yahweh (דבר־יהוה) then comes to him and asks a simple question, מה־לך פה אליהו, 'What are you doing here, Elijah?' At this point in the narrative, the question is reasonable, especially since the reader has received no direct indication of Elijah's reason for journeying to Mt. Horeb. Given the structure of vv. 4-8, in which Elijah appears to be weaned gradually from his intense fear of Jezebel and death, the reader expects Elijah to provide an answer describing some noble purpose for his trip to Horeb, a purpose tied to his role as a prophet of Yahweh. The writer has thus set up the reader for the surprising answer Elijah gives in v. 10: קנא קנאתי ליהוה אלהי צבאות כי־עזבו בריתך בני ישראל את־מזבחתיך הרסו ואת־נביאיך הרגו בחרב ואותר אני לבדי ויבקשו את־נפשי לקחתה, 'Indeed, I have been very zealous for Yahweh, the God of hosts, because the people of Israel have forsaken your covenant, torn down your altars, and slain your prophets with the sword. And I, I alone, am left, and they seek my life, to take it.' Now the reason for Elijah's trip to Horeb is clear. He has not come to Horeb to do Yahweh's will: rather, he is still fleeing from Jezebel and seeking Yahweh's pity (cf. v. 4). As Elijah's words make plain, the angel's twofold feeding of the prophet did not shore up Elijah's courage and renew his trust in the power of Yahweh as the God of life. Rather, he seems as despondent as he was in 19.3-4. He has come to Horeb to bemoan the downfall of Yahweh, the slaying of Yahweh's prophets, and his own sorry fate as one marked for death. It is as if the victory in ch. 18 had never taken place.

Elijah's assessment of the situation in 19.10 does not accord with the events described previously. He says that the people of Israel have forsaken Yahweh's covenant. That is very similar to Elijah's charge against Israel in 18.21. Yet, after Yahweh sent down fire to consume the offering, the people immediately fell on their faces and twice said יהוה הוא האלהים, 'Yahweh, he is God'. Thus, it looks as if Israel has been called back to the covenant relationship by Yahweh's decisive victory. Likewise, Elijah says that the people of Israel have thrown down Yahweh's altars. While it is true that 18.30 said that the altar of Yahweh on Mt. Carmel had been thrown down, Elijah had rebuilt the altar with 12 stones representing the 12 sons of Jacob (18.31-32). This, along with Israel's confession in 18.39, would seem to indicate that the throwing down of Yahweh's altars should no longer be a problem. Also, Elijah says that Israel has killed Yahweh's prophets with the sword. While 18.4 and 13 mention Jezebel's efforts to cut off the prophets of Yahweh, in 18.40 Elijah ordered the people of Israel to seize the prophets of Baal and not let one of them escape. All 450 were then put to death beside the Brook Kishon, as Ahab reports to Jezebel in 19.1. It is the prophets of Baal, not the prophets of Yahweh, who are killed by Israel. These events in the last half of ch. 18 depict Israel as a people prepared to re-commit themselves to a covenant relationship with Yahweh, and show Baal's forces reeling from the devastating slaughter of Baal's prophets at Elijah's command. Therefore, Elijah's assessment in 19.10 is totally unrealistic, especially if one takes into account the resumption of the rains by Yahweh in 18.41-46. The only reason Elijah has for such negativism is the threat by Jezebel to Elijah's life (19.2). Yet, that reason alone is powerful enough to reverse completely Elijah's assessment of the struggle between Yahweh and his foes. Here we have yet another example of the way in which the writer of chapters 17–19 presents death as a serious challenge to Yahweh's power. In this instance, death works through Jezebel to deny Yahweh the services of his most powerful and successful prophet.

Elijah's despondency is intensified by the last words in 19.10. He complains ואותר אני לבדי, 'And I am left, I, I alone'. The repeated use of the first person in each of these three words, and the emphasis on לבדי, 'I alone' highlights Elijah's sense that he is the only one still faithful to Yahweh. He then asserts that even this prophetic remnant is in danger, since ויבקשו את-נפשי לקחתה, 'they seek my life, to take it'. As with his previous words, Elijah's assessment of the situation is unrealistic. Elijah is not the last prophet left to Yahweh. 18.4 and 13 had referred to one hundred prophets of Yahweh whom Obadiah had hidden in a cave (מערה) to protect them from Jezebel. As if to remind the reader of that fact, in 19.9 the writer mentions Elijah's sleeping in a cave (מערה) on Mt. Horeb, also seeking sanctuary from Jezebel, and in 19.13 depicts Elijah going out to stand at the entrance to the cave. Yahweh later refers (19.18) to seven thousand people in Israel who have not bowed the knee to Baal. Thus, not only does Elijah in 19.10 fail to take account of the significant victory Yahweh had won in ch. 18; he also seriously underestimates the support left to Yahweh.

Were Elijah's words, which are filled with self-pity, designed to call forth another demonstration of Yahweh's power, as in the calling down of fire from heaven to consume the offering?[48] If so, the words fail, since Yahweh's answer is not given by means of power.

Yahweh commands Elijah (v. 11) צא ועמדת בהר לפני יהוה, 'Go out and stand on the mountain before Yahweh'. Earlier, when Elijah had announced to Ahab the coming of the drought (17.1), he had boldly proclaimed that he was speaking on behalf of Yahweh 'before whom I stand' (אשר עמדתי לפניו). As the words in 19.11 trigger the reader's memory of the words in 17.1, quite a contrast is evident. The prophet who had courageously presented himself to Ahab as Yahweh's prophet and had both ushered in the drought and subsequently destroyed the prophets of Baal is now to stand again before Yahweh after he has crumbled in the face of the threat of death posed by Jezebel. If, as elsewhere in the prophetic tradition (1 Kgs 22.19; Isa. 6), Elijah's claim to have stood in Yahweh's presence (17.1) signaled his call and commission as a prophet, 19.11-18 presents Yahweh's futile attempt to recommission a very intimidated prophet. Thus, the striking contrast between Elijah's first standing before Yahweh (17.1) and his second standing before Yahweh (19.11) convincingly emphasizes the success that Jezebel and death have had in undermining Elijah's courage.

As Elijah stands before Yahweh this second time, he experiences three awesome demonstrations of power. A great and powerful wind tears the mountains and breaks rocks in pieces. Then there is an earthquake, and finally a fire. Significantly, after each of these phenomena, there is the phrase לא ב . . . . יהוה, 'But Yahweh was not in the . . .'. The text clearly implies that, while there have been three demonstrations of power, Yahweh has chosen not to assert himself through any of them. Especially significant is the fact that fire, the last phenomenon to be mentioned, is precisely the means used in 18.38 to assert Yahweh's victory so emphatically in the contest with Baal. If Yahweh in 19.12 is not in the fire, as he was in ch. 18, the message to Elijah would appear to be that, as a prophet of Yahweh carrying out the struggle against Baal, he cannot always expect

dramatic divine intervention in support of his efforts, but rather
must learn to deal with the difficulties his role will present by using
more conventional means. If Elijah's negative attitude in vv. 4 and 10
reflects his despondency that Jezebel was able to express such a
powerful threat to his life even after the decisive victory of Yahweh
on Mt. Carmel, Yahweh's declining to be involved with the
demonstrations of power in 19.11-12 gives a clear message that Elijah
cannot expect routinely to call on Yahweh's power in order to
overwhelm his foes.

The point is strengthened by the words (19.12) ואחר האש קול דממה
דקה, 'And after the fire a calm, small voice'. After all the spectacular
demonstrations (vv. 11 & 12) in which Yahweh has had no part, he
chooses to speak to Elijah in a very calm, ordinary manner, away
from the masses of Israel and apart from any miraculous occurrence
that would counter Jezebel's threat. At this point, for Yahweh to
speak in a still, small voice is hardly what Elijah wants, for it is not
much better than what the impotent Baal was (un)able to muster in
the contest on Mt. Carmel. The prophets of Baal in ch. 18 had been
mocked for being unable to generate even a voice (קול) from Ba'al,
and now Yahweh seems barely able to do even that. Is it any wonder
that, by Elijah's standards, Yahweh seems helpless against the forces
of death, and Elijah subsequently (v. 14) feels it necessary to repeat
his earlier complaint from v. 10. It is as if he assumes Yahweh is no
longer able to help, or perhaps didn't understand Elijah's complaint
the first time.

Yahweh's response in a still, small voice corresponds quite well,
however, with Yahweh's earlier response to Elijah in 19.5-7. After
Elijah's words in v. 4, which appeared to be a direct challenge to
Yahweh either to take Elijah's life or to do something dramatic and
save him from his plight, Yahweh chose to do neither. Instead, he
elected to preserve Elijah's life simply by feeding him, an unspectacular
but nevertheless vital activity which directly parallels Yahweh's
efforts to preserve Elijah's life in 17.1-16 by feeding him during the
life-threatening drought.

However, the message conveyed in v. 12 through the still, small
voice falls on deaf ears as Elijah continues his complaining self-pity.
After Yahweh had countered Elijah's complaining by feeding him in
vv. 5-7, Elijah appeared to be strengthened and traveled all the way
to Mt. Horeb. However, once there, he resumed his complaining
(v. 10), Yahweh's efforts to sustain his life clearly having made no
impact. After Yahweh had made his point more emphatically by

declining to be present in the wind, earthquake, and fire, he repeated
word for word (v. 13) the question asked of Elijah in v. 9, מה־לך פה
אליהו, 'What are you doing here, Elijah?' The tone of the question,
especially when it is now asked for the second time, implies that
Elijah really ought not to be at Mt. Horeb complaining, but rather
back doing what he was sent to do among the people of Israel. By
repeating the question word for word from v. 9, the writer intensifies
its force, and creates in the reader an expectation that perhaps now
Elijah will have recovered sufficiently from his fear of death to be
willing to return to the land of Israel and continue his role as a
prophet. However, Yahweh's persistence in asking the question is
countered by Elijah's equally intense persistence in the way he
answers the question. Elijah repeats word for word in v. 14 the
response he gave in v. 10. In fact, Elijah's persistence appears to be
more powerful than Yahweh's simply because of the length and force
of his answer. As each word familiar to the reader from v. 10 is
uttered, the impression grows that Yahweh's efforts to convince
Elijah in vv. 11-13 have been completely in vain. Elijah fears death as
much as ever, and appears unwilling to trust a God who chooses to
speak not through power, but through a still, small voice.

The writer has chosen to use the words ויבקשו את־נפשי לקחתה, 'And
they seek my life, to take it' in both v. 10 and v. 14 as a key means to
underline the threat that death poses to Yahweh by its ability to
intimidate his followers and prevent them from doing Yahweh's will.
The writer uses end stress to heighten the impact of the words, since
in both v. 10 and in v. 14 this fear of death is the last thing Elijah
expresses. Despite Yahweh's attempts to reassure Elijah, his fear of
death is as strong at the end of Yahweh's attempts to shore up and
strengthen him (v. 14) as it was when he first expressed this fear
(vv.3-4).

A comparison of the Obadiah narrative of 18.7-16 with the
narrative in 19.3-14 indicates that Elijah's fear of death is just as
intense and persistent as was Obadiah's. Obadiah's fear of death did
not diminish as the dialog continued, but was as strong at the end as
it was at the beginning, as indicated by his concluding word (18.14)
והרגני, 'And he will kill me.' Likewise, Elijah's fear of death in 19.3-14
does not diminish, but is expressed quite forcefully in his concluding
words in v. 14. This direct parallelism between Obadiah in 18.7-16
and Elijah in 19.3-14 indicates that Elijah has switched roles. In 18.7-
16 Elijah's stony resolve in the face of the threat posed by death stood
in stark contrast to Obadiah's timorous pleading. In chapter 19,

however, Elijah has become Obadiah, being intimidated by the fear of death at the hands of Jezebel, just as Obadiah feared death from another royal figure, Ahab. In 19.3-14 Yahweh must play Elijah's former role, being the pillar of strength who ensures that others do not give in to the threat of death.

That Yahweh in 19.3-14 plays Elijah's role from the Obadiah scene may be seen by the use of the verb הלך and closely associated verbs in the two scenes. In 18.8 Elijah had used the imperative form לך, 'Go!' in commanding Obadiah to reveal Elijah's presence to Ahab. Twice (vv. 11, 14) Obadiah incredulously repeated this command, expressing his fear that compliance would lead to his death (see also 18.12). Only after Elijah takes an oath (v. 15), boldly declaring once again that he, Elijah, will confront the much-feared Ahab, does Obadiah go (v. 16, וילך, 'And he went') to deliver the message to Ahab. In the scene in ch. 19 Elijah also goes (וילך, vv. 3, 4), but his travel is a flight in terror from Jezebel. No longer is Elijah urging courageous action on behalf of Yahweh. Rather, Yahweh has to urge Elijah to rouse himself and abandon his despondency. Twice Yahweh commands the recumbent prophet to arise (קום, vv. 5, 7: note the imperative). In v. 11 he commands Elijah to go forth (צא, another imperative) to see the demonstrations in vv. 11 and 12. When even this last attempt by Yahweh to penetrate Elijah's resistance fails, Yahweh gets quite firm with Elijah (v. 15), commanding him to go (לך, in the imperative) anoint three figures who will oppose the Baal-sponsoring house of Omri, just as Elijah had earlier been firm with Obadiah and through an oath had forced him to go to Ahab.

These parallels between the fearful Obadiah in ch. 18 and the fearful Elijah in ch. 19 underline a key point in ch. 19. As the sequence of events had developed in the struggle against death, Yahweh seemed to have carried the day in ch. 18 with his decisive victory and his sending of the life-giving rains. Elijah, who had been bold and outspoken in his advocacy of Yahweh's cause, seemed to have crushed Baal and his prophets. However, with Jezebel's threat to take Elijah's life, the narrative suddenly reaches its nadir. Even the most devoted servant of Yahweh has crumbled under the impact of death's threat. The parallels between the Obadiah scene in 18.7-16 and the scene of Elijah's fear in 19.3-14 help emphasize the power of death's threat, since death has now been able to intimidate the very prophet who earlier had been a tower of strength and had resolutely, indeed, almost disdainfully, brushed aside Obadiah's very human fear of death and had insisted on carrying forward the struggle with

Baal and death. It may have taken death some time to undermine Elijah's resolve, but once Elijah's resistance to the threat of death weakens, his collapse is devastating. Thus, when the reader finishes 19.14, Yahweh's supporters seem vastly weaker than they had been earlier when Obadiah had been overcome by his fear of death.

As the reader moves to v. 15, where Yahweh gives his command to Elijah, the reader must wonder what can be done to provide supporters for Yahweh's cause. Despite the impressive victory on Mt. Carmel and the sending of the rains, death appears to have the upper hand, since it has claimed even the previously-impregnable Elijah. If Elijah's claim that he alone is left as a servant to Yahweh is true, his sudden but persistent weakness appears to be a grave blow.

In the context of Elijah's fear and hesitancy, Yahweh's words in v. 15 ring out with clarity and resolve: לך שוב, 'Go! Return!' Earlier, Yahweh had asked Elijah (vv. 9, 13) מה־לך פה אליהו, 'What are you doing here, Elijah?' implying, especially the second time the question is asked, that Elijah should be back in Israel doing Yahweh's work, rather than hiding in the wilderness and complaining. Elijah's words in vv. 10 and 14 give no indication that he intends to resume his mission, despite attempts by Yahweh in vv. 5-7 and 11-12 to redirect Elijah's thinking. Yahweh's words to Elijah in v. 15 are therefore quite directive, leaving no room for disagreement by Elijah. He is sent out of the wilderness and is given specific missions to perform on Yahweh's behalf. Thus, Yahweh's words 'Go!' and 'Return!' indicate that at this point Yahweh is tired of coddling the prophet. He demands some action.

Significantly, not a word is said to Elijah to reassure him about his personal safety. Just as Elijah had earlier brushed aside Obadiah's rambling objection to going to Ahab, so Yahweh brushes aside Elijah's often-repeated complaint that his life is in danger and sends him on another mission, fraught with as much danger as previous ones. He is directed to anoint Hazael to be king over Syria, and Jehu to be king over Israel. Anointing a new king would have been seen by the king currently in power as a revolutionary activity, and could result in dire consequences for Elijah. In light of Elijah's lack of resolve in ch. 19, it is not surprising that Elijah never carried out these two directives, leaving them instead to his successor Elisha (2 Kgs 8.13; 9.1-3).

Chapter 19, however, does not deal with Elijah's failure to anoint Hazael and Jehu, but focuses on the new means by which Yahweh will counter his foes. In ch. 17, where Yahweh first confronted Ahab through the words of Elijah, there is no talk about a termination of Ahab's dynasty. Rather, the focus is on demonstrating that Yahweh, not Baal, is god. That focus continues in ch. 18, as Yahweh wins the contest with Baal and Ahab seems to show tacit acceptance of Yahweh's victory. After Jezebel strikes back, however, in ch. 19, Yahweh demonstrates a different attitude toward Ahab's dynasty, commanding that a new king be anointed (19.16), predicting the downfall of Ahab's dynasty (21.21-24), and deceiving Ahab so that he will fall on the battlefield (22.19-23). While the last two references carry us beyond 1 Kings 17-19, the directions given to Elijah in 19.15-18 already signal a change in approach by Yahweh from earlier actions, a change which will continue through the end of the Elijah–Elisha cycle.

How does the command to Elijah in vv. 15-18 relate to Yahweh's speaking to Elijah earlier through קול דממה דקה, 'a calm, small voice?' Even if vv. 15-18 do not imply the use of the forces of nature, as in vv. 11-12, they do imply a great deal of force and violence. It would be almost impossible for new kings to be anointed and to reach for the throne without there being bloodshed and warfare. Verse 17 makes this explicit when, in discussing Hazael, Jehu, and Elisha, it states והיה הנמלט מחרב חזאל ימית יהוא והנמלט מחרב יהוא ימית אלישע, 'The one who escapes from the sword of Hazael will be killed by Jehu, and the one who escapes from the sword of Jehu will be killed by Elisha'. This is anything but a 'calm, small voice'. How are we to reconcile vv. 11-12 with vv. 15-18?[49]

The answer lies within Elijah. That Yahweh does not avoid the use of power and violence may be seen repeatedly in the Elijah–Elisha stories, as in 1 Kgs 18.20-40; 19.17; 21.23-24; 2 Kgs 9.36-37; and even the rather bizarre story in 2 Kgs 1.9-16. Elijah, however, appears to want victory without risk, and capitulates at the first sign of a serious threat to his own person. He is willing to challenge Ahab, mock the prophets of Baal, and slay 450 of them when he feels he has Yahweh's support, but he is not willing to carry the battle further if he himself is in serious danger. Even though Ahab and Elijah had been adversaries in ch. 17 and throughout most of ch. 18, Ahab had never directly threatened Elijah's life, and Elijah had been bold in Ahab's presence. Jezebel, however, does threaten Elijah's life, and very effectively brings into the open Elijah's innermost fears.

Thus, Elijah understands and desires the powerful side of Yahweh, the side which can dramatically defeat the enemy, but he cannot cope with the long term struggles and difficulties that must be handled, especially if these difficulties threaten his life. Elijah seems incapable of understanding that the forces of Baal will fight back, and will sometimes win. Elijah's words in 19.4, 10, and 14 imply that Elijah wants a victory that is immediate, unambiguous, and clear-cut, one that would give him unquestioned status as the victorious prophet who had earned a seat of respect in the king's court. Significantly, after the victory had been achieved in 18.36-38, and before Jezebel's blunt words burst his bubble and threw him into a panic, Elijah began to act like an accepted prophet in Ahab's court, giving Ahab explicit directions and displaying himself prominently in front of Ahab's chariot all the way back to Jezreel (18.41-46). The impression is that Elijah presumes that the struggle between Yahweh and Baal is over.

Unfortunately for Elijah, not only do the events of ch. 19 make it clear that the battle is not over; the theophany in 19.11-12 points out that Yahweh will not always be there with fire, wind, and earthquake to support his adherents, as the small, quiet voice in v. 12 indicates. The directions to Elijah in 19.15-18 declare that the battle with Baal will be bloody, dangerous, and long.

Verse 18 points out that, if Elijah has underestimated the difficulty of achieving complete victory, he has also greatly underestimated the resilience and number of Yahweh's adherents. The declaration in v. 18 that there are seven thousand left in Israel כל הברכים אשר לא־כרעו לבעל וכל־הפה אשר לא־נשק לו, 'all the knees which have not bent to Baal, and all the mouths which have not kissed him', strongly counters Elijah's previous claims that he alone is left as an advocate of Yahweh (ואותר אני לבדי, 'And I am left, I, I alone', 19.10, 14, and the slight variant in 18.22, אני נותרתי נביא ליהוה לבדי, 'And I, I am left, I alone, a prophet to Yahweh'). Thus, in 19.18 Elijah is shown to have thought too much of himself, not only by claiming that he alone is left as an advocate of Yahweh, but also by placing too much emphasis on his own role in the struggle against Baal, as if without him the struggle could not be carried on. Elijah's opening words in vv. 10 and 14, קנא קנאתי ליהוה, 'Indeed, I have been very zealous for Yahweh' had emphasized Elijah's high view of his own importance in the struggle, as is indicated especially by the use of the infinitive קנא. The words in v. 18 show, however, that the struggle with Baal will take place even if Elijah continues to demonstrate the fear and negativism he has shown throughout ch. 19. That the struggle can be carried on without Elijah is also indicated by the word תחתיך, 'in your place', which follows the instructions to Elijah to anoint Elisha as a prophet (v. 16).

Thus, in vv. 3-14 Elijah's view is that all is lost, and Yahweh might as well take his life (v. 4), since he is the only prophet of Yahweh left (vv. 10, 14). This negativism arises because Jezebel fights back effectively on behalf of the forces of Baal, undermining Elijah's view that the victory against Baal has been won and the struggle is over. The words of Yahweh to Elijah in vv. 15-18 declare that the struggle with Baal will be a long one, will entail the efforts of two new kings and a new prophet, and will be based on the solid support Yahweh still has among the 'seven thousand in Israel'.

If death has posed a serious threat to Yahweh through its intimidation of Elijah in vv. 3-14, vv. 15-18 emphasize once again Yahweh's power over death and his use of death to his purposes. This is accomplished not only by the command to Elijah to stop dwelling on the threat of death and take some action, but also by the stress on Yahweh's use of death against the supporters of Baal. Verse 17 emphasizes Hazael, Jehu, and Elisha's inflicting death on the enemy. Twice the attempt of the enemy to escape is mentioned (הנמלט, 'the one who escapes'), indicating that the foe will be fleeing from these three. Twice the sword (חרב) of these figures is mentioned, and twice it is indicated that they will slay (ימית, 'he will slay') the foe. This emphasis on Yahweh's use of death against the forces of Baal parallels the last half of ch. 18, wherein Yahweh also uses death as a tool against Baal. In both chapters 18 and 19 death initially poses a serious threat to Yahweh's power, but this threat is subsequently reversed as death becomes Yahweh's tool, in ch. 18 serving to express vividly Baal's condition (vv. 26-29) and being Yahweh's means of countering the threat posed by the prophets of Baal (v. 40), and in ch. 19 serving as the means whereby the three figures to be anointed will counter the forces of Baal.

The ability of Yahweh to counter the threat posed by death is also emphasized by v. 18. Even though Elijah implies that all Israel has forsaken Yahweh (vv. 10, 14), v. 18 makes it plain that 7000 persons have not gone over to Baal. Given Jezebel's intense efforts to kill and intimidate the followers of Yahweh (18.4, 13; 19.3), the figure of 7000 persons loyal to Yahweh despite that threat shows Yahweh's ability to counter the threat posed by death. He maintains a cadre of loyal followers even after Jezebel has done her worst. The combination of the numbers seven and 1000 in the figure 7000 adds to the impression of the large size of Yahweh's loyalists, since both seven and 1000 frequently serve as symbols of wholeness or completeness.[50] Thus, if death in 19.1-14 has countered Yahweh's victory from ch. 18 by immobilizing Yahweh's champion, in 19.15-18 Yahweh responds by choosing three new figures who will carry on the battle against the Baalistic Israelite dynasty and by calling on the strength of the many Israelites who are still loyal to him.

Elijah's role in ch. 19 has been very different than in ch. 18. In ch. 18 he appeared as the sole pillar of strength who was unbowed by the forces of Baal and the threat of death, while Obadiah and the people of Israel were portrayed as weak and wavering persons who did not have the courage to act on Yahweh's behalf. In ch. 19, however, it is Elijah who is weak, who stands intimidated, broken, and unwilling to carry the struggle any further. Strength and resolve to carry on Yahweh's cause come from the 7000 in Israel and from those Elijah is commanded to anoint. While Elijah will again become an active advocate of Yahweh (as in ch. 21), he does not do so within the context of chs. 17-19.

D. *Scene 4: Elisha the Son of Shaphat—1 Kings 19.19-21*

The motif of conflict between Yahweh and death and Yahweh and Baal, on the one hand, and the motif of conflict between Elijah and Jezebel, on the other, are not resolved within the three chapter unit of 1 Kgs 17-19. These three chapters are clearly delineated from the surrounding text, in part because Elijah, the chief character, does not come on the scene until 17.1, and disappears for a chapter after 19.21, and in part because the motif of conflict between Yahweh and death and Yahweh and Baal is carried on in a very intense fashion in chs. 17-19, in contrast to the preceding chapter and the subsequent one. Since chs. 17-19 form so cohesive a unit, one might expect the writer to bring to completion in ch. 19 the main elements within the story. However, to do this would be to undermine what has been said in ch. 19. A key point in this chapter has been Yahweh's message to Elijah that the battle will not be easy and brief, with Yahweh consistently intervening in a dramatic way to support his followers and defeat the forces of Baal. Rather, the battle will be lengthy and bloody, and will necessitate the recruiting of new persons to combat the forces of Baal. For the writer to wrap up the conflict between Yahweh and his foes in a decisive way would be to suggest that the victory was quick, easy, and unequivocal. Since both the writer and the readers know that the battle will be a long and difficult one, the writer points the reader beyond these three chapters to the continuation of the struggle, primarily through what is said in vv. 15-18 about Elisha, the revolution of Jehu, and the numerous faithful worshippers of Yahweh. The writer then winds the story down (vv. 19-21) by having Elijah take one of the three actions (vv. 15-16) commanded by Yahweh: the designation of Elisha as the prophet who will replace him.

The story of Elisha's selection may seem a bland ending to the three chapter unit after the high drama that has preceded it, but it does effectively point beyond chs. 17-19. We are told very little about Elisha at this point, only that he was a farmer, that he was eager to follow Elijah, that he wanted to kiss his parents before he left them, and that he killed the yoke of oxen and fed the people with their flesh before he went after Elijah. These words give hardly a clue about Elisha's later career. When coupled with the comments about Elisha in vv. 16 and 17, this concluding scene creates in the reader a sense of anticipation, a desire to know what great things Elisha will do as he continues the battle on Yahweh's behalf. This coordinates nicely with the sense of anticipation created by the brief mentioning of Hazael and Jehu in vv. 15-17. Thus, as the cluster of stories in chs. 17-19 ends, the reader's future attention is ensured. The three characters, especially Elisha and Jehu, will play out their roles in the ongoing struggle until Jehu has overthrown the Baalistic house of Omri (2 Kgs 9-10), having been anointed king of Israel on Elisha's initiative.

If vv. 19-21 do not end the three-chapter cycle in a dramatic way, they do repeat a motif that has been very important throughout chs. 17-19. Although in these chapters Yahweh has countered the challenge from death by the powerful demonstration in ch. 18 and has asserted his role as the true God of life by sending the rains, he has more frequently asserted himself as the God of life by feeding the hungry. First Elijah, and then the widow and her son were sustained during the drought (17.3-16), and Elijah was fed when he fled from Jezebel (19.5-8). In 19.19-21 Elisha, as the newly designated prophet of Yahweh, also feeds the hungry. He is introduced as a farmer, plowing his field with twelve yoke of oxen (v. 19).[51] In v. 21 he sacrifices[52] the yoke of oxen, and after boiling the flesh gives it to the people to eat (v. 21). He is portrayed in the same role of feeding the people that Yahweh has repeatedly filled in chs. 17-19. However, since this event is described tersely, with no explicit conclusions drawn, the reader's imagination is only teased as he anticipates the future career of Elisha. This fits in well with the tendency of the writer, at the end of ch. 19, to point the reader's attention to future events revolving around the three figures introduced in vv. 15-16.

Summary

My fundamental assumption throughout this study has been that the writer of 1 Kgs 17-19 was a skilled artist who selected his materials carefully and tightly structured the account in order to convey to the reader specific themes and ideas. No doubt there were sources on which the writer depended. The focus and perspective of those sources have, however, been subordinated to the more encompassing focus and perspective employed in composing 1 Kgs 17-19. I do not claim that this study exhausts the variety of imagery, the intricacy of narrative structure, or the wealth of ideas presented by the writer in these chapters. What I do claim to have presented in detail is one major theme that runs throughout these chapters: the struggle of Yahweh with Baal and, most especially, with death.

The struggle with Baal is intermittent, often implicit, and usually in the background (except for 18.17-40). It is, in fact, not really a struggle with Baal, but rather a struggle with those who are advocates of Baal. We learn in 16.31-33 that Ahab was a proponent of Baal. It is to Ahab that Elijah delivers the message about the impending drought, thereby challenging implicitly Baal's claim to be the sender of the rains. The ensuing drought lasting several years is certainly a challenge to Baal's power (although it can also be interpreted as a challenge to Yahweh's, as described above), but Baal is, interestingly, not mentioned by name in chs. 17 and 18 until the preface to the contest in 18.18. Before 18.18 only Jezebel's efforts, presumably on Baal's behalf (18.4, 13), are mentioned. We may surmise that the writer chose to ignore Baal as one means of expressing Baal's impotence. Once the contest with Baal is joined, Baal's advocates are the 450 prophets of Baal. It is through the mocking of their efforts to arouse Baal that Baal himself is mocked, and shown to be dead. The large number of the prophets of Baal helps accentuate their impotence: even with 450 ecstatic and bleeding participants, not a sound is elicited from Baal. Their demise at the hand of Elijah places them in the company of Baal, who has already been shown to be dead. Yahweh's returning the rains (18.41-46) firmly asserts his power in the realm that was supposed to have been Baal's. After this the only life left to Baal is through his advocacy by Jezebel (19.2, 10, 14), who seeks revenge for the death of Baal's prophets. Her advocacy is, nevertheless, formidable.

Yahweh's struggle with death is more pervasive, direct, and prominent than is the struggle with Baal. Once the implicit challenge to Baal has been made in 17.1, Baal recedes and the struggle becomes one with death. Sometimes the challenge of death to Yahweh and Elijah is expressed indirectly, as in Yahweh's command to Elijah to hide himself (17.3), the implication being that Ahab may seek to kill him. Normally, however, the challenge of death is expressed quite directly. Elijah, at Yahweh's command, is being sustained by the Brook Cherith. However, death asserts itself by drying up the Brook. Yahweh counters by sending Elijah to the widow of Zarephath. She proves, however, to be a poor source of sustenance, being herself out of food. Yahweh must sustain the widow, her son, and Elijah on the jar of meal and cruse of oil. Death then asserts itself powerfully by seizing the widow's son. Yahweh counters and achieves the victory by bringing the widow's son back to life.

Death, however, still holds sway. The famine is intense in the land (18.3), and the three lives preserved by Yahweh in ch. 17 seem tiny by comparison to the many who are starving. Ahab's cattle are starving, and he seems more concerned about them than about his people. Jezebel is systematically killing the prophets of Yahweh (18.4, 13). Even Obadiah, the 'servant of Yahweh', is so intimidated by death that he is petrified by the simple task of announcing Elijah's presence to Ahab. The people of Israel, fearful of the continuing famine, are reluctant to express any commitment to Yahweh (18.21).

If death is in the ascendancy in the first portion of ch. 18, the rest of the chapter is Yahweh's. In the contest between Yahweh and Baal, death wins a victory, but it is a victory over Baal, as in Canaanite mythology, and not over Yahweh. In fact, Yahweh's prophet Elijah is able to use death as an effective means of silencing the 450 advocates of Baal. Yahweh then asserts his power as the God of life and restores the rains to the land. Both Baal and death seem to be vanquished.

However, Jezebel, Baal's most powerful advocate, threatens Elijah's life, and death thereby gains an overpowering hold on Elijah, previously the most impregnable supporter of Yahweh. Elijah flees, displays a persistently defeatist attitude regarding Yahweh's recent victory, and balks at Yahweh's repeated attempts to get him to resume his role as Yahweh's advocate. Elijah is overpowered and rendered ineffective by his fear of death, just as Obadiah was earlier. At this point in the narrative the writer is setting the stage for one of his concluding points. The victory of Yahweh, decisive as it was, did not eradicate the power of the advocates of Baal, and did not remove the danger that Yahweh's followers would continue to be threatened by death. The struggle will continue. Elijah appears to want ongoing demonstrations of Yahweh's power in support of Elijah's role as a prophet, as his pitiable pleas make apparent (19.4, 10, 14). Yahweh, however, declines such demonstrations (19.11-12), and instead speaks to Elijah in a still, small voice. When Elijah continues to be reluctant about carrying forward Yahweh's tasks, and continues to be consumed with the prospect of his own death (19.14), Yahweh gets quite directive, ordering Elijah to anoint those who will carry on the struggle in Elijah's stead. In the final scene Elisha, one of those chosen, is introduced. His act of feeding the people with the twelve yoke of oxen, which parallels Yahweh's feeding of the hungry in chs. 17-19, points to his future role as an advocate of Yahweh, the God of life.

The writer of 1 Kgs 17-19 has thus presented a tightly written narrative which skillfully interweaves the struggle between Yahweh and Baal with the struggle between Yahweh and death. The writer has carefully selected his sources and has trimmed and focused them to present in dramatic fashion the power of Yahweh as the victorious God of life. The writer shows considerable skill at shaping scenes and sub-scenes to suit his purpose, as in the Obadiah scene (18.7-15), where he slows the movement to a standstill, using Obadiah's many words and his unwillingness to move as a means of emphasizing Obadiah's fear of death. Another example is the way he leaves the prophets of Baal ranting and bleeding while Elijah makes preparations for his part of the contest (18.29-30). The writer also demonstrates great care in his choice of words, as when he repeatedly uses חי (life) in the oaths to express implicitly the idea that Yahweh is the God of life, or when he repeatedly uses עלה (to go up; 18.41-44) to focus the reader's attention expectantly on the heavens from which the promised rain will come. The writer clearly knows how to develop and sustain a motif over a lengthy unit of narrative, and he knows how to build his narrative toward a dramatic climax. For example, he does not have Yahweh vanquish death in one intense scene. Rather, he carefully builds his drama, as in ch. 17, wherein death poses ever increasing challenges which Yahweh needs to counter. In light of these and the more detailed discussions presented earlier, it is safe to say that the various stories and traditions in 1 Kgs 17-19, whatever their origin, have not been loosely assembled and simply placed together in a roughly chronological order, but rather have been carefully and artfully woven into a narrative tapestry of considerable power.

Finally, the writer does not end these conflicts in a neat package, with Yahweh victorious and unchallenged against both Baal and death. Not only would that have been unrealistic, since these struggles continued well past the departure of Elijah and Ahab, but it would also have precluded the development of the struggle motifs in subsequent narratives. The discussion of those motifs past 1 Kgs 19 is, however, a task for another study.

NOTES

1. There are a number of reasons for treating these three chapters as a unit. One is Elijah's presence as the main character in the three chapters. He is introduced suddenly in 17.1, and dominates the scene until ch. 20, when the focus switches to the conflict between Ahab and Ben-Hadad. Elijah is never mentioned before 17.1, and after 19.21 he drops from the scene until 21.17. Another reason is the theme of the contest against Baal, which appears frequently throughout the three chapters, but disappears in ch. 20, when the focus is on the struggle against the Syrians. Yet another reason is the story of the drought and famine, which is repeatedly treated, especially in chs. 17 and 18, but drops from the scene after the end of ch. 19. Other thematic elements, such as the struggle of Yahweh against death, and the motif of eating or not eating, also link these three chapters, but their importance can only be assessed after the three chapters have been analyzed in detail.

The variety of proposals concerning the manner in which chs. 17–19 reached the form in which we have received them seems to be limited only by the imagination of interpreters. For example, Otto Eissfeldt in *The Old Testament: An Introduction* (trans. Peter R. Ackroyd; Oxford: Blackwell, 1966), 290-93 argues that chs. 17 and 18 form a unit to which 19.1-18 forms the logical sequel, with 17-18 being composed of 'originally independent narratives now skillfully woven into a sequence.' 19.19-21 is not counted as part of this complex because of its close association with later narratives. Georg Fohrer in *Introduction to the Old Testament* (trans. David E. Green; Nashville: Abingdon Press, 1965), 232-33 lists four 'original' narratives which formed the core of 1 Kings 17-19, to which five anecdotes were subsequently added. Fohrer discusses these traditions in more detail in *Elia* (Zürich: Zwingli-Verlag, 1957). Other discussions of the literary sources of 1 Kings 17-19 include: Rudolf Smend, 'Das Wort Jahwes an Elia: Erwägungen zur Komposition von 1 Reg. xvii-xix', *Vetus Testamentum* 25, 525-43; Otto Eissfeldt, *Der Gott Karmel* (Berlin: Akademie-Verlag, 1954); Odil Hannes Steck, *Überlieferung und Zeitgeschichte in den Elia-Erzählungen* (Neukirchen-Vluyn: Neukirchener Verlag, 1968); and H. Gunkel, *Elias Jahve und Baal* (Tübingen: Mohr, 1906).

Whatever the sources for chs. 17-19, my study of these chapters leads me to view the final editor as a skilled writer who shaped the text into the polished whole we now have before us. I am content to let the unravelling of sources to others while I study the structures, motifs, and literary devices used by the writer to convey his message.

2. For a detailed discussion of the Baal traditions in Canaanite literature and their relevance to the stories of Elijah and Elisha, see Leah Bronner, *The Stories of Elijah and Elisha as Polemics Against Baal Worship* (Leiden: Brill, 1968). Michael David Coogan, in *Stories from Ancient Canaan* (Philadelphia: Westminster, 1978), 84 discusses the cycle of the struggle between Baal and death, claiming that the cycle refers not to the yearly cessation of the rains during the summer months, but rather to the failure of the winter rains every few years. Since 1 Kgs 18.1 indicates a three year duration for the drought, thereby involving the failure of several successive winter rains, Coogan argues that what is described in 1 Kgs 17–19 is clearly more than the annual cycle of rains followed by the dry season. Nevertheless, it would seem unwise to propose, as Coogan does, that the Baal cycle was seen by the Canaanites to refer only to the more pronounced, devastating droughts. The annual agricultural cycle in Palestine is most readily understood as an alternation of rain and drought, and thus of death and life, so that the periodic, long term droughts may well have been seen simply as more severe cases of what occurred annually.

3. Compare the sequence of stories in Exodus 5–15. Presumably, one plague would have been enough to get Israel out of Egypt. However, in order to allow the story to build to a climax, and to provide ample opportunity to relish the defeat of the Egyptians, ten plagues are listed, with Yahweh repeatedly confronting the Egyptians.

4. As Alexander Rofé correctly points out in his article 'Classes in the Prophetical Stories: Didactic Legenda and Parable', *Supplements to Vetus Testamentum* 26 (Leiden: E.J. Brill, 1974), 148, the question of the literary *source* for 1 Kgs 16.29-33, which may well indicate a different source for these verses than for 1 Kgs 17.1ff, is quite a separate question from the issue of the current relationship of the two in the edited text of 1 Kings. I agree with Rofé that 1 Kgs 16.29-33 is closely linked to 1 Kgs 17–19 (even though I do not agree with all of his reasons), as opposed to O. Eissfeldt, 'Die Komposition von 1 Reg 16.29–2 Reg 13.25', in *Festschrift L. Rost* (BZAW 105) 49-58.

5. Chapter 17 forms a cohesive sub-unit within the broader structure of 1 Kgs 17–19. It is delimited by the two brief scenes (17.1, 18.1-2) which serve as turning points to structure and focus the narrative. Its setting is basically intimate, domestic, and remote, while the next major unit (ch. 18) involves the king and all Israel in the decisive contest on Mt. Carmel. Chapter 17 builds to a climax in the final scene (vv. 17-24), wherein the authority of Yahweh as the God of life and of Elijah as his prophet are established. Once that climax has been reached and Yahweh's authority asserted, the intimate

setting of ch. 17 is left behind and Yahweh's power is again challenged by death, now on a much broader scope.

There has not been much written in recent years on the literary structure of 1 Kgs 17-19. The most helpful treatment I have seen is Robert L. Cohn's 'The Literary Logic of 1 Kings 17-19', *JBL* 101 (1982), 333-50. While I have problems with aspects of Cohn's analysis, such as his inclination to carry too far his 'cumulative logic' patterns in chapters 17-19, his work has been helpful as I have developed my own analysis of these three chapters.

6. See Bronner, 23-24 for a discussion of the origin and significance of Elijah's name.

7. Examples of חי as part of an oath may be found in Judg. 8.19, 1 Sam. 14.39, and 1 Kgs 2.24. Examples apart from oaths wherein חי expresses animation and life may be found in Gen. 6.19, Exod. 21.35, 2 Sam. 12.18, and Eccl. 9.4.

8. נסתרת is, technically speaking, a Niphal perfect but, when preceded by the ו, it acts as an imperfect.

9. That כול has a more inclusive meaning than simply 'to feed' may be seen in Gen. 50.21, where Joseph promises to care for his brothers and their families after the death of Jacob, in 2 Sam. 19.33, where David offers to sustain Barzillai in his court with him in Jerusalem, and in 2 Sam. 20.3, which describes David's providing for the ten concubines he had left behind in Jerusalem when he fled from Absalom.

10. Examples of the way in which נשמה, 'breath' is used to express the difference between life and death may be found in Gen. 2.7, 1 Kgs 15.29, Job 27.14-15, and Isa. 42.5.

11. That ch. 18 is a separate section within the overall structure of chs. 17-19 may be seen by the contrast of its content with that of ch. 17 (discussed above in n. 5), and with the content of ch. 19. In ch. 19 Elijah will once again be mainly by himself in remote places, very much as in ch. 17, whereas in ch. 18 he is in the forefront of national attention. Also, in ch. 18 he is confident and bold in his function as a prophet, whereas in ch. 19 he flees in terror from Jezebel and death, and wants to abandon the struggle on behalf of Yahweh. Chapter 19, like ch. 17, has the preservation of the prophet's life in the forefront of the reader's attention, whereas that is not the case in ch. 18. Finally, there are the small transitional units which the writer has used to divide from each other the major sections of the text: 18.1-2, wherein Elijah is told to appear to Ahab, and 19.1-3, wherein the victorious prophet flees from yet another threat by death.

12. See, for example, Gen. 38.12 and Exod. 2.23.

13. The beginning of verse 12 focuses the reader's attention on Obadiah: והיה אני אלך, 'And it shall come to pass when *I, I* go. . . ' The focusing of the danger on Obadiah is accomplished both by reversing the usual verb-subject word order, and by including אני, 'I', which really is not necessary, since the verb is without question first person singular.

14. Robert Alter, in *The Art of Biblical Narrative* (New York: Basic Books, 1981), 73 discusses the way in which Obadiah's many words, which 'seem to stumble all over each other', help to express his grave fear of the risk he will take if he does as Elijah commands.

15. For example, Gen. 4.8; 27.42; Exod. 2.14; Ps. 78.31; Amos 9.4.

16. See Cohn's discussion, 339.

17. Note the reference in 19.18 to the 7,000 in Israel who have not bowed to Baal. See Cohn's brief discussion, 338-39.

18. Intriguingly, this threat posed by death will even affect Elijah in ch. 19.

19. She will again act suddenly and with murderous intent in 19.2, in that case very effectively threatening Elijah.

20. I disagree with the suggestion by A. Jepsen in 'Librum Regum', *Biblia Hebraica Stuttgartensia* (Stuttgart: Deutsche Bibelgesellschaft, 1967), 603 and James A. Montgomery and Henry S. Gehman, *A Critical and Exegetical Commentary on the Books of Kings* (ICC; Edinburgh: T&T Clark, 1951), 297 that וביתה, 'and her household' in 17.15 should in fact be ובנה, 'and her son'. The widow's household is again mentioned in 17.17, where the widow is described as the mistress of the house, בעלת הבית. The textual evidence is not sufficient to warrant an emendation.

21. Note, for example, the way in which the threefold reference to the possibility that Ahab may slay Obadiah (vv. 9, 12, 14) builds in the reader a growing anticipation of the evil that may befall Obadiah when he goes to Ahab. Also, as noted previously, the word הרגני, 'He will kill me' is the last word spoken by Obadiah, and therefore sticks in the reader's mind.

22. One need not look very far for other examples of Israelite prophets who were treated harshly for speaking a word that aroused the wrath of a king and/or others. Jeremiah suffered considerably during Zedekiah's reign, when Jerusalem was under siege (Jer. 37-38), and sought an oath from the king before he would reveal further words to him (38.14-16). Jeremiah's contemporary Uriah was brought back from Egypt and executed for speaking prophetic words against Jerusalem and Judah (Jer. 26.20-23). The prophet Micaiah was cast into prison for speaking a word anticipating Ahab's death in battle (1 Kgs 21.15-28).

23. The verb עכר can refer both to someone or something that is taboo or an outcast, as in Gen. 34.30 and Josh. 6.18, and to someone who causes trouble, as in Judg. 11.35 and 1 Sam. 14.29. Ahab's words to Elijah appear to incorporate both meanings. Elijah is certainly seen as a troubler because of his role in causing the drought. But he is also an outcast in that he has fled from Ahab's presence and hidden himself while Ahab has pursued him in all of the surrounding kingdoms. Is there perhaps in Ahab's question to Elijah a bit of sarcasm aimed at Elijah's fleeing Ahab's presence and not being willing to face up to Ahab's wrath? The words האתה זה, 'Is it you?' could be seen to

imply sarcastically that Ahab has not seen Elijah in so long he can hardly recognize him.

24. Note that Jezebel is not present or even mentioned from 18.13 until 19.1.

25. See my earlier discussion of Ahab's passivity after v. 20.

26. While פסח can mean to pass over in the sense of sparing, as in Exod. 12.13, 23, 27, it can also refer to limping or being lame, as in 2 Sam. 4.4. See Francis Brown, ed., *The New Brown, Driver, and Briggs Hebrew and English Lexicon of the Old Testament* (London: Oxford, 1907), 820; H.H. Rowley, 'Elijah on Mount Carmel', *Bulletin of the John Rylands Library* 43 (1960), 204.

27. סעף is frequently used to refer to boughs or branches, with the extended meaning here of crutches made from branches, or perhaps even unequal legs, *ibid.*, 703–704. That this root can refer to people of split loyalties or divided opinions may be seen in Ps. 119.113.

28. See Bronner for a detailed discussion of Baal portrayed as a god of fire and lightning in Canaanite mythology. James B. Pritchard, *The Ancient Near East in Pictures relating to the Old Testament* (2nd edn, Princeton: Princeton University Press, 1969), 168, 307 presents the Ras Shamra stele, and discusses the object in Baal's left hand as either a stylized bolt of lightning or a tree. I see no reason why it could not have been intended to represent both.

29. Note that the writer intensifies the people's ambivalence by means of the words וקראתם בשם אלהיכם, 'You call on the name of your god' at the beginning of v. 24. He thereby implies that the people have wavered so much from the worship of Yahweh that they are actually leaning toward Baal's side.

30. Ludwig Koehler and Walter Baumgartner, eds., *Lexicon in Veteris Testamenti Libros* (Leiden: Brill, 1958), 243, 1030.

31. I have not translated וכי in the clauses וכי שיג לו and וכי דרך לו. While the recurrent וכי is important to the structure of the last half of v. 27, in these two clauses it translates rather awkwardly into English, which does not tolerate as readily as does Hebrew the repetition of key words.

32. Koehler-Baumgartner, 919.

33. *Ibid.*

34. As Montgomery and Gehman indicate, 302, 310-11, שיג most likely is a euphemism for 'he is relieving himself'. In light of that, שיח would be taken to refer to the business or musing one does in a privy and, as Rashi noted, וכי דרך לו is to be taken as referring to a trip to the privy. See also I.W. Slotki, *Kings: Hebrew Text & English Translation with an Introduction and Commentary* (London: Soncino Press, 1950), 132; and Rowley, 'Elijah', 206.

35. Another example of the mocking of an enemy by means of base and earthy prose can be seen in Gen. 19.30-38, where the writer destroys any

credibility the Moabites and Ammonites might have by declaring that they arose out of an incestuous relationship between Lot and his two daughters.

36. J. Robinson, in *The First Book of Kings* (The Cambridge Bible Commentary; Cambridge: Cambridge University Press, 1972), 209 points out that the waking of the fertility god from his slumber would be expected by those offering sacrifices at the beginning of the growing season. In this context, the prophets' expectation that Baal will come to life makes his lack of any response even more devastating.

37. For example, see Lev. 17.10-14; Deut. 12.23; and Gen. 4.10-11.

38. In the earlier period of Israel's life in Palestine, נבא is frequently used to describe ecstatic prophesying, as in 1 Sam. 10.5-13; 19.20-24; and 1 Kgs 22.10-12.

39. The prophets of Baal raved on 'until the offering up of the oblation' (עד לעלות המנחה, v. 29). They thus are continuing to prophesy while Elijah makes his extensive preparations (vv. 30-36), since he does not call on Yahweh until the time of 'the offering up of the oblation' (בעלות המנחה, v. 36).

40. See Bronner, 16.

41. In ch. 17, the honorific title איש האלהים, 'man of God' is twice applied to Elijah by the widow in the scene where her son is raised from the dead (17.17-24). Like 18.30-40, where the title הנביא, 'the prophet' is applied to Elijah (v. 36), 17.17-24 constitutes the climax of the chapter, where Elijah wins his most significant victory in the chapter unit. It is therefore quite appropriate for the writer to apply the titles to Elijah at these points in the narrative.

42. Koehler–Baumgartner, 960.

43. Note how Elijah's imperatives, עלה, 'Go up!' אכל, 'Eat!' and שתה, 'Drink!' are balanced by Ahab's obedience, יעלה, 'He went up', לאכל, 'to eat', and לשתות, 'to drink'.

44. Even though Elijah's posture in v. 42 might be understood as one connoting prayer, the writer says nothing to lead the reader to conclude that, not mentioning even a single word of Elijah to Yahweh requesting rain.

45. Note once again the use of an imperative when Elijah speaks to Ahab.

46. Compare Jonah's words in Jonah 4.3, 8, 9. See my article 'Jonah: In Pursuit of the Dove', *JBL* 104 (1985), 34-37.

47. Robert E. Coote, in 'Yahweh Recalls Elijah', in *Traditions in Transformation: Turning Points in Biblical Faith*, ed. Baruch Halpern and Jon D. Levenson (Winona Lake, Indiana: Eisenbrauns, 1981), 115-120 discusses parallels between Elijah's trip to Horeb and Moses' trip there. He raises some interesting points, but at times is perhaps too enthusiastic in his quest for parallels. Slotki, *Kings*, 138-39 also notes these parallels.

48. Note that in 18.22, immediately before he began the contest in which Yahweh dramatically displayed his power in the victory over Baal, Elijah had

used the words אני נותרתי נביא ליהוה, 'I, I alone am left a prophet to Yahweh', which are similar to ואותר אני לבדי, 'and I, I alone, am left' in 19.10.

49. I disagree with Ernst Würthwein, 'Elijah at Horeb: Reflections on 1 Kings 19.9-18', in *Proclamation and Presence: Old Testament Essays in Honor of Gwynne Henton Davies*, ed. John I. Durham and J.R. Porter (Richmond, Virginia: John Knox Press, 1970) 152-66, who argues that the theophany in vv. 11-13a is secondary and therefore should not be taken into account in attempts to interpret 1 Kgs 19. There are no convincing stylistic reasons for omitting the theophany and, as I argue in my discussion of these verses, the theophany provides an apt answer to Elijah's complaints in vv. 4 and 10.

50. אלף (1,000) is commonly used as a means of designating a complete unit such as a clan or tribe, and in one case (Ps. 144.13) the verbal form of אלף is used to describe the generation of offspring in abundance (Koehler-Baumgartner, 56-57). שבע is also used to designate a complete unit, as in Gen. 1-2, 4.15, and Num. 23.1. In Prov. 3.10 שבע is used to designate abundance.

51. It is interesting that Elisha is plowing behind twelve yoke of oxen, which would seem an unusually large number of animals for plowing a field. Might this not be an allusion to the twelve tribes of Israel (as in Elijah's use of the 12 stones to rebuild Yahweh's altar, 1 Kgs 18.31-32)? This reference could then be seen as a brief hint by the writer at Elisha's future role as a prophet to the tribes of Israel, as one who will reconstitute Israel as a people under Yahweh.

52. Despite the impression given by some translations, זבח does not mean simply to kill, but rather implies killing as part of a sacrificial ritual (Koehler-Baumgartner, 249).

IRONY AND THE UNMASKING OF ELIJAH
Russell Gregory

Chapter 1

THE IRONIC STRUCTURE OF 1 KINGS 17–19

You wanted to descend like a storm wind
And to be mighty in deed like the tempest,
You wanted to blow being to being
And bless human souls while scourging them,
To admonish weary hearts in the hot whirlpool
And to stir the rigid to agitated light,
      —You sought me on your stormy paths
And did not find me.

You wanted to soar upward like a fire
And wipe out all that did not stand your test,
Sun-powerful, you wanted to scorch worlds
With sudden force to kindle a young nothingness
      —You sought me in your flaming abysses
And did not find me.

Then my messenger came to you
And placed your ear next to the still life of my earth,
Then you felt how seed after seed began to stir,
And all the movements of growing things encircled you,

Blood hammered against blood, and the silence
    overcame you,
The eternally complete, soft and motherly
      —Then you had to incline upon yourself,
Then you found me.

              Martin Buber (trans. Maurice Friedman)

It is the pattern of the impeccable which makes the average
possible. It is the attachment to what is spiritually superior: loyalty
to a sacred person or idea, devotion to a noble friend or teacher,
love for a people or for mankind, which holds our inner life

together. But any ideal, human, social, or artistic, if it forms a roof
over all of life, shuts us off from the light. Even the palm of one
hand may bar the light of the entire sun.

Abraham Heschel

Elijah's story, as recounted in 1 Kings 17-19, stands as one of the
many monuments on the plain of Old Testament narratives which
reflect the life and thought of an ancient culture. Yet, this narrative
does not merely review the events of yesteryear, but comes to life and
engages the interested observer as the tatoos of the illustrated man
rose up and constructed a narrative world.[1] The text opens as a stage,
the words introduce characters and events as the story is reread and
imagined, perhaps lived, anew. And with the tale comes the
interpretation.

This span of narrative, which is bounded on one side by the
deuteronomistic evaluation of Ahab (1 Kgs 16.29-34) and on the
other side by the narrative recording of the war between Benhadad,
the king of Syria, and the king of Israel, Ahab, has been variously
divided into constituent segments.[2] Aware of the numerous diachronic
analyses of this material, this study sought the controlling design
which held these segments or episodes together. The subsequent
discovery of that design rewarded my efforts, directed what other
methods or information were required, and directed the remainder of
the study.[3]

For reasons that will soon be evident, the story under scrutiny
unmasks a disingenuous Elijah by means of a carefully crafted ironic
presentation. Evidence abounds for both verbal and situational
patterns of irony. Accordingly, this assertion demands that interpreters
acquaint themselves with the characteristics of irony so that they may
understand more completely the techniques, the purpose, and the
power of this composition.

The Ironic Perspective: Theory and Practice

To many, irony is a statement or an event which carries the opposite
meaning.[4] Furthermore, as Wayne Booth observes:

> For both its devotees and for those who fear it, irony is usually seen
> as something that undermines clarities, opens up vistas of chaos,
> and either liberates by destroying all dogma or destroys by
> revealing the inescapable canker of negation at the heart of every
> affirmation.[5]

Such a definition, based on opposites, proves too simple on two counts. First, irony does not necessarily mean that the opposite message is intended; it means that something other or more complex than what is literally represented is proposed.[6]

Second, irony in this sense would be interpreted thoughtlessly and mechanistically once it was detected. The ironic content or elements would be lined up and the corresponding opposites would be derived. Booth points to another popular idea held about irony when he suggests:

> Since irony has this power to deceive the unwary, it is often talked about as something designed to deceive some readers and thus make other, shrewder readers feel proud of themselves. I think this view is in part mistaken, but we should begin by admitting just how often irony does get itself misunderstood.[7]

This idea of selective deception fails as an overarching definition for it magnifies one facet of irony, perhaps out of fear that the irony will slip past, or out of pride, that the irony in all its manifestations never slips past: the clever reader never finishes compiling all the signs and instances of irony.[8] Neither the subtlety nor the intention of irony in general, or in a particular narrative, is fully appreciated by these restrictive views.

Irony as a general category eludes a precise definition, yet exhibits constantly the contrast between appearance and reality. Paul Duke, in a fine treatment of irony in the gospel of John, defined irony as 'a leap from what seems to be to what is'.[9] Cognizant in his own way of this contrast, D.C. Muecke proposes the 'elements, properties, or features' which appear to be basic to all forms of irony, notably verbal and situational irony.[10] First, he notes the element of 'innocence' or 'confident unawareness'.[11] He adds:

> The victim of irony does not need to be, though he often is, arrogantly, wilfully blind; he need only reveal by word or action that he does not even remotely suspect that things may not be what he ingenuously supposes them to be. The basic element is a serene, confident unawareness coloured, in practice, by varying degrees of arrogance, conceitedness, complacency, naivety, or innocence. Other things being equal, the greater the victim's blindness, the more striking the irony. . . The victim of irony is serenely unaware that his words or actions convey a quite different meaning or assumption the ironist 'innocently' pretends to have this serene unawareness. . .[12]

Duke enlarges this perspective by drawing on the classic Greek understanding of irony. He writes:

> As played by Socrates, the character of the eiron was both assassin of pretension and midwife of truth... It is this first, more negative function of the eiron that was emphasized in Greek comedy. The eiron's counterpart and enemy in the drama was the alazon. While the eiron presented himself as less than he really was, the alazon vaunted himself as more. As the classic distinction has it, the eiron dissimulates, the alazon simulates. In the Greek comedies alazons were invariably swaggering imposters in one of two ways. Either they claimed honorable positions or professions which in fact were not theirs, or they claimed privileges and pleasures which they did not deserve. The result was usually some hilarious disaster in which the pompous quack was exposed for the pretender he was. Alazony in comedy is the exact counterpart of hubris in tragedy: downfall follows. The agent of this downfall, the wily one who triumphs over the pretender, is the character who seemed so little and emerges so large—the eiron.[13]

Second, Muecke underscores the contrast of reality and appearance, then observes:

> ... the ironist presents an appearance and pretends to be unaware of a reality while the victim is deceived by an appearance and is unaware of a reality.[14]

Third, he suggests that the comic element in irony arises naturally from the first two elements—'the basic contradiction or incongruity coupled with a real or a pretended confident unawareness'.[15] Fourth, Muecke describes the element of detachment which refers to the 'ironist's pretended manner and sometimes to the real attitude of the ironist or the ironic observer'.[16] He continues:

> The ironic observer's awareness of himself as observer tends to enhance his feeling of freedom and induce a mood perhaps of serenity, or joyfulness, or even exultation. His awareness of the victim's unawareness invites him to see the victim as bound or trapped where he feels free; committed where he feels disengaged; swayed by emotions, harrassed, or miserable, where he is dispassionate, serene, or even moved to laughter; trustful, credulous, or naive, where he is critical, sceptical, or content to suspend judgement. And where his own attitude is that of a man whose world appears real and meaningful, he will see the victim's world as illusory or absurd.[17]

Fifth, Muecke highlights the intentional character of irony. He comments:

> The art of irony, in its slighter manifestations, resembles that of the wit of the raconteur, which relies largely upon arranging, timing, and tone, and it does not abandon these cares as it grows more ambitious.[18]

In some degree, all these elements are present when the ironical twist is attempted or discovered.

The concept of irony is further delimited by the discussion of stable irony by Wayne Booth. He stresses the conscious effort of the ironist to equip his piece with enough clues so that the ironic intent can be discovered by almost anyone. Nevertheless, irony is not overt, but remains disguised. For this reason misunderstanding or complete oversight continue to jeopardize the interpretation of an ironic passage or piece. Yet, the basic meanings

> ... are stable, in the sense that once we have reconstructed a solid platform out of the unstable surface meanings, we have a right to feel some confidence that the author shares our new position.[19]

Subsequently, the audience or reader has every right to assume that the irony is finite, i.e., that the new meaning is not infinitely expansive but allows a firmly worded, perhaps somewhat lengthy, but precise statement.[20]

Two different categories of irony share the focus of this study: verbal irony and situational or dramatic irony.[21] Verbal irony refers to the design of a narrative; the author or editor structured the whole piece to contribute to a particular awareness and a hierarchy of meanings[22] that only become visible when this design is detected.[23] The events and characters depicted in the story may be exceptionally believable until the story's nature forces a reassessment. Situational irony includes those narrative events where the anticipated occurrence or result is replaced surprisingly by another. The diving instructor who runs to the board, springs high into the air while barking instructions to the students behind, and looks down only to discover an empty pool is the victim of situational irony. Neither of these forms is dependent on the other, though they are not mutually exclusive.

Certain conditions exist for irony to be employed as a reaction. Primarily, the author judges reality by means of a vision of existence. The resulting composition reveals a tension between the appearance (what is apparently happening in the story) and the result (what is really happening). This visionary writer may be the victim of a collapse of meaning,[24] the spokesperson for a group critical of the status quo,[25] or someone who wishes to clarify or to protest certain incongruities.[26] Paul Duke relates:

> A Critic once called irony 'the shoe-horn of new ideas', for in the indirect whispering way of irony there is both gentle beckoning and a powerful persuasion.[27]

Whatever the reason for the employment of irony, the bearing of the vision of truth must be seen as a determining feature. From this feature one may determine what change is being provoked or what situation is being redeemed.[28] In addition, this vision practically guarantees that the criticism will not stoop to condemnation but will favor the emancipation of those enslaved in the old world (status quo) to a new world (status quo redeemed by the vision).[29]

The advantage of irony as an instrument of criticism resides in the economy and incisiveness of irony. This economy arises in a literary technique charged with purpose but necessarily guarded. The message, usually complex, must be discovered by an audience who may not remain passive either during the discovery by reading or hearing, or the reflection that naturally follows. In addition, the message that has been nowhere stated but rather embedded in the narrative design of the story, is extraordinarily difficult to state simply. In fact, Wayne Booth, who claims he does not 'decode' the hidden messages but 'reconstructs' a stable platform for interpretation out of the unstable surface meanings, warns:

> The art of reconstruction and all that it entails about the author and his picture of the reader becomes an inseparable part of what is said and thus that act cannot really be said, it must be performed.[30]

In another context, he notes:

> If in describing it 'straight' I try to include some account of the cultural preconceptions on which the silent communion depends, I find that I need two to three hundred words at a minimum, and even then, of course, the emotional force has been dissipated.[31]

Duke enlarges this understanding of reconstruction when he relates:

> In using irony an author invites the reader to reject an ostensible structure of meaning. The meaning to be rejected is often far more

than the literal meaning of a particular sentence or expression, but rather a whole structured 'world' of meanings or values which the author spurns. Those who do not share the author's perception may choose to remain in such a structure.[32]

The reliance on audience participation in the discovery of meaning promotes a much closer communion between the critical position of the author and the transforming/transformed position of the enlightened audience than possible through non-ironic statement. Paul Duke concludes:

> If irony has this power to win people more fully into the ironist's camp, it has another agreeable effect as well: irony rewards its followers with a sense of community...' As we will see, then, irony's relation to community is circular. It aims at drawing people more fully into its camp, but its fullest force is with those already within. Indeed irony may often be not so much a call to community as the sure sign of its presence.[33]

This communion forms the context for the generation of interpretation and any subsequent change which begins with the reader.

The quality of incisiveness arises primarily from the ability of irony to get behind the reader's defenses. 'Signs' of the real world are used in the story:[34] the literal level of the story maintains a familiarity that comforts. Yet, at some point, some clue convinces the audience that these 'signs' are not the real story but the front which camouflages the real story. In the same manner, the characteristic mixture of the familiar and the strange, which is found naturally in narrative,[35] contributes to this power. Here the mixture does not assist in the transition to the 'other world' alone, but engenders the transformation of that 'other world' into a conscious critical messenger. What begins as clear, merely a new 'world-in words',[36] becomes momentarily cloudy, only to clear under the reconstructive energies of the attentive audience.[37] So the audience has actually discerned and mastered two clues: the narrative hint offered by the text as 'an index or emblem of the whole—as a guide to our reading of the whole'[38] and the ironic clue which signals the purpose of the author or editor. The person who finally understands the ironic intention experiences a sense of accomplishment and an extraordinary awareness of the message of the originator.

Obviously, an ironical story depends upon the detection and reconstruction by an alert audience. This detection occurs when one of several classes of clues is noted: straightforward warnings in the author's own voice; obvious errors; conflicts of facts within the work; clashes of style; or conflicts of belief.[39] In the event that one or more of these clues triggers a cautious rereading of the work, Wayne Booth has outlined four steps in the transformation of meaning.[40] First, the audience, now wary, is required to reject the literal meaning. Second, alternative interpretations or explanations are tested against the text. Third, a decision must be reached about the knowledge or beliefs of the editor. The question of intention, a treacherous issue in literary criticism,[41] stands in the foreground of this operation. Irony both requires and allows this attention, for by its nature, irony entails the attempt by someone to shape a potentially disconcerting message in a circumspect manner. Fourth, the audience must choose a new meaning or cluster of meanings which truly accords with the unspoken beliefs that the audience has decided to attribute to the author. The intricacy of this step, is reflected in Booth's statement:

> ... you had to reconstruct what my real meaning was, with nothing but your hunches about my hunches about your hunches to go on.[42]

And yet, upon the arrival at this new manner of viewing and understanding the narrative, its true stability is indelibly stamped upon the mind of the audience.

Needless to say, an instrument of such subtlety and power is subject to the danger of misinterpretation which commonly falls into two categories.[43] Some may fail to detect the ironic bent; these persons just 'do not get the point'! This failure may arise from ignorance concerning the 'signs' or the genre of the narrative. The farther removed the reader from the milieu or the literature, the more difficult the detection. At the same time, this failure may stem from a blind spot in the audience's perception; they may be those being criticized and may accept the 'signs' as a fine description of the status quo—what ought to be. In either case, when the story ends, so does the opportunity for conversion or redemption. The other danger of overstating the ironic content balances the account. Certain persons may multiply the ironies of a particular story beyond acceptable limits. Most likely, these interpreters have ceased to pay attention to the limits suggested by the story and have invented the excess out of their own design. Others, acting out of a variety of motives, find irony where there is none. Rather than finding a subterranean, but essential, meaning, these persons import a meaning that perverts the piece. In each of these cases, the text must constantly be consulted along with credible interpretations for balance and feasibility. With practice and care, these dangers will form a boundary rather than a mined field and the study of that literature which confesses its ironical identity will be enriched and enriching.

The Levels of Irony in 1 Kings 17–19

Undoubtedly, the three chapter narrative comprised of 1 Kings 17–19 exhibits three levels of ironic involvement.[44] Elijah's mockery of the prophets of Baal forms the first, though minor level. This is suggested by the narrator's use of the verb התל (to mock). This word, in addition to several others, assures the audience that Elijah is doing something other than dispensing helpful advice. The second level of ironic involvement lies in the events that take unexpected turns.[45] Elijah's encounter with Obadiah (1 Kgs 18.2bff.) exhibits the clash of expectation and actuality, inevitably present in ironic accounts, when Obadiah searches for water throughout the kingdom, but instead finds Elijah who announced the drought to the king then immediately disappeared from the royal presence. This, and other twists provide assistance for the inquiry into the meaning of the story and the movement of the plot. Subsequently, the messages of this narrative surface. Finally, the design of the whole account transforms this complex and gripping story into an examination of one prophet of God, Elijah, and by implication, all prophecy.[46]

The Ironic Design of the Whole Narrative

The first verse of this three chapter narrative, for all the abuse that it has borne as the sign of the truncation of a larger, more understandable account, ushers Elijah on the scene, introduces him, and portrays him as an imposing figure *in medias res*.[47] In the middle of this narrative and personal introduction, the self-characterization by Elijah as one who 'stands before Yahweh (also 18.15)', a designation frequently assigned to Elijah and Elisha,[48] sets him apart as a very special and fervent follower of Yahweh. This figurative use is maintained until chapter 19. There, in verses 11 and 13, the command of Yahweh to stand, actually stand, before HIM astounds those who see this demand as an awesome and risky honor and who read this apart from the earlier mention.

What these verses await is the catalytic effect which occurs when the alert audience holds them in tandem. The consideration of the two verses in chapter 19 which contain the command of Yahweh and the tentative response of Elijah, leads one to wonder about this fiery prophet 'who stands before Yahweh'. When the self-characterization that Elijah encased in an oath and labored under crashes against Yahweh's imperative, or the figurative designation is demanded in literal currency, Elijah is called into question and the whole story requires a reconstruction that treats the gap between what is being depicted ostensibly and what actually is being relayed. The subsequent review, starting at the very beginning, underscores the impression that the surface appearance adeptly provides all the signal quality of reality. Yet, as soon as the key is placed inside the lock, these 'signs' burst free and relate their true story. Elijah is seen as he really is; he is a prophet plagued by his own ego and exaggerated importance. His punishment is the relinquishing of his mantle, the symbol of his individuality and his mission. He is unmasked and undone at the same time.

His name, ever electrifying, suits him for the task which apparently forms the primary concern of the narrative. Whether one unscrambles the name to mean 'Yahweh is my God' or 'Yahweh is God',[49] the import is clear; this prophet's loyalty appears unshakeable for his own name stands as a testimony. He lives his name; he is recognized and lauded repeatedly as the prophet of Yahweh or the man of God. Nothing could be more fitting than the man who proclaims by the utterance of his name, Elijah, an exclamation of faith, calling a divided people back to covenant loyalty and fidelity to their god. Yet, this very Elijah usurps one of the epithets of Yahweh; he calls himself 'jealous' or 'zealous' (cf. Exod. 34.14), once when arriving at Horeb (1 Kgs 19.10) and once while lifting his mantle over his face to avoid the level stare of the deity (1 Kgs 19.14). The prophet who stood before the Lord now places himself before the Lord. The insistent glorification of his significance eclipses his god. His task, like his name, ceases to be seen as joyous proclamation and begins to be recognized as the service of self-gratification.

Elijah assuredly bears the signs of the prophetic office as manifested in the Israelite content.[50] He is guided by the directives of Yahweh at every major juncture of the story except one. On that occasion, recounted in 1 Kgs 19.3ff., Elijah senses Jezebel's response to his victory on Carmel and fails to await a word from his Lord. He regularly swears his oaths by the God he claims to hold in the center of life. He pronounces an oracle in the standard manner: 'Thus says the Lord (... כה אמר יהוה—1 Kgs 17.14)'. He serves as the very conscience of the king, the burr that remains under the saddle of Ahab's reign, just as other prophets played this role risking great personal danger.[51] On one occasion, in this role, he says: '"I have not troubled Israel; but you have and your father's house, because you have forsaken the commandments of the Lord and followed Baals" (1 Kgs 18.18b)'.[52] He berates the wayward people in language that is reminiscent of other prophets' addresses to God and people: 'How long' (... עד־מתי—1 Kgs 18.21). Here stands the consummate prophet of Yahweh, imploring God and people to repent.

Elijah's conduct, for the most part, places him squarely in the role of prophet, not only by what he does but how successful he is in the accomplishment of his tasks. When the widow's son falls ill for some mysterious reason, Elijah takes charge. He dominates her and even instructs Yahweh about the best means to bring wholeness to this household. His subsequent success proves his worth to the mother. In a similar situation, on the top of Carmel where the production of a flaming sacrifice was the measure of victory, Elijah again implored Yahweh, in a manner which suggests begging (1 Kgs 18.36b-37), to demonstrate a dynamic efficacy, and, concomitantly, Elijah's effectiveness. These events mark Elijah as one who apparently enjoyed the good pleasure of Yahweh and served him well. Elijah acts and sounds like a prophet but the vindictive words of Jezebel (1 Kgs 19.3ff.) will reveal the nothingness behind his sound and fury.

Following the linking of the brash defense of Elijah in 19.10, 14, and the unrehearsed ease in his identification in 1 Kgs 17.1, the struggle of Elijah for self-gratification and the true source of his strength and mission bobs to the surface. When he made the renewal of rain dependent upon his word, he exchanged his prophetic commission for an egotistical challenge. Certainly, he repeatedly claimed the support of Yahweh, God of Israel, and received the benefit of the Creator's cooperation, but embedded in his oath was the *double entente* of egotism. Elijah could and did overstep his bounds. A moderating voice does introduce an equilibrium appropriate to a working relationship between prophet and God. In 1 Kgs 17.16, after the widow, her son, and Elijah have weathered numerous days of the drought without any depreciation of their stock of food, the narrator remarks: 'The jar of meal was not spent, neither did the cruse of oil fail, according to the word of the Lord which he spoke by Elijah'. Similarly, after the miraculous cure by Elijah empowered by the life-giving impulse of Yahweh, the woman exclaims: 'Now I know that you are a man of God, and that the word of the Lord in your mouth is truth' (1 Kgs 18.24). The hint of Elijah's pride is hidden to the audience reading the narrative on the surface, but those who study or scrutinize the Elijah leaning tentatively on the cave wall at Horeb, somewhat like the Elijah who waited at the gate of the city to see when the widow would appear, reassess this prophet.

The second chapter of this story portrays the natural complement to the first. The chapter opens with Yahweh's instructions to Elijah: 'Go show yourself to Ahab; and I will send rain upon the earth' (1 Kgs 18.1). After a dramatic interruption, brief in story time but protracted in discourse time,[53] that builds suspense, gives information, secures this scene, and sets up a contrast between the reception of Elijah by Obadiah and that of Elijah by Ahab, Elijah indeed appears before Ahab. In fact, Elijah moves beyond the terse commission of Yahweh and initiates a full-scale competition between the prophets of Baal and himself to decide what cult deserves the undivided attention of the people.[54]

While this narrative unfolding fits the Hebrew style which allows a story to grow as it will,[55] sometimes taking surprising turns and revealing hidden characters, this turn engenders suspicion. For the most part, Elijah's obedience is thoughtless; what Yahweh commands, he does. When Yahweh sends him to Cherith, he follows the command exactly. When Yahweh sends him to Zarephath to receive succor from a widow, he follows his instructions fairly closely. The gap between command and execution grows wider though, like a crescendo mark which prescribes a gradual, but constant, increase in volume until the maximum intensity is reached. In chapter 18, he springs again to fulfill the command, but the question arises as to the extent of Yahweh's involvement in the calling of this contest. No doubt, Yahweh carries the day following the prayer of Elijah (1 Kgs 18.36ff.), just as he listened to Elijah on another day as Elijah leaned over a lifeless boy, but the suspicion of manipulation, though not the kind that occurs through feeble magic, lingers. When the rain finally comes and Elijah runs, enlivened by the spirit of Yahweh, little does Elijah know that the next test, a test which he sets up for himself by the failure to wait for Yahweh's word while he waits outside the royal domicile, will be the hardest test. He will fail this test and will remain only temporarily in God's service but he will never leave God's care.

The formidable courage displayed by Elijah in the presence of Ahab, or on Carmel, becomes more suspect as this review continues. Originally, the statement of Elijah uttered on Carmel (1 Kgs 18.22) exhibited a great deal of propriety; he was the only designated prophet of Yahweh there. On Horeb, that same claim, in the midst of the examination by his commissioner, Yahweh, became a hollow defense. As Kenneth Gros Louis aptly remarks:

> He was never as isolated as he thought he was. He should not have made his isolation his virtue, and then that virtue his despair.[56]

This hollowness is proved undeniably by Yahweh's final tally at the conclusion of Elijah's new commissioning (1 Kgs 19.18). Yahweh's assertion resembles an afterthought which grinds the message home with greater force, and recalls that meeting with Obadiah in 1 Kgs 18.7-15 where Elijah encounters one discreet benefactor of Yahweh's prophets. There Obadiah's confession (1 Kgs 18.13), underwritten by the narrator (1 Kgs 18.3b-4), remained only a whisper while Elijah cleared the way for his rendezvous with Ahab. Besides, Obadiah was suspect to Elijah and the audience for he served his lord, Ahab. This naturally placed him in the camp of those appropriately frightened by Elijah, the servant of Yahweh, God of Israel.

Obadiah's sincerity in retrospect holds true; his rescue efforts fit in the larger plan of Yahweh even if Elijah seems a threat to him. Until chapter 19, these earlier clues were held in suspension. Obadiah's assistance to the prophets was treated in much the same vocabulary as the divine assistance to Elijah. Obadiah fed (כלכלם—1 Kgs 18.4, 13) the prophets much the same food that Elijah was fed by the ravens and the widow. This verbal association, the aspect of hiding, and the grisly historical events that Obadiah recounts, suggest that the linear plot testifies to parallel events. While Elijah was being cared for by Yahweh's instruments, Obadiah was serving as Yahweh's comforter to another group. Obadiah, 'servant of Yahweh', was earning his name. Obadiah's admission further anticipates the announcement of the remnant in 1 Kgs 19.18. He claims he hid one hundred 'of the Lord's prophets' (מנביאי יהוה—1 Kgs 18.13b) and thereby implies that there were others to be aided. To listen to Elijah, one would think that the extinction of the covenant community was a breath away;[57] to attend to the account offered by Obadiah, especially after the unmasking of Elijah, one could praise Yahweh for the beneficence of his servants.

When one perceives this ironic structure, the uncontrollable fear of Elijah in the face of Jezebel's threat should come as no surprise. Furthermore, this liberates the explanation of his sudden depression from speculation on Hebrew psychology.[58] The design of the narrative, in concord with the content, prepares and ushers Elijah into this time of reckoning (1 Kgs 19.3-14). He is there, at Jezreel, to be installed as a spiritual hero; he is uncovered as a faithless, and therefore, fearful man. Later, at Horeb, after the justice of the reckoning has been meted out and the new commission has been detailed (1 Kgs 19.15-18) the time for real anxiety arrives. Elijah, instructed to initiate the lasting extermination of this abominable Baal cult, a plan that excludes him in favor of a successor, waits to see his status in the waning days of his assignment. His continued, though temporary, status as spokesman for Yahweh is subtly assured in his command to Elisha. He repeats the earlier command from Yahweh verbatim: 'Go, return. . . ' (. . . לך שוב לדרכך—1 Kgs 19.15 and. . . לך שוב,—1 Kgs 19.20) and continues in words which could have been intoned by Yahweh at Horeb. A sobered Elijah speaks a word of decision so that his successor, Elisha, will possess an undivided allegiance which is what Yahweh requires from people and prophets alike.

The Situational Irony within the Narrative

There is another level or kind of irony that threads through the pattern of this overall design and provides a constant interplay between anticipation or expectation and realization. This situational irony influences the plot in a more immediate manner than the previous sort; these narrative turns generate the action which propels the characters. Undoubtedly, the presence of this irony strengthens the ironical import of the total story.

One example of these generative sequences consists of the two appearances Elijah made before royalty and the subsequent hasty departures (1 Kgs 17.1ff., 19.1ff.). Although the first location remains unknown (1 Kgs 17.1), one may assume that the king was in his territory, whether at one of the royal residences or 'by the way' (1 Kgs 20.38). So these ventures of Elijah took him from a fellowship that in ideal times should be the height of the care-taking of the covenant faith in monarchic Israel, i.e., king and prophet together, to places and persons insensitive to, if not unacquainted with, the faith of Israel. In the first case beginning in 1 Kgs 17.8, especially with the greeting of the widow in 1 Kgs 17.12, one must mirror the question of Jean Steinmann:

> Que le fugitif aille se cacher en plein milieu du royaume d'Ittoball, le beau-père d'Achab, n'est-ce pas d'une ironie suprême?[59]

Others, like Leah Bronner,[60] emphasize the affront this poses to other gods and their domain, but do not highlight the simple humor and incongruity of Elijah's need to travel far away from Israel in order to enjoy the solace and safety of his God.

The incursion of a Yahwistic prophet into a country dominated by the worship of Baal and Elijah's acceptance and recognition by a woman apparently linked to another cult do not exhaust the irony. Elijah, who is dependent completely on the good graces of Yahweh, is sent from a depleted stream to this widow for basic sustenance. Elijah cautiously but deftly identifies the widow by a short series of tests.[61] Yet, he discovers that his rescuer is not eagerly awaiting his arrival or her time of service, but planning her last meal to be shared with her son before they slowly starve. Elijah offers an alternative plan and the success of that plan eclipses the woman's scheme. For this reason the protective care of Yahweh continues to sustain Elijah and includes these 'aliens' with whom Elijah resides.

Almost as soon as that situation stabilizes, the plot allows another complication. Like the stream that dries up from the lack of rain, the woman's son becomes so ill that no life remains (לא נותרה־בו נשמה—1 Kgs 17.17). This woman who had consigned so recently herself and her son to death, now berates their saviour for his presence; his presence and his link with the deity has brought an apparently fatal calamity to her son. Elijah assumes control to enliven her son. He questions Yahweh's extension of the curse of the drought to this life (הגם על־האלמנה—1 Kgs 17.20). Her gratefulness extends to a confession of faith in which she defines the designation—'man of god' (איש האלהים—1 Kgs 17.24)—she earlier used pejoratively to refer to Elijah (1 Kgs 17.18). Clearly, one cannot anticipate the sequence of events, for circumstances and the reaction of this woman divert the story in surprising directions.

The beginning of the second chapter of this narrative consists of a scene in which Ahab and his chief advisor, Obadiah, confer.

Obviously, Obadiah serves his master well, yet the adversative nuance of the preposition על (1 Kgs 18.3—can mean 'over' and 'against') grants to Obadiah an unstable role which is borne out in his public and private lives. Ahab instructs Obadiah to search throughout the land for any wells or streams which contain enough water to sustain the royal herds. The conditions are worsening, the narrator notes (1 Kgs 18.2b), and part of the strength and boast of Ahab is threatened.[62] This search possesses an urgency witnessed in Ahab's message and involvement in the search.

Obadiah's search is interrupted by the sudden appearance of Elijah. During the ensuing conversation between an assured Elijah and a traumatized Obadiah, an earlier search for Elijah, obviously to punish him for the curse that had precipitated this drought, is mentioned. Even though every nation and kingdom was scoured and every citizen was questioned for any sign of this recalcitrant prophet (1 Kgs 18.10), the search failed. Indeed, an oath was exacted which detailed the consequences of lying and harbouring this testy fugitive. When Obadiah stumbles upon Elijah, that earlier oath becomes his curse, especially when he is selected by the fugitive as the one to tell Ahab of the whereabouts of this testy, vanishing prophet. Obadiah persistently declines the task by detailing his fears and outlining the possible consequences which parallel the punishment that the prophets of Yahweh, some of whom he saved, met. Obadiah remains unmoved until Elijah, in the same form that he began this accursed drought, swears that he will appear to Ahab and, by implication, that Obadiah's life will not be jeopardized (1 Kgs 18.15—חי יהוה צבאות אשר עמדתי לפני ...).

In this short span of narrative time, several ironic twists have occurred. Obadiah has been sent to search for water and has found the subject of an earlier search. Yet, in finding Elijah he has also found water, for the audience knows that the appearance of Elijah will bring the end of the drought. The danger of the animals perishing from thirst has been exchanged for Obadiah's possible death by the sword for giving Ahab potentially false information. Elijah's pronouncement and disappearance was the cause of the original peril, and subsequently, the search for water, and his appearance is the genesis of the peril to Obadiah's life. However, Elijah's oath mitigates all those threats and initiates events which lead to a resolution of these tensions; he will appear to Ahab and rain will come in due time. One takes for granted that Obadiah, like the widow who earlier weathered the drought by means of Elijah's oath which promised unending supplies (1 Kgs 17.14ff.), maintains his position of responsibility and continues to fare well.

Two instances of ironical technique have been noted in the contest between Elijah and the prophets of Baal on Mount Carmel. Both arise in the part where Elijah is preparing his altar after the prophets of Baal have failed. The first occurs when Elijah completes the specified requirements of the contest altar which he had set apart by digging a trench about it. He then asked that four jars of water be poured upon the prepared offering. He asked that this be done a total of three times. Whether one believes that this represents a noticeable mixing of this account with the original drought account,[63] an example of sympathetic magic,[64] an act of faith by Elijah who used the water of the gathered people in anticipation of the victory of Yahweh and the ensuing rain,[65] the storyteller's manner of enhancing the story,[66] or the appropriation of available water for some purpose Elijah has in mind,[67] this use of water jolts one's expectation. The second instance, as Dennis Baly notes, relates to the

> remarkable fact that what the people were crying out for was rain, but the contest was about fire, and this contest was approved by people whose scorched fields must have caused them to dread the very word 'fire'.[68]

Two contrasting phenomena, fire, the nemesis of drought, and water, the conqueror of drought, appear suspensefully juxtaposed. The water douses a wholly prepared but unlighted sacrifice on the altar yet the fire not only overcomes the smothering capability of the water but laps it up like some thirsty dog.

The beginning of the third chapter of this story, famous for the hasty turnabout of Elijah, harbours, as expected, ironical events which supplement the action. As Ahab finishes the last word of his report, Jezebel composes a message to be hurled into Elijah's face: 'So may god do to me, and even more, if I do not make your life as the life of one of them by this time tomorrow' (1 Kgs 19.2).[69] There is no indication that Elijah considers waiting for a word from the Lord to instruct him; there is no hint of the strong-minded prophet who flung Ahab's insult back into the king's face as a stinging indictment (1 Kgs 18.18). The victory which Elijah planned and anticipated never materializes; Jezebel remains resolutely counter to Yahweh's will and Ahab doesn't resist her. What the narrator recounts in the ensuing events is a prophet who tries to bring her curse to pass. The Hebrew text suggests that on the morrow during a rest stop when he had traveled a day's journey (דרך יום—1 Kgs 19.4), he begged Yahweh to take his life. Elijah asked Yahweh to forsake the role of sustainer for that of killer.

Certain vocabulary places Elijah in a wider context, one he seems to deny, in which his despair becomes more pathetic. The first instance lies in Elijah's description of himself as being 'no better than my fathers' (1 Kgs 19.4).[70] This naturally contrasts with the phrase: 'as the life of one of them (כנפש אחד מהם—1 Kgs 19.2), and awakens the sense of consternation one feels at this broken prophet striving to effect Jezebel's curse. And yet, to die places Elijah not in the camp of the faithful, but in the heap with the slain prophets of Baal. Faithful Yahwists struggle to remain alive in order to stamp out apostasy and reform Yahwism. Two similar usages in 1 Kgs 18.5 and 1 Kgs 18.13 set up further contrast for they present concern for the continued vitality of the animals of the king and the prophets of Yahweh. In regard to this latter group, Elijah's request to die moves against the current of Yahweh's purposes. In addition, the collocation of certain words, namely מות and נפש, recall the sudden threat to the widow's son and his rescue by Elijah in 1 Kgs 17.17-24, especially verses 18, 20, 21f. Elijah lobbied on that occasion with a resolve that would have pleased Abraham. Now, this lifesaver exchanges that role for its opposite, that of arbiter for the taking of his own life (ישאל... למות—1 Kgs 19.4). Later, Elijah's defense on Horeb will be a reminder of this moment and that of Obadiah's defense in 1 Kgs 18.10, as Elijah claims that his life is sought by those who want to snatch it. Elijah's plea for death is a pitiful act. Yahweh's response to Elijah's request, carried by a messenger (1 Kgs 19.5, 7), comes indirectly but remains consistent with Yahweh's call to fidelity and, therefore, life.[71]

Accentuation of Ambiguity

Ambiguity particularly accentuates this instance of ironical incident, though it plays a part in other cases.[72] The primary equivocal element occurs in the curse of Jezebel whose intense anger erupts upon hearing about the events at Mt. Carmel. She shrieks: 'so may the gods [or the god] do to me...' (1 Kgs 19.2). Before the rain of death on the prophets of Baal, the prophets of her god, the people exclaimed the blessed equation: 'Yahweh is (the) God; Yahweh is (the) God' (1 Kgs 18.39).[73] This exclamation is the source of the indeterminacy of Jezebel's curse. Though one might say that she is swearing by her god,[74] Baal, in this context, after Carmel, she effectively binds herself by the god who proved to be a god—Yahweh. Therefore, she asks Yahweh's blessing on her murderous intent which forms a predominant part of her reputation. Curiously enough, Elijah calls upon his god, Yahweh, to take his life and this petition seeks to make Yahweh into Jezebel's god who would condone his murder. Yahweh, 'the god', remains unambiguously committed to his prophet and ignores this plea.

Another uncertainty, found in 1 Kgs 19.5, guides the suspense of the plot and supplements this ironical bent of the earlier part of chapter 19. Originally, Jezebel had dispatched a messenger to present Elijah the message of doom. Elijah immediately panicked, fled, begged death, and lay down to die like the old Indian, Old Lodge Skins, in the film, 'Little Big Man'.[75] A messenger, destination undesignated and overseer undisclosed, touches him. One expects the messenger of Jezebel who bodes death. Yet, that messenger bending over Elijah brings a message of life when he provides sustenance. The tension temporarily remains—the message associated with Yahweh, the messenger commissioned by Jezebel. The second appearance of the messenger to the sleeping Elijah dispels the tension, for this messenger is called specifically the messenger of Yahweh (מלאך יהוה—1 Kgs 19.7). The message, the messenger, and the dispatcher are in the same camp. In this case the ambiguity is resolved.

The Carmel scene (1 Kgs 18.19ff.) manifests ambiguity which complements the irony that pervades that charged scene. Before the contest, Elijah bids Ahab to 'send and gather all Israel to me at Mount Carmel, and the four hundred and fifty prophets of Baal' (1 Kgs 18.19). In the text, Ahab responds by sending to all the people of Israel, and gathering the prophets together at Mt. Carmel, a neat and significant separation of the verbs. At that point, Elijah approaches all the people (אל־כל־העם—1 Kgs 18.21).[76] The definite terms relating to the two groups ('all Israel' or 'all the sons of Israel'—'prophets of Baal' or 'prophets') are dropped for this general term. The picture is not all that surprising; all the people present gather around the convener. Yet, the usage of this broad term suggests the inclusion of the representatives of the other faith, the prophets of Baal, who bear alongside the people of Israel the rebuke by Elijah concerning the mixture of cultic practices or the abandonment of sole allegiance to

Yahweh for a schizophrenic faith, and later, watch the repair of the altar of Yahweh (1 Kgs 18.3). This vagueness assumes a comic effect as 'the people' are held up to Yahweh by Elijah in prayer so that Yahweh might cordon off his people once again. Finally, after the fire of Yahweh falls and consumes everything to the edge of the trench, all the people fall on their faces and say: 'Yahweh is (the) God; Yahweh is (the) God!' Although reason draws one to assume that this is the people of Israel adoring their God who has reclaimed their allegiance by means of a dazzling and well-timed theophany, imagination recognizes those frustrated, bleeding, fearful prophets of Baal in the back of that kneeling, praising bunch of repentant Yahwists. At that point, Elijah separates the group and calls them (specifically, the people) to seize the prophets of Baal and to kill them. The people that remain belong to Yahweh.

One other fascinating equivocal relation demands attention. The reader is told twice, once in a narrator's aside and once in the narration of Obadiah, that Obadiah hid 100 prophets of Yahweh 'in the cave' (1 Kgs 18.4, 13).[77] The location of the cave and the advisability of hiding these prophets in two groups of fifty remain untreated; that information is not particularly germane. Yet, the significance of this cave and these prophets increases because of its connection to a subsequent incident in the story. Much later, after Elijah has trod forty days and forty nights to Horeb, he comes to 'the cave' (1 Kgs 19.9). Regardless of the external narrative referents to this cave,[78] this internal correlation necessitates a juxtaposition of these two notices. Both of these contexts attest the sustenance associated with the divine care. In the Obadiah sequence, the bread and water were provisions during the length of the intense persecution which Jezebel instigated. Elijah arrives at a cave after a long journey which was fueled by a two-course meal of 'a cake baked on hot stones and a jar of water' (1 Kgs 19.6). In both cases, the persecution of Jezebel triggers, or at least precedes the tenure at the cave. Obadiah performs a courageous act of compassion for the prophets of Yahweh in the face of Jezebel's malicious acts; Elijah completes a cowardly pilgrimage of fear in respose to Jezebel's threat of death. Elijah's action and his stay at the cave subtly identify him with those prophets and make his forthcoming claim of being the only prophet ludicrous. The structure and design of this narrative does not allow one to forget the contrast between Elijah and these prophets and the contrast between Elijah and Obadiah. The courage and faithfulness of Yahweh's servant who ministered to these hunted prophets judge the conceit and fearfulness—or faithlessness—of Elijah.

Elijah's Use of Irony

The third type of irony evidenced in this material bears a resemblance to the verbal irony that structures this whole story, yet here Elijah is not the victim of the irony. Elijah addresses the prophets of Baal ironically. Gunkel, years ago, noted the irony contained in Elijah's bidding: 'Choose for yourselves one bull and prepare it first, for you are many; and call on the name of your god' (1 Kgs 18.25bc).[79] He exposed the reality behind this comment; Elijah is alone because all his kind, prophets of Yahweh, are dead in contradistinction to the prophets of Baal who share the favor of Jezebel and Ahab. His statement thus poignantly and pointedly picks up the earlier accounts of the persecution of the prophets and the earlier contrast of Elijah as one against the four hundred and fifty prophets of Ba'al.

Elijah's sardonic strategy, paralleling the increasing fervor and frustration of the prophets of Baal, ultimately spills out into the open, and, in fact, is marked in the Hebrew text by the most obvious means; the text states that Elijah mocked them (ויהתל—1 Kgs 18.27).[80] Elijah said: 'Cry with a great voice, for he is (a) God; either he is musing, or has gone aside, or has gone on a journey, or perhaps he is asleep and must be awakened'.[81] Although all these references are not completely clear, one can be assured that Elijah, like the ironist who shaped Elijah's story, takes the 'signs' from the trappings of Baalism and constructs an encouragement that no true Yahwistic sympathizer, in the crowd or in the audience, could allow to stand as literal statement.[82] Elijah's allegiance, his confidence, and his vocabulary here, especially 'because he (is) God' (כי־אלהים הוא—1 Kgs 18.27b), anticipate the final victory rung in by the people when they shout: 'Yahweh is (the) God; Yahweh is (the) God' (יהוה הוא האלהים—1 Kgs 18.39).[83] In addition, he is poking fun at a god tied to the earth and its rhythms (natural and personal) and inattentive to the cries of these prophets. Odd, indeed, that this prophet who belittles these prophets and their god, Baal, should soon flee a day's journey into the wilderness and fall asleep awaiting death. Yet, the discontinuity of Elijah's behavior is surpassed by the tragedy of this faithless prophet.

The Plot's Support of the Ironic Structure

The ironic cast of this narrative, though it provides the primary means of organization, relies on the support of the plot. From start to finish, the plot flows temporally in a straight line with direct and indirect references to past and future events which endow the narrative with necessary detail. At the same time, the events of chapters 17–18 generally correlate to those included in chapter 19.[84] This correlation supports in turn the ironic design of these three chapters.[85]

Both halves, though the twenty-one verses of chapter 19 do not measure up in length to the seventy verses of chapters 17–18, begin punctuated by a curse. The occasion of the second curse is very specific: Elijah has killed the prophets of Jezebel's faith. Likewise the content is very clear: Jezebel intends to have Elijah assassinated, for he is a prophet of Yahweh and he is the very one responsible for the deaths of the prophets of Baal. On the contrary, the first curse or oath, of which Elijah is the subject not the object, is shrounded in mystery for some time. The story begins suddenly, *in medias res*, with a general and somewhat cryptic introduction to a prophet who circumscribes the whole domain by his curse, slow death by privation or drought. Only later, in 1 Kgs 18.18 does the reason for the curse surface.

In both instances, Elijah quits the location and travels to another place. Early in the story, his movement is guided by the word of the Lord to an obscure hideaway where food and water are provided until the effects of the drought affect his source of water, the brook Cherith. At this point, he is again notified of a place where he may obtain food and water in a safe setting. After Jezebel's threat, Elijah flees, *sans* the word of the Lord,[86] to a place a day's journey from civilization, to a place of foreboding, to the wilderness. Sustenance, however, will soon arrive there, but what characterizes this scene is the fear and despair in contrast to the confidence and comfort earlier, especially evident in the contrast between 1 Kgs 19.3a and 17.10a.

No one can doubt the depth of Elijah's despair as he asks his life to be taken. Perhaps he longs for the death that almost came to the son of the widow of Zarephath. Elijah experiences a curious recovery tutored by a messenger who takes the very words of despair (רב עתה—1 Kgs 19.4), and incorporates them into a vivifying, yet challenging directive of Yahweh (כי רב, in addition to ממך הדרך—1

Kgs 19.7). Attentive once again to the designs of Yahweh, Elijah moves towards action.

The third correlative sequence, with regard to the wilderness despair of Elijah, is the meeting with Obadiah. Gunkel realized that the meeting with Obadiah, and, later, with Ahab constituted a significant parallel. He called this the style of amplification (der ausführender Stil), in which first one meets with the representative and then with the king or God.[87] Similarly, Gressmann commented on 1 Kgs 18.2b-15 in terms that praised the narrator's art when he wrote:

> Das Unwichtige geht voran, wie in der Horebgeschichte (c. 19) zuerst der Engel, dann Jahve erscheint, damit durch die bedeutsamere Fortsetzung der Eindruck gesteigert wird. Die Kunst des Erzählers, die Personen zu charakterisieren, entfaltet sich hier besonders glänzend, und die Art, wie er die Ereignisse am Königshof 'nachholt', ist äusserst geschickt. Statt der Reihe nach zu berichten, was unterdessen geschehen ist, begnügt er sich zunächst mit dem Notwendigsten, um die Trennung des Königs von seinem Minister erklärlich zu machen.[88]

In both cases, the messenger—Elijah to Obadiah, the nameless messenger to Elijah—pierces the hesitation of the receiver in order to spur the latter on his way. In the first instance, Elijah, who delivers a message to Obadiah in order to arrange a meeting with Ahab, eventually trades insults with Ahab and argues about their fidelity to Yahweh. With the weight of the Yahwistic faith on his side, Elijah overwhelms the waffling Ahab. In the second cse, the messenger stirs Elijah and sends him on his way to Horeb to meet Yahweh. The earlier pattern shifts to fit the particular scene, but remains significantly the same. Elijah, not the messenger who spurred him on, has the last word with Yahweh, but Elijah is as strident as he was with Ahab. Elijah appears here, as there, to claim that the one who stands before him is 'the troubler of Israel' (compare 1 Kgs 18.18 and 1 Kgs 19.10, 14). On Horeb, Elijah's boast is defused both by the silent sound[89] and the pronouncement of God's commission that never depends upon any one person, but upon submission to the will of Yahweh.

Just as the ironical design of the story forces one to begin the narrative anew with the knowledge of Elijah's pride, the last two episodes of the story, the Horeb sequence and the calling of Elisha, invite one back to the Carmel scene and the coming of the rain where the tension in the first section of the narrative is resolved. In short, the Horeb scene recalls the ordeal upon Carmel and the coming of the rain; the events upon Carmel anticipate the Horeb scene. Likewise, the appointment of Elisha is compared best to the Carmel scene. However, in this case, not only does the last scene of 1 Kgs 17–19 hark back to this triumph on Carmel, but it anticipates a future victory and closes this story of the important, but prideful prophet, Elijah.

This relation between Horeb and Carmel surfaces most readily in three instances. First, both are mountains where Yahweh chooses to reveal the divine intention in theophanic style. At Carmel, the manifestation occurs at the proper time and in the proper form. At Horeb, the god 'who is who he is' varies the appearance in both timing and form in regard to both Elijah's and traditional expectation.[90] Second, the completeness of the annihilation of the prophets of Baal after their defeat at Carmel (איש אל־ימלט מהם—1 Kgs 18.40) anticipates the total devastation of the followers of Baal that is to come at the hands of Hazael, Jehu, and Elisha (הנמלט מהרב—1 Kgs 19.17).[91] Undoubtedly, this indicates that Elijah knew the goal of Yahweh's plan; he just wanted a larger share of the management. Third, the prominent role of the word *qol* (קול) presses the comparison or contrast of the use of this word in two arenas. *Qol* applies only to Baal at Carmel and the word emerges in a context that underscores the impotency, the inattentiveness, or the disinterested character of Baal. Any of these attributes in such a contest with Yahweh, who claimed undivided attention from the faithful, meant that this other god was not god for Israel.[92] The voice that comes at Horeb after the powerful displays of natural forces is qualified not by the negative particle *lo'* (לא), or, the sound of absence, but characterized by the silence of close presence, of a being so close that the stare and the wafer-thin whisper, whether gentle and soft or charged and liquid, are all that is needed. Carmel reveals the sound of silence (Baal); Horeb witnesses the sound of silencing (Yahweh).

The theophany and the commission delivered to Elijah possess a pointed ordering.[93] First come the three marvelous, but terrifying natural features which rest in the memory of all Israelites. Then, comes that voice or sound wherein lies a mysterious revelation to the awaiting Elijah. In the assignment of Elijah, twice a three-fold figure is employed. Elijah is to anoint three key figures and these three persons are to form a three-link chain through which no follower of

Baal may burst. Just as the silence slipped out of the tumult, after the raging execution will remain a zealous group, apparently unknown by Elijah, whose steady faith, sustained by Yahweh, outlasted the drought of pure Yahwism.[94] Elijah's thunderous zeal is silenced by the fervor of these silent faithful.

The same word, *qol*, that linked in part the Carmel scene to the Horeb scene, ties the Horeb scene to the coming of the much needed rain. There, in the earlier scene, Elijah sends Ahab to the top of Carmel as he hears the roaring sound (קול המון—1 Kgs 18.41) of a violent torrential rain. A short time later, after the seven trips of the youth to look toward the sea, Elijah sends this nameless helper to warn Ahab of the hazardous effect of this rain. Ahab, however, will not be swept away by this welcome end to the accursed drought, but this sound points on to the time when Yahweh declines to sound his will through nature, but commissions Elijah to legitimate the reigns which will sweep away the dynasty of Omri and the syncretism which so characterized that family, and will leave seven thousand faithful.

The final scene (1 Kgs 19.19-21) loosely corresponds with the last episode in chapter 18. Elijah runs before Ahab and Elisha runs after Elijah (רוץ—1 Kgs 18.46 and 19.20). Yet, this activity, in addition to the comparison between an unnamed youth who appears practically out of nowhere and follows Elijah's every command and this hesitant successor, Elisha, underscores the difference between Elijah triumphant and Elijah humbled.[95] At the close of chapter 19, Elijah no longer manages the whole affair. He remains somewhat within the will of Yahweh and mirrors Yahweh's will as he hastily empowers a successor who ministers to Elijah not out of obligation or obedience, but out of the natural relation between prophet and successor.

The final scene (1 Kgs 19.19-21) actually corresponds with the Carmel scene. This correlation is cemented by means of the scene which details the end of the drought (1 Kgs 18.41-46) and the final verse of the Horeb scene (1 Kgs 19.18). Elijah was told by Yahweh: 'Yet I will leave several thousand in Israel, all the knees that have not bowed to Baal, and every mouth that has not kissed him' (1 Kgs 19.18). This recalls Elijah's enigmatic bowing on the peak of Mount Carmel while Ahab ate a meal and points to Elisha's surprising request to be allowed to return to kiss his mother and father. The difference between fidelity to Yahweh on the part of Elijah and the hesitancy on the part of Elisha, underscored by those seven thousand who display their fidelity to Yahweh by disdaining Baal, places the decision or the choice that Elisha must make on a par to that which the people were instructed to make on Carmel. To stand with Elijah in either place, on Carmel, or beside this tilled field, is to side with the faithful; this last episode makes that perfectly clear. Furthermore, Elisha's subsequent sacrifice and inclusion of the people quickly and astonishingly fulfills the triumph at Carmel and prefigures the coming triumph when the dynasty of Omri and the worship of Baal will be overturned. 'The people', that ambiguous group, finally refined to the people of Israel at Qishon (1 Kgs 18.40), but neglected in the regal celebration at the top of Carmel, are included here. Elisha, when he chooses to follow Elijah, to forego his former way of life, and to leave behind his twelve yoke of oxen for the man who built an altar with twelve stones, includes the people in the celebration. The full victory of Carmel—Yahweh's triumph, not Elijah's victory—is realized at last. Furthermore, Elisha is selected as a successor who will assist in a victory that will be more glorious and more enduring than that of Carmel.

Chapter 2

THE THEME OF DECISION AND ITS INFLUENCE
AS THE SUPERSTRUCTURE OF
1 KINGS 17-19

God is not alone when discarded by man. But man is alone.
Abraham Heschel

We stand, brethren, where we stand, in our impossible and often
mischievously idle jobs, on a boundary of opposing urgencies
where there is often not space enough to set one's feet—we so stand
as steeples stand, as emblems; it is our station to be visible and to
provide men with the opportunity to profess the impossible that
makes their lives possible. The Catholic church in this at least was
right; a priest is more than a man, and though the man disintegrate
within his vestments, and become degraded beyond the laxest of
his flock, the priest can continue to perform his functions, as a
scarecrow performs his.

John Updike

In addition to the ironic design, the parallel structures, and the
repeated vocabulary, whether single words or longer phrases, these
three chapters cohere by means of certain themes and motifs.[1] R.A.
Carlson, an outspoken scholar, argues that 1 Kings 17-19 should be
considered as two acts of one drama.[2] This drama, according to
Carlson, speaks of the struggle between Yahweh and Baal and its
unity and power finally rest in this theme that guides and enriches
the action, together with numerous framing motifs.[3] He mentions
specifically the motifs of the death of the prophets, the servant (נער)
of the prophet, the theophany, and the remnant. These are supplemented
further by the obvious *verba associandi* peculiar to each motif.[4] As
the drama unfolds, he claims that the unity and effect of the
narrative rely upon the complex interrelation of these several
elements.

Carlson's article, not solely based on the perceptive analysis of this
material as a dramatic whole, manages to provide certain insight. His

conclusions generally accord with the traditional interpretation of this segment of the Deuteronomistic History. Undoubtedly, the eradication of Baalism fuels Elijah's vigorous attempt to be the one who finally stamps out that wretched faith which divides his people. But this goal is controlled literarily and thematically by the theme of choice—deciding to serve Yahweh or to serve Baal (not Yahweh). This theme radiates added power for the ironic structure reveals that Elijah needs to make that choice, too. Ultimately, therefore, Carlson eclipses the guiding theme and confuses the subject matter with the theme. The final test, of course, of the centrality of this theme consists of the ease with which it fits with the previously delineated design.

The theme of choice, which additionally focuses this narrative, accords with the parallel structure of these three chapters (17–18 with 19) for the one major decision made in the first part, the people's choice to follow Yahweh, is completed in the major decision in chapter 19, Elisha's decision to follow Elijah. These two decisions are linked by the remaining choice, Elijah's decision truly to serve Yahweh. The theme of choice automatically fits with the ironic tenor of these three chapters as it follows the indomitable Elijah who forces two of these decisions and struggles with himself in the third. Other themes and motifs, which fall lower on the hierarchy of importance, primarily connect the different episodes to one another. Finally, there are themes, motifs, and expressions which connect parts in a relatively short span, i.e., during episodes and at transition points in the narrative. All these march the narrative forward like some practiced band which moves rapidly back and forth, in and out, intermingling almost chaotically from the spectator's viewpoint, until the full plan has been executed and the band stops, expertly arranged.

The choices distributed through this three chapter span likewise display a range of types. All of the key choices—that of the people on Carmel, that of Elijah on Horeb, and that of Elisha by the field—are linked. The most portentous choice, that of Elijah's eventual determination to submit wholly to the strictures and calculations of Yahweh, proves most subtle in its development; yet this struggle and its resolution rests in the midst of the other two decisions. A second level of decisions, not as far-reaching as the others, still entails a high level of risk. These decisions demand a clear answer from the person solicited. The widow and Obadiah make such choices. The third level of decision, as in all the others, is prompted by Elijah, but these choices do not allow for real thought or hesitancy, just response. Here Elijah commands or instructs and the person of group—Ahab, the servant, the prophets of Baal, the widow, the people—immediately, almost mindlessly, obey. The time for the decision proves brief for the story speeds on its way. Finally, there are decisions made by Jezebel and Ahab, indirectly goaded by Elijah or his actions, which appear in the plot. On the whole, these decisions testify to the centrality of Elijah and magnify his need to unify his motives and to serve Yahweh wholly.

The First Level of Decision

The choice made at Carmel illustrates this first order of decision. The contest at Carmel arose in the face of an interruption in the spiritual development of Israel. Whether the king had accommodated his queen and in turn the people had become comfortable with the syncretism, or, the syncretism, notably prevalent in the north, made the accommodation by the people and king more acceptable is not the question. The confusion or the fusion of Yahwism and Baalism was unacceptable to those who were steeped in pure Yahwism. The Carmel scene is certainly one place where Elijah is portrayed as one of those zealous Yahwists[5] who directs the people in a dramatic determination to become holy unto Yahweh alone, again[6] if just for one testimonial moment.

Elijah excels in the management of this necessary determination on Carmel.[7] The scene is cut into two major sections by the appearance of the verb נגשׁ (1 Kgs 18.21, 30).[8] In the first instance, Elijah faces a tentative group and exercises the initiative; he approaches the people. In the second, he calls for action and the people respond. Between these two occurrences, Elijah rebukes the people for their participation in the mixing of the faiths,[9] calls for decisive action, devises a contest when his plea confronts unresponsive people, and goads his opposition with instructions and mockery until their failure becomes overwhelming.

Although one might think that Elijah followed the unsuccessful prophets of Baal in this context because of his confidence,[10] that sentiment should not deny the tension that resides in this encounter at this point. However, the signs which indicate the people's edging toward the embrace of Yahwism are equally present. David Jobling provides convincing evidence that the acceptance of Yahweh as the true god is prefigured in the people's willingness to obey Elijah when he commands them to draw near (18.30).[11] The second half of the contest begins with this obedience of the people and the rising tide of support.

The account of Elijah's elaborate preparation slows the narrative, signaling the uniqueness of his preparations. Part of these procedures parallel those of the prophets of Baal. He follows in the space of one word (יעשו—1 Kgs 18.26), with two notable exceptions, the rules that were followed by the opponents. First, he builds an altar befitting an Israelite sacrifice; the altar contains twelve stones representing the twelve tribes. The similarity between the preparations of the prophets of Baal and Elijah, and yet the difference, is underscored paronomastically. The prophets of Baal cut themselves as is their custom (כמשפטם—1 Kgs 18.28), and Elijah builds the altar according to the number (כמספר—1 Kgs 18.31) of the tribes of Israel. Second, he surrounds the altar with a trench which enables the altar to be a place where the Holy One may act exclusively. In addition, the completed altar and sacrifice is drenched with water, twelve full containers, until the altar is soaked and the trench is filled. Whatever the reason for this last preparation,[12] it complicates the task. Signaled by the final appearance of the verb נגש (1 Kgs 18.36), Elijah, like the prophets of Baal, calls upon his god, Yahweh, pleading that Yahweh answer by fire. The response is immediate; Yahweh's fire consumes everything—the offering, the wood, the stones, the dust, and the water (ואת האבנים . . . את-תעלה ואת-העצים—1 Kgs 18.38)—to the border of the altar area. After all the waiting, 'the god' replies and so do the people.

The prayer of Elijah, both for its length and its content, holds special interest.[13] The first third of the prayer follows the expectation; Elijah calls on the special name of his god and requests that Yahweh seal his sovereignty over Israel with fire. Then, Elijah attaches a rider to his plea. This rider has the effect of tying Elijah's position and authority to the anticipated manifestation of the deity.[14] Curiously enough, the phrase in 1 Kgs 18.36—כל-הדברים האלה—ties this Carmel scene with an earlier scene which was introduced by the phrase אחר הדברים האלה (1 Kgs 17.17). The raising of the widow's son was also a scene where the efficacy of Elijah and the worth of his word were at stake. While this may be seen as a normal affirmation of a powerful prophet's word and deed, this may be interpreted alternatively as the devising of a self-serving prophet who has lost sight of who is sovereign.[15] Elijah continues to mirror the unsuccessful priests of Baal as he pleads for an answer that will break the impasse of this situation—the people's waffling and the silence of the gods: 'Answer me, O Yahweh, Answer me, so that this people may know that you, O Yahweh, are the god. . . ' (כי־אתה יהוה האלהים—1 Kgs 18.37a). The story teeters for a moment between the failure indicated by silence— the silence of the people when Elijah first approached and the silence of Baal when Baal's prophets called upon him—and the success brought by Yahweh's earlier action-the raising of the lad. Finished with his primary request, Elijah hastily adds: '. . . then you may surround their heart afterward' (1 Kgs 18.37b).[16] The fiery response which came as Elijah drew in his breath, concludes the prayer and the contest along with the unashamed exclamation by the people, a people who began stone silent.

The two sections of this Carmel encounter are set apart by one other fascinating and crucial literary feature—the prevalence of two images that reflect the dynamics of the predicament of the people of Israel. In the first half, 1 Kgs 18.21-29, the word פסח connects the people to Baalism and images the confusion that Elijah links with the people's blatant denial of Yahwism's exclusive claim upon them. In the latter half, 1 Kgs 18.30-39, with the approaching success of Elijah and the growing inclination of the people to assert Yahweh's supremacy, סביב and its root verb סבב (*hiphil* in 1 Kgs 18.37) provide the material for a new image.[17] The new reality is an Israel once again circumscribed by the true faith and practice. As Elijah sets the altar apart from the rest of the space on Carmel, so he asks that Yahweh declare by fire his supremacy and then encompass this people once again.[18] Just as the fire will consume all that is within the boundaries, Yahweh, when he has fulfilled the instructions, will engulf Israel with his sovereignty. These two images—Israel confused and Israel consumed—guide the progress of this contest and Elijah's vision. Ultimately, the people are engulfed by a passion for the god who answered and their fiery acclamation is fanned by Elijah who incites them to devour the prophets of Baal by the sword. Yahweh once again has encircled his people; he has yet to corner his prophet.

Elijah's decision, in chapter 19, proves more troublesome to outline than the decision at Carmel. At Carmel, the issue, aggravated by a curse from the lips of Elijah and the subsequent drought, was explicit—Yahweh or Baal—and the opponents clear. Aligning oneself with Elijah meant aligning oneself with Yahweh. Yet this mighty prophet slowly disclosed his true allegiance, to himself, and, in his own way, jeopardized the purity and continuance of Yahweh's plan.

The obvious components of the decision, skillfully displayed in the Carmel episode where Elijah called for a choice, fail to surface in the long narrative that trails a mighty Elijah, later a dejected Elijah, down the road to decision. The subtlety of this movement derives from his central role, apparently in the forefront for Yahweh, and the complexity of his idolatry, the pride and power inherent in his role. For him, the call to decide comes through his fear, his despair, but ultimately, his arrogance when he encounters Yahweh's unnerving presence on Horeb. Yahweh's questions, the theophany, and the new commission weigh down this pretentious prophet; Elijah suffers under the insult of Yahweh's plan which excludes him. His subsequent decision, evident in his acceptance of the commission, means that he has affirmed the people's choice—Yahweh is (the) God![19]

No doubt, certain vocabulary that winds through this narrative undergirds Elijah's feeling and claim that he is the single defender of the faith. The words אותר, אני and לבדי, concentrated in 1 Kgs 19.10 and 14, reveal once more Elijah's arrogance.[20] These words emphasize the singularity that existed sometimes in fact and always in the mind of Elijah. From the conflict on Carmel where Elijah acted as the sole representative of the faith to the defense on Horeb where he represented himself as the sole actor in the drama of faith, even relegating Yahweh to the less zealous of the two, Elijah's perception of how he stood alone and what he would do now startles. One receives the impression that the wilderness scene plays with this solitude. Elijah sleeps under one broom tree. The lone prophet in the wilderness sleeps under the lone shade tree in the no man's land between the acclamation on Carmel and defamation on Horeb. Yet, when the only one meets the Holy One on Horeb, he discovers what the audience knew long before; Elijah is not alone in any respect.

Although the realignment of Elijah's fidelity releases the constant tension that stemmed from Elijah's hubris (alozony), the implementation of the plans of Yahweh must be passed to a faithful successor. Elijah, the one sought by Ahab in every nation and kingdom and found by Obadiah or the one who described himself as the one sought after (1 Kgs 19.10, 14), finds Elisha engaging in the activities of a livelihood. Elijah interrupts Elisha's work and calls him in a manner which easily carries the proper symbolic meaning; he casts his cloak upon him (1 Kgs 19.19).[21] Elisha's response is immediate. He runs after Elijah. However, this gesture is not as revelatory as it seems. Elisha runs after Elijah not to take a place of apprenticeship, but to request a short reprieve, one last glance homeward.

In two short verses, 1 Kgs 19.20-21, a decision as momentous as that on Carmel and as basic as that taken by Elijah occurs. Just as on Carmel, to follow Yahweh's representative, Elijah, is to follow Yahweh's sanctioned way which leads to victory. Elisha's reticence is countered by a command and a question that rebuke him and pose a threat to him. The first part of Elijah's reply, לך שוב, rebukes for it reflects Yahweh's abrupt message on Horeb (1 Kgs 19.15) to an as yet unrepentant, prideful prophet.[22] In an instant, Yahweh had jerked Elijah from his pedestal and fitted him into a larger frieze. The second part of Elijah's reply, כי מה-עשיתי לך, truly searches for an answer as it recalls two earlier instances where Elijah's presence brought consternation and threat.[23] The widow had said: 'What have you against me, O man of God? You have come to me to bring my sin to remembrance, and to cause the death of my son' (1 Kgs 17.18). Later, Obadiah had inquired: 'Wherein have I sinned, that you would give your servant into the hand of Ahab, to kill me?' (1 Kgs 18.9). Here the man of God queries and reverses these former instances by placing the burden of action and decision upon Elisha, just as Yahweh had done to him on Horeb. If Elisha turned back to kiss his parents, he would decide against the plans of Yahweh and would render himself ineligible for the task; Yahweh wants those who do not pledge themselves to another (1 Kgs 19.18).

Elisha's response incites the worst of fears in the audience as he turns back (וישב מאחריו—1 Kgs 19.21), but that initial impression fades as he sacrifices the symbol of his life and connection to the past—the yoke of oxen.[24] Then, Elisha shares this act with 'the people' (1 Kgs 19.21) who are linked by means of vocabulary (לעם), with those instrumental, but not immediately included, in the ceremony afterwards on Carmel (1 Kgs 18.39). Appropriately, with the prophet who will complete the purge of Baalism, the people now share. For Elisha, the return for this sacrifice represents a decision to honor the plans of Yahweh and to guarantee the eventual victory.[25] Finally, in words reminiscent of Elijah's earlier acquiescence to

Yahweh's command (1 Kgs 17.10, but also 19.3), Elisha follows Elijah and ministers unto him (וישרתהו). Like the people and Elijah, Elisha has selected Yahweh exclusively; Elisha will now care for Elijah until his turn to serve. With the victory guaranteed and the succession in transition, the story closes.[26]

The Second Level of Decision

Another set of choices which structure and fill the narrative prove more earthbound. These involve a decision to trust Elijah, this overbearing man of God, this elusive spokesman for Yahweh. The widow must make two such determinations: one to save her and her son's lives while sustaining Elijah and another to save her son's life. Obadiah need only make one decision, but he interprets that decision as one that could mean his death if Elijah does live up to his reputation. Ultimately, both choose to trust Elijah and reap not only the benefits of their trust, but enhance the prestige of Elijah.

These choices solicited from the widow and Obadiah are linked by more than the common connection to Elijah and the possible benefit or harm that his sections might bring them. Certain Hebrew phrases accord with one another and thereby encourage a comparison by the audience. For example, upon being asked by Elijah to provide a small morsel of bread to overcome his hunger, the widow maintains: 'As the Lord, your God, lives, I have nothing baked, only a handful of meal in a jar, and a little oil in a cruse' (חי־יהוה אלהיך אם־יש־לי ... —1 Kgs 17.12). Upon first hearing the command of Elijah to inform Ahab of Elijah's whereabouts, Obadiah exclaims: 'As the Lord, your God, lives, there is no nation or kingdom whither my lord has not sent to seek you' (חי יהוה אלהיך אם־יש־גוי ... —1 Kgs 18.10). Moreover, in the second incident detailing the widow's dealings with Elijah, when her son becomes lifeless, she says to Elijah: 'What have you against me, O man of God? You have come to me to bring my sin to remembrance, and to cause the death of my son!' (מה־לי ולך ... להזכר—1 Kgs 17.18). Obadiah links Elijah's perilous request to his sin when he says: 'Wherein have I sinned, that you give your servant into the hand of Ahab, to kill me?' (חטאתי ... —1 Kgs 18.9). Elijah treats both similarly. To the widow, he counters with an oracle promising deliverance from the injurious effects of the drought; to Obadiah, he swears by the very life of his god that Obadiah's life will be spared (כה אמר יהוה אלהי ... —1 Kgs 17.14 and ... חי יהוה צבאות

—1 Kgs 18.15).[27] In each case, the trust is repaid with success, a truly precious return, and Elijah is rewarded with an ever-increasing credibility.

The Third Level of Decision

The third level of choice, seen in numerous places, plays a lesser part in the theme of choice and primarily influences the flow of the story. These are the cases in which Elijah, or some other character, suggests or commands a certain manner of proceeding and the other person(s) acts accordingly. For example, Elijah demands that Ahab gather two groups to Carmel. Ahab complies and this compliance signifies a decision; yet there is no particular emphasis on this decision like those displayed in the larger discourse. On the other hand, the command of Elijah to the widow to hand over her son to him, meets with either indecision or rejection. So Elijah makes her decision for her or overrules her objection by acting firmly. Both of these types of decision contribute to the movement of the plot, speeding it up or slowing it down, so that the points of greater narrative emphasis may stand out even more.[28]

The Characters as Alternative Models

Choice naturally entails two or more alternatives. The decisions outlined above require either a yes or no reaction or the choosing of one point of view over another,—saying yes to one and no to the other. No decision allows both; one must rest on one side or the other.

The antitheses, witnessed in the two poles of the decision, spill over into the larger narrative in a most peculiar and fascinating manner. The story offers alternatives in the people portrayed, and like the primary loyalties they symbolize, to choose one of them or to emulate one of them is to be identified with them. The audience thereby not only confronts the decisions portrayed, but participates in the making of those choices.

One opposition which arises within this narrative is that between the widow of Zarephath and Jezebel. Jean Steinmann observes:

> . . . la veuve de Sarepta est le parfait antitype de Jézebel. Elle est Phénicienne, comme la reine; mais elle pratique la grande vertue orientale d'hospitalité, qui est la plus belle approximation de la

charité. Et si Jézebel a provoqué la mort dans le royaume de Iahvé,
Elie, héraut du Dieu vivant, va porter la vie dans le royaume de la
Phénicienne en ressuscitant le fils unique de la pauvresse. Ce
miracle... est un signe tangible de l'universalisme grandissant de
la prédication prophétique, mais aussi signe de la nature d'un Dieu
qui rend la vie á un enfant, au moment où les crimes d'une reine
précipitent un royaume dans la mort! Comme la première exclamation
de la veuve: 'Par Iahvé vivant ton Dieu!' reçoit une singulière
justification! L'auteur du texte semble jongler avec les mots 'vie' et
'mort'. C'est le triomphe de la vie jusqu'à la profession de foi finale
de la femme: 'Je sais que tu es homme de "El" et que la parole de
Iahvé est vraiment dans ta bouche!' On pourrait jeter ce credo à la
face de la Phénicienne Jézebel![29]

As one can imagine, such an opposition invites a comparison and
contrast that can only deepen the significance of this narrative.
However, in a narrative in which the primary theme is that of
picking the more acceptable alternative, it becomes imperative to
notice this comparison.

Another major opposition is that between Obadiah and Ahab. This
one is both more subtle and more obvious. More subtle, for Obadiah
was the trusted first servant of Ahab; he managed all the affairs of
Ahab (על—1 Kgs 18.3a). More obvious, for in the same verse in
which Obadiah's job description occurs, there begins a description of
him that documents his covert activity as protector of the Yahwistic
prophets (1 Kgs 18.3bff.).[30] Later, he recounts what the audience has
learned earlier of this subversion and includes an addition that
magnifies significantly the level of commitment exhibited by
Obadiah ('and your servant has feared Yahweh from my youth'—1
Kgs 18.12c), i.e., he maintains that his faith in Yahweh is all he has
really known. Moreover, his great fear about bearing the news of
Elijah's appearance, if indeed Elijah is dealing honestly with
Obadiah, arises in part from the necessity to keep from jeopardizing
his credibility with Ahab. Without his office and Ahab's trust, his
double service is over. He must dance between two worlds to
preserve the true faith. The opposition that resides in the relationship
of Ahab and Obadiah is reflected in the narrative by the division of
the territory and their going their separate ways. Ahab's concern for
the redemption of the animals (ולוא נכרית—1 Kgs 18.5) contrasts
readily with the painstaking care of Obadiah for the salvation of the
threatened prophets (בהכרית—1 Kgs 18.4). In addition, it is the
person who favors Yahwism, Obadiah, who succeeds in finding

Elijah (water).[31] Obadiah's initial greeting to Elijah records one
further indicator of this contrast. He welcomes Elijah as his lord
(האתה זה אדני—1 Kgs 18.7c), whereas Ahab, echoing the reaction of
Obadiah, greets him as the one troubling Israel (האתה זה עכר ישראל—
1 Kgs 18.17). To the audience the opposition appears clear; to Elijah,
engrossed in his plans, the opposition between Obadiah and Ahab
remains unknown.

An interesting dynamic appears in this confrontation between
Elijah and Obadiah in their antagonistic roles. The designation 'lord'
plus a number of pronominal suffixes ('your' and 'my') embue this
figure of address and this dialogue with the necessary seriousness to
make the shifts more than a mere thoughtless change. Elijah early
places Obadiah in the other camp and tells Obadiah to tell Ahab
('your lord'—1 Kgs 18.8) about Elijah's impending appearance.
Obadiah counters by designating himself as Elijah's servant ('your
servant'—1 Kgs 18.9). In the very next verse, however, Obadiah tells
of the great search and how Ahab ('my lord'—1 Kgs 18.10) sent him
out. After repeating his fearful account of the instructions of Elijah,
Obadiah launches into his vision of what would happen. When he
arrives at the confession of his faithfulness to Yahweh, he irrevocably
signals who his 'lord' is and in whose camp he stands. If this
information had been told to the 'lord' to whom Elijah attributes
Obadiah, the latter probably would be dead. When this word is told
to the 'lord' whom Obadiah now beholds, Obadiah should be
respected and treated as a comrade. Yet, death or threat of death
remains the fear of Obadiah and Elijah remains unconvinced.
Subsequent to this outburst, Obadiah returns to his repetition of the
original command as his refusal to obey (1 Kgs 18.14). Only with the
oath of Elijah does Obadiah become convinced that he may risk his
life and ministry.

As Ahab and Jezebel are wedded both in fact and in deed, Obadiah
and the widow are wedded by means of vocabulary, especially in
their opposition to the slaughter of the prophets. The first instance
consists of the mention in chapter 17 (vv. 4, 9) of the command of
Yahweh to the ravens and the widow to feed Elijah, this threatened
iconoclast (לכלכלך—1 Kgs 17.4, 9). The standard fare for Elijah was
bread and water.[32] Obadiah is credited with offering the same solace
and provision to certain prophets (כלכלם/ואכלכלם—1 Kgs 18.4, 13).
This correspondence would certainly support his claims that he
feared Yahweh greatly or from his youth, for he performed faithfully

the same service as the divinely ordained ravens and hesitant widow.

Interestingly enough, Obadiah seems linked temporally to the ravens' and widow's service. Of course this is not immediately obvious but Obadiah's mercy which occurred when Jezebel was 'cutting off' the prophets of Yahweh (בהכרית—1 Kgs 18.4) certainly corresponds to the time that Elijah was at Cherith (כרית—1 Kgs 17.3, 5) and afterwards. In this way, the narrator witnesses to the broad scope of Yahweh's action and prepares the audience for the truth of the claim in 1 Kgs 19.18. This protective care at Cherith is documented by Obadiah himself when he tells Elijah of the search that failed (1 Kgs 18.10ff.); Elijah was in the care of Yahweh and thereby protected from factions that would harm him. The ravens, the reluctant pagan widow, and the minister of the syncretistic king, three unlikely allies, work together, even while separate, to foil the royal alliance.

Elijah's loyalty, evident from many features in the text, remains problematic; he is a strange middle figure. One would expect a prophet to represent a special group, perhaps the pinnacle of the Yahwists, but Elijah winds up between these two groups—the ravens, the widow, and Obadiah on one side, and the royal couple on the other side. In the first half of the narrative, chapters 17–18, he ostensibly champions the cause of Yahwism and is therefore definitely in the camp with those opposed to the policies of state. Indeed, the only time Elijah exhibits any semblance of cordiality toward the royalty, i.e., the king (for Elijah never harbors anything but contempt for Jezebel, the pagan fanatic), is after the victory on Carmel when Elijah assumes that the faithless one, Ahab, who received the curse of drought from him, now will be blessed with undivided faith. Yet, the uneasiness that characterized the encounter of Obadiah with Elijah suggests a lack of concord of Elijah with Obadiah's group. Almost the whole second half of the narrative, until 1 Kgs 19.19, Elijah hovers close to the Ahab–Jezebel camp simply for the reason that he seems unsympathetic with Obadiah's group. He flees without instruction from Yahweh, begs death, and ultimately goes to Horeb, the foundation place of the covenant, to have a showdown with Yahweh. The only indication that Elijah is open to membership in the Yahwistic group is his acceptance of the meal, which, for Elijah, has always stemmed from Yahweh's beneficent care, that will sustain him until he gets to Horeb. At Horeb he finally describes the bounds of his group of one (1 Kgs 19.14) and Yahweh smashes those bounds. In his own way, Elijah has killed all the other prophets and faithful adherents of Yahweh. Yahweh's commission demonstrates that the group which Elijah has populated with himself is narrow, exclusivistic, and unnecessary: it precludes the essential decision allowed by Yahweh—to serve Yahweh or not to serve Yahweh. When Elijah makes that essential decision, he finally and wholly enters the company of the Yahwists.

Repetition as a Reflection of the Theme of Choice

The division that comes with decision has left one other mark upon this narrative text. Carlson was correct in emphasizing the repetition of two members and the purposes that these could serve.[33] There are certain repetitions which seem odd or superfluous, yet in the context of this intricate tale they supplement the choices being undertaken. What these recurring words and phrases require is the notice of the similarities, shifts, or changes. What comes first supplies information so that what comes later develops into an empathic moment.[34]

The first instance, the oath which essentially precipitates the whole story and its complement in 1 Kgs 18.15, provides a neat demarcation of the beginning and ending of this drought. The first oath, a curse (1 Kgs 17.1), whatever its cause—that information surfaces after the drought's end is assured (1 Kgs 18.18)—hangs over the narrative like some hot, scorching sun so that the search for sustenance remains primary. The second oath (1 Kgs 18.15), building on the efficacy of the first to bring hardship, mitigated for Elijah and for others helped by Yahweh, unmitigated for those without that connection, promises to bring an end to the hardship, and the audience awaits the fulfillment of this credible message. In other words, this second oath recalls a day when Elijah did appear before Ahab; now he is to come with the shadow message to the earlier one. In addition, these two oaths are a certain counterpoint to the powerful Elijah; they underscore the consequences of the drought and the success of the Yahweh-empowered exile for Elijah.

The information offered by the narrator in 1 Kgs 18.3b-4 and later by Obadiah himself (1 Kgs 18.13) comprises the second example. Here the differences are slight, one expected, some surprising. The expected variation is the shift from narration to first person presentation. Although significance resides in Obadiah's telling his own story, the greater significance resides in other changes. In his intense anxiety, Obadiah (translating his name as 'servant of Yahweh') briefly changes his name to convince Elijah of this *esprit de corps*; he calls himself 'your servant' (עבדך—1 Kgs 18.12). Whereas the narrator stressed the present intensity of the faith of Obadiah, Obadiah emphasizes the constancy over a long period of time. Again, the narrator freely offers the information to the audience so that they may possess information to orient them to his character and the time in which he did his heroic task, while, at the same time, the narrator delivers an important message of Yahweh's beneficence which encompassed more persons than Elijah. In a time of threat, Obadiah tries to suggest his part, however covert, in the larger plan of Yahweh. Finally, the shift from the temporal clue of the narrator (בהכרית—1 Kgs 18.4), or the language used to refer to the murderous activity of Jezebel, to a different verb (בהרג—1 Kgs 18.13) anticipates a time when someone else, Ahab, might kill him (והרגני—1 Kgs 18.14) and a time when Ahab informs Jezebel of the killing of the prophets (הרג—1 Kgs 19.1). The ultimate effect of this correlation is to prove to the audience that an alliance exists between Obadiah and Elijah. However, Elijah remains aloof and acknowledges only the manner in which Obadiah may serve him now.[35]

The third repetition hinges upon the word וירא which wavers in its meaning like the terms noted earlier for their fertile ambiguity. After the fire of Yahweh falls, the text reads: 'And when all the people saw it, they fell on their faces. . .' (1 Kgs 18.39a). Not too many verses later, after Jezebel has issued a damning oath, the text reads: 'Then he saw and he arose and went for his life' (וירא or the same form as before—1 Kgs 19.3a).[36] In both of these verses, the verb וירא could also be translated 'feared' though the manuscript evidence seems to support that maneuver only in 1 Kgs 19.3. Yet, the same translation in both instances commends itself. The account in 1 Kgs 19.1-3 portrays the action within the confines of Jezreel.[37] Somewhere between the queen and the entrance where Elijah was waiting, Elijah realized that this approaching messenger was bringing bad news. Perhaps he thought his convincing theory would persuade the king and queen to appear and reward him. However, in the twinkling of an eye, Elijah's memory of the people's acclamation vanished along with his confidence and his attention to the guiding word of Yahweh.

The clever transformation of the plea for death by Elijah in 1 Kgs

19.4 (רב עתה יהוה) to the message of the messenger of Yahweh in 1 Kgs 19.7 (רב ממך הדרך) comprises the fourth instance of double repetition that enriches this theme of decision. This sign of hopelessness and resignation poignantly summarizes Elijah's feelings concerning Yahwism and his dramatic but ineffectual attempt to stem the tide of Baalism. The messenger draws Elijah back to the present and prepares him for the future when Elijah's way will indeed be difficult (לדרכך—1 Kgs 19.15). Elijah, according to the messenger, is not in a position to offer his last words; he still must endure more. What the audience eventually discovers is a future which holds promise, maybe not as much for Elijah, who is to be replaced, as for those who endure faithfully until the plan of Yahweh is worked out completely. Elijah's decision is voided, therefore, by a reply that challenges him to view the progression of history from outside the purview of his own experience and plans.

Within the bounds of that repetition just discussed, lies another two-part repetition which at the same time includes the activity of the messenger (three total appearances—one from Jezebel and two from Yahweh). This duplication builds by addition, the first instance (1 Kgs 19.5) recording an almost instantaneous touching and appearing of the messenger with the message and tokens of sustenance. This verse essentially places the narrative in a state of suspension. The next verse reviews quite cleverly the Carmel contest which preceded Elijah's despair which sent him scurrying. Elijah looks (1 Kgs 18.43) toward his head's resting place (1 Kgs 18.42) and there lies a cake baked on hot stones (1 Kgs 18.38) beside a container of water (1 Kgs 18.34). Immediately, the water and the hot stones recall the water which Elijah poured on the stone altar only to be lapped up by the fire of Yahweh. The next time the messenger appears (1 Kgs 19.7), the time for reflection is past. The message is elongated; the action is more deliberate. First, the angel seems to return and, then, this messenger touches the sleeping Elijah. Elijah's decision to beg death is swept away by the pressing demand of the messenger who possesses the power to turn Elijah's word of resignation into a word of motivation.

Perhaps the most scrutinized of all these twofold repetitions is that in 1 Kgs 19.9b-10 and 19.13b-14.[38] In many cases, this exact repetition has propelled exegetes to maintain that in one or the other place, someone mistakenly inserted or purposefully, though needlessly, replicated the earlier passage. Yet, the spotlight of 1 Kgs 17-19 focuses so intensely upon Elijah, his decision and his destiny, that this jarringly exact repetition proves remarkably appropriate. The first time this statement of defense is presented to the audience, the emphasis falls on Elijah's feelings (informative) but the precise reiteration exhibits Elijah's inflexibility and egocentrism (elucidating).[39]

A familiar phrase sets up a crucial shift in this context: 'the word of the Lord came to him'.[40] Later, after Elijah's blunt and proud reply, the theophany which concludes with a qualified silence, and Elijah's distinctively individual manner of hovering close to the opening of the cave, that phrase drops out. Now, a voice (קוֹל) suddenly rifles the question asked earlier. The same question is asked but in a different context, at least for Yahweh. Now Yahweh inquires about Elijah's part in the larger design for Elijah has become rooted in his own interpretation. Yahweh's question in 1 Kgs 19.13 recalls the repeated queries of Yahweh witnessed throughout the Hebrew Bible, whether that be in Gen. 3.9 ('Where are you?') or, here, in 1 Kgs 19.13b ('What are you doing here, Elijah?'). In addition, this voice resonates with the varied appearances of 'voice' or 'sound' in this whole narrative—the absence of the voice of Baal; the sound of rain; the sound that is less than silence; and this voice that literarily replaces the 'word of the Lord' but reflects continuing interest in the activity of Elijah—and offers one more chance for Elijah to answer the question. In this charged moment, Elijah meets a Yahweh distanced from the elements of the Horeb theophany[41] in addition to the dramatic event upon Carmel. Yahweh addresses Elijah simply, stripped of the fanfare, devoid of the authority inherent in the messenger formula, so that the message will be intimate and direct. In this sense, the shift from word to voice is crucial,[42] the story mounts in seriousness; the stakes are high again. Soon, Elijah's capacity to help shape the strategy of final victory will be stripped on account of his intransigence and he will only be able to stand on this holy mountain and look over into the future to a time when the eradication of Baalism will be complete.[43]

The final pair consists of Yahweh's reply after Elijah's second defensive response (1 Kgs 19.15) and Elijah's retort after Elisha's plea to return to pay proper homage to his parents (1 Kgs 19.20). As has already been suggested,[44] these rebukes communicate an interchangeable disdain. Concerning the first instance, the future planned by Yahweh is about to be displayed. The future of Yahwism will be assured through other servants of Yahweh, Elijah will be replaced, and his faithfulness will be discredited, though he will perform one final mission for Yahweh. Concerning the second instance, Elijah in his own way proclaims the word of Yahweh, and its subversion, threatened in Elisha's response, brings a resultant harshness, which mirrors that earlier response of Yahweh. Only the choice that Elisha ultimately makes—the reactualization of Carmel in the meal and discipleship to Elijah, who is now undeniably following Yahweh's schedule—pays homage to the god who brooks no rivals, neither God nor man.

Chapter 3

ELIJAH IN HISTORY: TEMPERED JUDGMENT

The revolution is dead said little Willie to Joe
just like a balloon that's been flying high the revolution's
gone and lost all its air and fell on the ground
Folks done stomped it so its almost buried in the dirt

I tell you, Joe, little Willie said,
Black is as tired as it is beautiful.

The 'revolutionaries' is whispering so low
you cant git over or under em
Looks like to me the women, pimps and dope fiends is gon run
it
I tell you, the revolution is dead, my man, dead.

Naw, said Joe the revolution aint dead
Sometimes when you be flying in the sky in them airplanes,
you move so fast dont seem like you be moving at all/
And you go up and down hitting air pockets, you dig?
You be hitting hard like a boxer
like a heavyweight boxer that the wite folks got in a monkey
ring
boxing wid a different person every hour of the day
now you's be tired, Little Willie if they had you in that bag
        wouldnt you?
You'd have to either stop fighting altogether or ease up
        change or tighten your strategy or you'd fall out from
        pure exhaustion.

        Naw Little Willie, Joe said,
I looks at it this way, man man. . .
        the Revolution aint dead
        its tired,
        and jest resting.

                                        Carolyn Rodgers

> I asked, then, has God rejected his people? By no means! I myself
> am an Israelite, a descendant of Abraham, a member of the tribe of
> Benjamin. God has not rejected his people whom he foreknew. Do
> you not know what the scripture says of Elijah, how he pleads with
> God against Israel? 'Lord, they have killed thy prophets, they have
> demolished thy altars, and I alone am left, and they seek my life'.
> But what is God's reply to him? 'I have kept for myself several
> thousand men who have not bowed the knee to Baal'.
>
> Paul the Apostle

Elijah is obviously judged; the whole narrative is an uncovering of
his self-service. Yet, to heed only this direct assessment of Elijah's
activity and attitude shortchanges the full range of the evaluation of
Elijah proffered in this narrative. As the land of Israel had many holy
places and historic monuments, so this story possesses its signposts.
The narrative invites the audience, through numerous allusions, to
examine this prophet over against certain of the great events and
individuals in Israel's history. Against this background, the career of
Elijah, portrayed in these three chapters, leaves a mark both
triumphant and tragic.

Kishon and the Victory of Yahweh

Certainly the book of Deuteronomy, which provides a practical and
theological umbrella for the Deuteronomistic History, offers one
solution to the riddle of the harsh judgment executed on the prophets
of Baal; these prophets lured the people away from the true faith and
deserved to die.[1] Yet, another avenue opens at the same time to place
this experience at the foot of Carmel square in the middle of the
stream of Israelite history. This avenue, marked by the signpost
Kishon, leads through the terrain where Yahweh triumphed in
Israel's story.

Kishon was associated supremely with Deborah, the judge, and
her struggle against Jabin, king of Canaan. The prose account of this
struggle represents this river as the site for the climactic battle which
would decide the outcome of the conflict. The poetic version, a
vibrant song of victory, elevates this river to a torrent which wars,
along with the rest of creation, against Yahweh's foes. In both
accounts, this river is the place where the cruel reign of Jabin is
overturned.

The distance between Deborah and Elijah is registered in years and events—the establishment of a united monarchy and its division, but the narrative distance is fractional. At the mention of the name Kishon, the expectation of the annihilation of the enemies of Yahweh emerges. After the great confession of faith by all the people, Elijah commands that no prophet of Baal be allowed to escape (איש אל־ ימלט—1 Kgs 18.40); Baraq, Deborah's reluctant general, pursues his task until none of his enemies remains except Jabin (לא נשאר עד אחד—Judg. 4.16). In both cases, the river Kishon marks a decisive intervention of Yahweh and the destruction of an alien force in Israel's midst.

Psalm 83 contains the only other reference to this location in the Hebrew Scriptures. This psalm exhorts God to break his silence and to rout the enemies who threaten the very existence (name) of Israel.[2] Following a description of the present danger and the recital of some of the decisive victories of Yahweh during the time of the judges, including the defeat of Sisera, the psalm suggests, in theophanic flurry,[3] the manner in which Yahweh might destroy these present enemies. The final phrase proclaims: 'Let them know that you alone, whose name is Yahweh, are the Most High over all the earth' (Ps. 83.18). This lamentation which knows both Yahweh's silence and Yahweh's mighty deeds implores the deity to display his grandeur so that his name and the name of his people will be secure.

The situation in the psalm finds narrative application in 1 Kgs 17–19. This psalm mirrors the sense of the Carmel event. There, too, the issue is the response of God in a time of threat. The prayer of Elijah (וידעו העם הזה כי־אתה יהוה . . .)—1 Kgs 18.37) reflects the language of this psalm (וידעו כי אתה שמך יהוה לבדך)—Ps. 83.19) and aligns the sentiment of this psalm with the sentiment of the narrative. In 1 Kgs 18.39, after the incredible, immediate action of Yahweh, the people acknowledge this wonder by shouting: 'Yahweh is (the) God'. Immediately after their outcry, the people slaughter every last prophet of Baal just as Barak's army had killed every Canaanite soldier commanded by Sisera. Although the response has not come by the time the psalm ends, the attitude of confidence and praise provide surety. In the context of the contest on Carmel, though, the message rings true; Yahweh has shown in deed that he alone is Most High over all the earth.[4]

The second part of this psalm shares its expression with the second mountain scene in the Elijah story. The psalm speaks of whirling dust and chaff (כגלגל . . .—Ps. 83.14b), fire and flame (כאש . . .כלהבה—

Ps. 83.15), tempest and hurricane (בסערך ובסופתך—Ps. 83.16). 1 Kgs 19.11ff. speaks of wind (רוח—1 Kgs 19.11b), earthquake (רעש—1 Kgs 19.11c), and a fire (אש—1 Kgs 19.12a); all of these failed to reveal a message from Yahweh. However, in both instances the revelation of Yahweh's primacy remains the point. On Carmel, that message was flashed to all present—king, people, and prophets of Baal—while on Horeb the message was imprinted in the aftershock on Elijah. Elijah, who feels that he alone is left, must relearn that Yahweh, alone, supremely reigns.

Beersheba and Death in the Wilderness

The narrative complex in 1 Kings 17–19 accords with the narrative found in Gen. 21.1ff., especially vv. 14ff. On account of the ill will of Sarah, Abraham sends Hagar and her son, Ishmael, into the wilderness. She is given some provisions—bread and water (לחם וחמת מים—Gen. 21.14)—but these soon fail. Overcome by her affection for her child, she places him under a tree and moves far away so that she does not have to witness the death of her child. As the child's cry rises to the heavens, a messenger of God calls to her and says: 'Do not fear for God has heard the voice of the youth who is there' (Gen. 21.17). She is commanded to retrieve the child for he is to be the beginning of a nation. At the same time, God opens her eyes so that she sees a well which brings an end to their brush with death.

The resemblance of this incident with the experience of Elijah recorded in 1 Kgs 19.3ff. invites the audience to compare and contrast these cases.[5] Hagar is ejected along with her son whom she places under a bush (אחד השיחם—Gen. 21.15) in order to escape the necessity of watching him die. Elijah, as he flees, leaves his companion in Beersheba. He places himself under a bush (רתם אחד—1 Kgs 19.5) and cries out in desperation, but his voice begs for death. The earlier story from the patriarchal cycle has been altered; Elijah begs for the death that Hagar dreaded for her son and herself. Finally, characteristic to the particular stories, the messenger of Yahweh provides sustenance to these despairing persons—a well of water for Hagar and the boy, bread and water for Elijah.

The influence of the Hagar episode remains just as strong, even in its subtlety, on the earlier part of 1 Kings 17–19. In Gen. 21.17, the text states:

And God heard the voice of the lad and the messenger of God called unto Hagar from the heavens and said to her: 'What's the matter (מה־לך), Hagar? Do not fear (אל־תיראי) for God has hearkened unto the voice of the lad (קול הנער) who is there'.[6]

In 1 Kgs 17.(8)8-16, the widow of Zaraphath is faced with death by starvation along with her son as the drought continues to take its toll. To this woman appears Elijah who bears a promising message prefixed by the phrase: 'Do not fear' (אל־תיראי—1 Kgs 17.13). In both instances, life results.

1 Kgs 17.17 reports the sudden and inexplicable illness of the son of the widow. The mother responds by blaming the presence of Elijah for the death of her son when she says: 'What have you against me (מה־לי ולך), O man of God? You have come to me to bring my sin to remembrance and to cause the death of my son' (1 Kgs 17.18). Elijah wrenches the child away from her, takes him upstairs, and calls to Yahweh, his God, in a manner that represents both the woman's complaint and his own request. Yahweh obeys Elijah and returns the life to this boy who is then returned to his mother. Upon returning the son to his mother, Elijah remarks: 'See, your son lives', a response which recalls the experience of Hagar who received comfort from the messenger of God only to have her eyes opened to see a well of water that meant life. A Phoenician woman and her son in the time of Elijah experience the same salvation experienced by Hagar and her son.

Although the comparison and the contrast between 1 Kgs 17.(8)9-16, 17-24, and Gen. 21.1ff. enrich Elijah's reputation as the powerful and unpredictable messenger of God, the more direct correlation between Gen. 21.14ff. and 1 Kgs 19.3ff. remains the more important. Elijah is not commanded by Yahweh to run off; he chooses to flee into a barren waste. After separating himself from his young helper, he finds a tree under which to lie and asks that his life be taken. He effects no pity, but self-pity. Yet his request is met with the same response as Hagar's fear of death for her child; he is offered sustenance and encouragement. Elijah's moan of failure is overshadowed by a mother's despair, and both of these emotions are overcome by the larger design of God.

Jacob and the Struggle with God and Man

The clue for the connection between Elijah and Jacob occurs during the Carmel episode, or, more specifically, in 1 Kgs 18.31. In this verse the narrator includes the reason for the twelve stones— 'according to the number of tribes of Jacob' (1 Kgs 18.31)—and further reminds the audience that this Jacob incurred a name change at the Jabbok ford (Gen. 32.23-33). Later, consistent with that information, Elijah prays to the god of Abraham, Isaac, and Israel (1 Kgs 18.36). This connection provides additional overtones to the story of Elijah's struggle on Carmel and strengthens the counterpoint in the mind of the audience.

In Genesis, the narrator describes Jacob as being totally alone (לבדו . . . ויותר—Gen. 32.24) when a person begins to wrestle with him. In three places, though two of these occur as exact repetition, Elijah describes himself in the same terms (אותר אני לבדי—1 Kgs 18.22; 19.10, 14). Jacob, looking forward in uncertainty to the meeting with Esau, remains absolutely alone after sending his clan ahead. Elijah, on Carmel, seems the only single-minded, identifiable representative of Yahweh. As a result of his success in struggling with God and men (Gen. 32.28), God changes Jacob's name. Interestingly, at Carmel Elijah contends with a people and a group of prophets who claim a rival God and Elijah prevails.

In accord with the particular structure of the Elijah narrative, Elijah strives with Yahweh at Horeb after a short, extremely important stay in the wilderness. There an angel touches (נגע בו—1 Kgs 19.5) the sleeping, depressed Elijah in order to prepare him for his encounter with Yahweh on Horeb. At Horeb, Elijah once again maintains his absolute prominence as the only prophet left. Just as the result of the angel's touch slowed Jacob, but enabled Elijah, i.e., the outcomes were opposite, the result is different on Horeb. Elijah strives with God and loses. The claim of singularity is exaggerated; Elijah's importance is fleeting. Elijah's name remains the same but the name of the commissioned messenger of Yahweh changes. Elisha, not Elijah, will direct the final victory of Yahwism over Baalism. Jacob's wonder and surprise after a night struggle with God face to face shifts with Elijah to a belligerent refusal to stand before Yahweh. In every way Elijah proves himself no better than his fathers (1 Kgs 19.4).

Gideon and the Defeat of Baal

The struggle on Carmel receives additional narrative commentary from Gideon's story in the book of Judges. One striking clue, among several, consists in the similarity of the sequence of events, and specifically, the comment of Joash, Gideon's father, who says of Baal: 'If he is God' (אם אלהים הוא—Judg. 6.31), a phrase that closely resembles Elijah's sarcastic statement: 'For he is God' (כי אלהים הוא 1—Kgs 18.27).

However, the correspondences are much broader. Elijah's suggestion of a contest between himself, the prophets of Baal, and syncretistic people quickly elevates this struggle from the terrestial realm and sets it in the celestial. The final verdict rests with the gods; they must contend for themselves (Judg. 6.31; 1 Kgs 18.23ff.). In the contest he has initiated, Elijah allows the others to precede him; therefore, he acts secondly, necessarily getting the second bull. Gideon, in his unilateral endeavor, has no choice. Yahweh instructs him to take the second bull belonging to his father and to sacrifice it upon an altar he is to build after he destroys (והרסת—Judg. 6.25) the altar of Baal. In addition, Yahweh maintains that this altar must be built with the stones arranged properly (במערכה—Judg. 6.26). Interestingly, Elijah, on Carmel, builds an altar upon the foundation of a destroyed altar of Yahweh (את־מזבח יהוה ההרום 1—Kgs 18.30) out of a specified number of stones 'according to the number of the tribes of Israel' (1 Kgs 18.31). Then Elijah completes the preparation by the addition of the wood, the bull, and, curiously enough, twelve containers of water, all of which the heavenly fire consumes. Early in the story of Gideon, he places some meat and matsoth upon a rock (Judg. 6.20) at the instruction of a messenger of God. Subsequently, Gideon pours broth over it all. The messenger reaches out with a staff and touches (יגע—Judg. 6.21) the meat and matsoth. Immediately a flame arises from the rock and consumes the drenched offering (תאכל—Judg. 6.21). Preparation and defeat in Gideon's day strongly resemble the same in Elijah's time; ultimately, Baal's silence and Yahweh's involvement recommend the true God.

As in other instances above, the Gideon story provides correspondences to more than one episode. Gideon complains about the recent paucity of the acts of Yahweh when compared to the deeds that his 'fathers recounted to us' (Judg. 6.13). They spoke of a marvelous exodus. All Gideon could narrate was the oppression of the

Midianites. Elijah's sentiment in 1 Kgs 19.4 accords with that of Gideon, but his meaning is the opposite. He mourns his concord with his fathers who struggled with a faithless people and failed. Similarly, in contrast to the Gideon narrative, the angel touches Elijah so that Elijah may eat the divine provisions. The reversals continue as the Gideon account relates his seeing the angel of Yahweh face to face, like Jacob, and surviving. Elijah will be invited into the presence of Yahweh at Horeb, but his refusal to meet Yahweh face to face distances him from those who have seen God face to face and lived. Gideon, like Jacob, is given another name. Perhaps Elijah, had he not been so recalcitrant, would have received a new name in the desert or upon the mountain of Horeb. At least that appears as an expectation. Instead, Yahweh changes the man; Yahweh accepts the resignation of Elijah and promotes Elisha.[7]

Moses—True Prophet, Mediator, and Servant

Of all the allusions and narrative comparisons, the connection with Moses remains the most extensive and significant.[8] The role of Moses among the willful and transient Israelites on the way to Canaan, especially that section found in Exodus 32–34, is reflected in the Elijah story.[9] Primarily on the basis of these allusions, but also on account of the high esteem in which the Deuteronomistic History and its basis, Deuteronomy, holds Moses, the comparison of this material with Elijah's struggle becomes absolutely necessary.

The people of Israel, in Moses' or Elijah's time, are unimaginatively similar. While under the leadership of Moses, even while he is obtaining the law on Sinai, the people dilute their faith by building a golden calf (Exod. 31.1ff.). They become a confused, divided group which enrages their jealous God to the point that Yahweh is about to destroy them completely and to begin anew with Moses and his descendants (Exod. 32.9ff.). Moses successfully dissuades Yahweh, but the people are purified by the brandished swords of the sons of Levi who go through the camp killing the unfaithful (Exod. 32.25ff.), a scene much like that witnessed on the top of Carmel and by the river Kishon. With that purification effected, Yahweh eventually delivers instructions for the continued guiltlessness of the people; they are to tear down the altars, the pillars, and the Asherim of the peoples in Canaan (Exod. 34.11f.). The bases for this demand are the redemption from the Egyptian bondage and the jealous nature of Yahweh.

Obviously, the people to whom Elijah speaks on top of Carmel have allied themselves with peoples, prophets, and religious practices which represent a breach of the covenant. However, the demarcation of the good from the bad differs slightly; only the prophets of Baal, the pure representation of alien faith, are killed. Interestingly, Elijah, the only prophet for Yahweh on Carmel and the only prophet left, or so he maintains on Horeb, applies the crucial characteristic of Yahweh to himself, i.e., jealousy, implying that only one may exhibit such fervor. Perhaps this vicious remark, twice hurled at Yahweh, clears up some of the mystery surrounding Elijah's suicidal emotions in the desert. From Moses onward, the people constantly tested their leaders and Yahweh. Never did the situation change. Now Elijah was truly alone for he felt his jealousy oustripped Yahweh's, and Yahweh's estimate of Elijah's position expressed in the wilderness and on Horeb—'kill me and get rid of everyone else for I am the only faithful person'—is evident in our story; he replaces Elijah with Elisha. Held up to the person of Moses, Elijah's insolence and arrogance are magnified. Moses stops Yahweh from destroying the people and setting up a new nation beginning with Moses alone. Moses claims that if indeed Yahweh destroys the people, Yahweh must include him in the pogrom. Furthermore, Moses senses the mixture of the faithless and faithful people, designs a strategy whereby the two may be separated, and follows the plan to its execution. After this great purge, Moses returns to Yahweh to atone for the people; his determination to maintain his solidarity with them continues to contribute life and hope to the people, honor and glory to Moses.

The contrast with Elijah is severe. Certainly, Elijah and the significance of his struggle against Baalism under the mandate of the covenant, stand in the tradition of Moses.[10] His enigmatic trek to Horeb caps a troubled history of a covenant people cemented in the time of Moses, shattered in the time of Elijah. At the least, this scene calls to mind the former actions of Moses; Elijah has been made in the mold of Moses. Yet, he breaks the mold. He rightfully accuses the people of subverting the covenant faith, but he fails to intercede for them before Yahweh.[11] Instead, he vies with Yahweh for supremacy. As a result, Yahweh upturns the traditional theophanic occurrence.[12] In a manner that deprecates Baalism and refines Yahwism, Yahweh does not resolve this situation by means of a theophany; Yahweh issues a covenantal reminder to his prophet, and, by implication, to the people. In the grit of faithfulness and history, Baalism will be defeated. Elijah does not budge, so Yahweh intercedes for his faithful and excludes Elijah from the final victory. For all his vanity, Elijah is granted a foretaste of the victory but not participation; pride and blinding anger have kept another of Yahweh's leaders from entering fully into the time of promise.[13]

The subversion of the Mosaic picture is witnessed in the two accounts of the presentation of the deity to the two men. Moses asked to see the 'glory of Yahweh' (Exod. 33.17ff.), but Yahweh protectively denied his wish. Instead, he stated that his glory would pass by (בעבר כבדי—Exod. 32.22) while Moses was hidden in the cleft of a rock and Yahweh would proclaim his name (Exod. 33.19b; 34.6-7). Moses' response is to worship and to intercede for the people. Elijah is invited to view the deity (צא ועמדת . . . לפני יהוה—1 Kgs 19.1) and to witness the events which accompany such an appearance. Elijah responds tentatively and covers his face. Afterwards, he remains unchanged, unrepentant, and set against his people.

Undoubtedly, the use of Mosaic traditions served as a backdrop. Elijah was a prophet unashamed to confront Ahab and to judge him. He was a messenger unafraid to face the prophets of Baal who destroyed the covenant purity. Yet, somewhere in the enactment of his commission, he overturned his allegiance by sacrificing the people to his ego and thereby discarded the Mosaic model. In the wilderness and on Horeb, Elijah requires intercession. For this lapse, Yahweh reinstitutes the divine plan and dismisses this narrow-minded prophet.

Jonah—A Prophet Like Elijah

Elijah and Jonah share the dubious distinction of entertaining suicidal sentiments.[14] Critics generally agree that Elijah was justified and Jonah was unjustified.[15] The difference resides in the exhaustion of Elijah who had been zealous for Yahweh but had been threatened by the wicked queen, Jezebel, and the anger of Jonah who had been enraged by Yahweh's mercy. In my view, this contrast misses the mark; Elijah, in fact, fits alongside Jonah. Jonathan Magonet senses this accord and details the mechanics of their likeness, especially related to the use of Exod. 34.16. Indeed, both stories consider the effect of the mercy of God on an overzealous prophet of God. The creator of the book of Jonah additionally used elements of Elijah's troubled period to shape his tale. First, Jonah's creator mirrors the sleep of Elijah. Elijah slept after the threat to his life; Jonah slept during a threat. Second, both exhibited a suicidal state of mind when they discerned their plan of action had been subverted. Third, both stories exhibit the use of certain numbers to fit their plot. Elijah fled one day into the wilderness; Jonah walked one day into the city. Jonah's message of judgment mentioned forty days until the reckoning; Elijah travels forty days and nights to reach the mountain of God, Horeb, where his reckoning occurs. Fourth, Elijah and Jonah shared the pride that allowed each of them to judge the people to whom they were sent. Elijah's flight, as Jonah's flight, is an escape from the necessity to attune himself to the will of God who shows mercy and judgment. Fifth, Elijah and Jonah must finally realize that Yahweh goes beyond the boundaries that they have set for him. Elijah appears to grasp that realization after he no longer maintains the prophetic commission; Jonah remains suspended in this thought as Yahweh challenges him and the audience to widen their circle of compassion.

Chapter 4

CONCLUSION

How glorious you were, O Elijah
   in your wondrous deeds!
And who has the right to boast
   which you have?

                        Joshua ben Sira

If you meet the Buddha on the road, kill him.
                       Zen Proverb

Historical-critical research has displayed a fascination with the biblical traditions contained within 1 Kings 17-19. Yet, this interest and the historical-critical orientation have attained a certain predictability. On the one hand, scholars search for the historical information that will complement or complete our knowledge of Israelite history. In this regard, the narrative in 1 Kings 17-19 is separated into anecdote and historical reminiscence so that the actual occurrences may be detailed. At the same time, the stages of composition are outlined to obtain a sense of the history reflected in the amalgamation of these varied traditions. The various schemes multiply, but one concern remains constant—the quest for the historical. On the other hand, scholars generally neglect the narrative character of this material. This neglect runs ⸢s⸣o deep that many who comment on the creative narrative techniques still brush them aside to extract the contents of the text.

   Others, more influenced by the fictive quality rather than the historical appearance of Hebrew narrative, treat the literary aspect more seriously. These scholars know that the content and structure are linked in every way. Biblical studies, in its ongoing generation of methods, has renewed its appreciation of literary criticism. This perspective appreciates but tempers the momentum of historical-critical research. The concomitant disadvantages reside in the criticism this method obtains from other historical-critical perspectives and the low place it holds in the hierarchy of methods.

Literary criticism is not without its difficulties. Not so long ago, prominent literary figures protested the idea of examining biblical narrative in the same manner as one would survey a fictive creation. Besides, it was argued, many literary critics do not possess an adequate understanding of the language and culture of the Hebrew scriptures, concepts provided by linguistic studies, history of religions, historians, and theologians. For a time, no one dared to blend respect for the biblical world and regard for the textual world, but that time drew to a close and literary critics began to share the labors and rewards of biblical exegesis.

This researcher, excited by the application of literary-critical principles to biblical interpretation, sensed the possibility of understanding 1 Kings 17–19 by means of literary criticism. To be sure, historical research provided necessary background but literary criticism remained the major focus. In this way the narrative was offered the chance to tell its own story.

The perspective of this study emphasized the world pictured in the narrative, or, the 'world-in-words', rather than the world behind the words. This perspective guaranteed that the story would not be neglected in the search for historical referents. At once, the patchwork anecdotes of historical criticism were recognized as the medium of literary creation subject to the literary critic's craft of interpretation. Research into the structure and meaning of this particular narrative revealed a web of complementary relations. The presence of irony in several forms and the theme of decision directed the plot in order to communicate a poignant struggle and judgment.

The most helpful, if not surprising, discovery was the ironic cast of this whole account. Elijah exhibited all the attributes ('signs') of a mighty prophet, but certain inconsistencies ('hints') subverted this image, and this led to a truer picture of this important prophet. This ironic composition ultimately challenged Elijah's motives or laid bare the true motivation of Elijah. Elijah wanted to be the only prophet of Yahweh; he coveted the place reserved for the triumphant. Yet, true to form and this narrative, Yahweh allowed only one master in Israel—not Baal, not human design, not Elijah. The other forms of irony, witnessed throughout this narrative, undergirded this major irony, supplemented the plot, and assisted the theme by intensifying and lessening the narrative ferment.

Undoubtedly the plot mustered its share of excitement. Characteristic to Hebrew narrative, the small repetitions, scattered everywhere, were matched in a grand scale; the first act which built slowly to a mighty climax and apparent victory on Carmel was mirrored in the second act where victory turned into defeat and defeat into victory. The correlation was forged by means of corresponding places in the flow of the plot and the similarity of vocabulary. At the same time, the dissonance which resulted from contrasts within the analogous parts, filled this narrative with suspense as the struggle of a disingenuous prophet surfaced.

This prophet contended with the same decision that the people on Carmel and Elisha by the field faced—whether or not to serve only Yahweh. The people chose to serve Yahweh, not Baal. Elijah decided to respect the plans of Yahweh, not his own. Elisha, in a manner which furthered the decision of the people, resolved to leave behind the comfort of security in order to implement Yahweh's plan. Elijah's decision remains the most crucial; Elisha's determination remains the most final. All three decisions lead to a consonance between God and Israel necessary for continued communion between them.

The confluence of the major features of this story affected the characters and the very structure of the smaller sections of the narrative. Strangers who were allies, enemies who were allies, and allies who were enemies threaded through this story. Only the person who followed the plot, tallied the actions of the characters, and paid attention to the recurrence of vocabulary and similarity of incidents realized the true alliances.

This narrative finally judges Elijah in the midst of his peers. By deciphering the narrative hints, which referred to stories from the Hebrew memory, the judgment which weighed Elijah down emerged. The slaughter at Kishon recalled the battle at which, the song of Judges 5 proclaims, Yahweh won the victory. The sojourn of Hagar and her son at Beersheba awaiting death contrasted with a prophet begging death. The immediacy of the Jacob story and Jacob's true solitude countered the willed singleness of Elijah who permitted no other, even Yahweh, to share his place. The experience of Gideon, his struggle against Baalism, witnessed to the persons who in Elijah's day and in former times (not to mention the coming times) fought against other gods, namely Baal, with the assistance of Yahweh. Gideon's strict adherence to the instructions of Yahweh exploded the apparently masterful, obviously overbearing behavior of Elijah. The comparison to Moses capped this series of comparisons which left little doubt in the mind of the audience about how far Elijah had fallen from the model. On the one hand, Elijah and Moses shared honor and disgrace—prophets of God excluded from the fulfillment of the promise. On the other hand, one crucial difference stood out; Elijah lacked compassion and failed to mediate for his own people. This judgment was so powerfully implanted that later stories, like Jonah, which spoke of prophets who tried to displace Yahweh, mirrored Elijah's experience.

The judgment recounted in this three chapter narrative is unequivocal. Elijah is not who he seems to be or who he ought to be for Yahweh's sake. As oneness characterizes Yahweh, so oneness must typify his people and his prophets. In this narrative, Yahweh overwhelms his people and overpowers his prophet. Because of this divine initiative, Yahweh's representatives, the prophets, Elijah and Elisha, and his people, Israel, move nearer that elusive goal of covenant fidelity and farther away from divided loyalties. Elijah, truly like his fathers, a mixture of faith and doubt, pride and conceit, begins to recede in the shadow of his successor who strives to serve Yahweh so that Israel moves even closer to the service of Yahweh.

NOTES

Notes to Chapter 1

1. Ray Bradbury, *The Illustrated Man* (New York: Doubleday, 1951), pp. 1ff.

2. Generally, the various episodes in this three chapter segment of the Deuteronomistic History (sometimes 1 Kings 19-21 escapes treatment with these three chapters by scholars who believe these verses belong with the Elisha cycle) are considered a mixture of anecdotes and historical narratives. See Odil H. Steck, *Überlieferung und Zeitgeschichte in den Elia-Erzählungen*, Wissenschaftliche Monographien zum Alten und Neuen Testament 26 (Neukirchen-Vluyn: Neukirchener Verlag, 1968), pp. 6ff.; Rudolf Smend, 'Das Wort Jahwes an Elia: Erwägungen zur Komposition von 1 Reg 17-19', *VT* 25 (1975), pp. 525ff.; John Gray, *1 & 2 Kings: A Commentary*, 2nd edn, The Old Testament Library (Philadelphia: The Westminster Press, 1970), pp. 371ff.; Georg Fohrer, *Elia*, 2nd edn (Zürich: Zwingli, 1968), pp. 33ff.; Johannes Fichtner, *Das erste Buch von den Königen*, Die Botschaft des Alten Testaments XII/1 (Stuttgart: Calwer 1964), pp. 242ff.; Hermann Gunkel, *Elias, Jahwe, und Baal*, Religionsgeschichtliche Volksbücher für die Deutsche Christliche Gegenwart II/8 (Tübingen: J.C.B. Mohr, 1906), pp. 5ff.; Hugo Gressmann, *Die älteste Geschichtsschreibung und Prophetie Israels*, Die Schriften des Alten Testaments von Gressmann, Gunkel, Haller, Schmidt, Stark, und Volz, vol. 2 (Göttingen: Vandenhoeck & Ruprecht, 1910), pp. xivff.; Otto Eissfeldt, *Der Gott Karmel* (Berlin: Akademie, 1953), pp. 32ff.; or Eissfeldt, *The Old Testament: An Introduction*, trans. Peter Ackroyd (New York: Harper & Row, 1965), pp. 42ff. Eissfeldt, *The Old Testament*, p. 48, maintains that the ancient Hebrews did not distinguish between the two, but moderns can because the two different attitudes to the world are presented. This is not undisputedly true. This project does not consider the sifting of the parts primary to its progress. The struggle with the genre of this material may be seen vividly in A. Rofe, 'Classification of the Prophetical Stories', *JBL* 89 (1970), pp. 427ff., or Burke Long, '2 Kings 3 and Genres of Prophetic Narrative', *VT* 23 (1973), pp. 337ff. In the case that one wants to represent the composite nature of 1 Kings 17-19, the genre might be 'narrative complex' (Eissfeldt, *Der Gott*, p. 31), 'constructed narrative' (a broadening of the term fostered by Armin Schnitt, 'Die Totenerweckung in 1 Kön XVII: 17-24: Eine Form- und Gattungskritische Untersuchung', *VT* 27

(1977), p. 473, or 'narrative association' (Smend's Erzählungszusammenhang found in 'Das Wort', p. 543). Those labels are acceptable, but I have chosen to use 'story' or 'narrative' for the most part. This choice is based upon the supposition that the research should be free from predisposition.

3. The last episode of this text, 1 Kgs 19.19-21, provides a curious, but interresting example of this search for information or tools which may help me understand the text. Many regard these verses a horrible intrusion and an awkward ending to this series of events. Wondering what makes a good or correct ending, I studied Barbara Smith, *Poetic Closure* (Chicago: University of Chicago Press, 1968). Her study and the interconnections between 1 Kgs 19.19-21 and the rest of Elijah's story recounted in these chapters, revealed to me the appropriateness of these verses.

4. Terence Fretheim, *The Message of Jonah* (Minneapolis: Augsburg, 1977), p. 51.

5. Wayne Booth, *A Rhetoric of Irony* (Chicago: University of Chicago Press, 1961), p. 10.

6. Edwin Good, *Irony in the Old Testament* (Philadelphia: Westminster, 1965), p. 10.

7. Wayne Booth, 'The Pleasures and Pitfalls of Irony: Or, Why Don't You Say What You Mean?' *Rhetoric, Philosophy and Literature: An Exploration*, ed. Don Burks (West Lafayette: Purdue University Press, 1978), p. 2.

8. Booth, *Rhetoric of Irony*, p. 44.

9. Paul Duke, *Irony in the Fourth Gospel* (Atlanta: John Knox, 1985), p. 15.

10. D.C. Muecke, *Irony* (Norfolk: Methuen, 1970), pp. 25ff. Paul Duke labels these extended and local irony, respectively, in *Irony in the Fourth Gospel*, p. 43.

11. Muecke, *Irony*, p. 25.

12. *Ibid.*, pp. 28ff.

13. Duke, *Irony in the Fourth Gospel*, p. 9.

14. Muecke, *Irony*, p. 30.

15. *Ibid.*, p. 34.

16. *Ibid.*, p. 35.

17. *Ibid.*, p. 37.

18. *Ibid.*, p. 45.

19. Booth, 'The Pleasures', p. 4.

20. Booth, *Rhetoric of Irony*, p. 29. However, Booth firmly maintains that irony builds in many cases a larger community with few outsiders than would have been built by non-ironic statement. Irony hosts multiple interpretations reconstructed by the audience from the story rather than one indisputable message. The excitement of searching for a message and the range of possibilities comprise a large share of irony's attractiveness.

21. Paul Duke uses 'extended irony' for verbal irony and 'local irony' for situational or dramatic irony. Furthermore, Duke splits his local irony into

at least four different categories: Irony of Events which explores the particular incongruity arising when events bring the unexpected; Irony of Self-Betrayal which reveals the disparity between what a character claims to be and what he or she really is; Irony of Imagery which contrasts the images portrayed with the action taking place; and Irony of Characterization which creates a clash between a character's ultimate personality or behavior and the behavior that character previously displayed. I find the first two—Irony of Events and Irony of Self-Betrayal which overlaps with the Irony of Characterization—very germane to this study. See Isaac M. Kikawada, 'A Comment on Irony: Observations of Luis Alonso Schökel's "Narrative Structures in the Book of Judith"', *Narrative Structures in the Book of Judith*, ed. Luis Alonso Schökel (Berkeley: The Center of Hermeneutical Studies in Hellenistic and Modern Culture, 1975), pp. 38ff.

22. Booth, *Rhetoric of Irony*, p. 44. See Muecke, *Irony*, p.49.

23. See Alonso Schökel, 'Narrative Structures', p. 47.

24. James G. Williams, 'Irony and Lament: Clues to Prophetic Consciousness', *Semeia* 8 (1977), p. 53.

25. *Ibid.*, p. 52. See Terence Fretheim, *The Message of Jonah*, pp. 51ff.

26. Good, *Irony in the Old Testament*, pp. 24, 32.

27. Duke, *Irony in the Fourth Gospel*, p. 37.

28. Fretheim, *The Message of Jonah*, pp. 51ff. See Booth, *Rhetoric of Irony*, where he describes the process as exploration or extension rather than repudiation or reversal. Paul Duke, commenting on Booth on p. 41, said: 'There remains in irony, if not always the hope of correction, at least a touch of identification with the victim, and so quite often a element of sorrow. From such a mixture of mirth and sadness can stem a degree of redemption'.

29. Good, *Irony in the Old Testament*, pp. 27ff.

30. Booth, *Rhetoric of Irony*, p. 39.

31. Booth, 'The Pleasures and Pitfalls', p. 12.

32. Duke, *Irony in the Fourth Gospel*, p. 34.

33. *Ibid.*, p. 39.

34. See Muecke, *Irony*, p. 7. He illustrates this point by referring to the Romantic landscapes of Caspar David Friedrich, the noted painter. Muecke claims that certain qualities in the paintings of this man or any artist of the Romantic movement have become 'signs' of Romanticism. These 'signs', in turn, are the raw material for the ironical painter.

35. See Wesley Kort, *Narrative Elements and Religious Meanings* (Philadelphia: Fortress, 1975), pp. 13ff., or Owen Barfield, *Poetic Diction*, 3rd edn (Middletown: Wesleyan University Press, 1973), p. 120.

36. J.P. Fokkelman, *Narrative Art in Genesis* (Amsterdam: Van Gorcum, Assen, 1975), pp. 5ff.

37. See Muecke, *Irony*, p. 5.

38. John Frank Kermode, *The Genesis of Secrecy: On the Interpretation of*

Narrative (Cambridge, Mass.: Harvard University Press, 1979), pp. 131ff.

39. Booth, *Rhetoric of Irony*, pp. 51ff.

40. Ibid., pp. 10ff.

41. W.K. Wimsatt, Jr., and M.C. Beardsley, 'The Intentional Fallacy', *Sewanee Review* 54 (1946), pp. 468ff.

42. Booth, 'The Pleasures and Pitfalls', p. 6.

43. Booth, *Rhetoric of Irony*, pp. 222ff., provides his 'five crippling handicaps'. Our assessments somewhat overlap; however, I have organized mine according to extremes, i.e., too little and too much.

44. Robert Cohn, 'The Literary Logic of 1 Kings 17-19', *JBL* 101 (1982), pp. 333ff., addresses the question of irony in this narrative. However, he fails to recognize the pervasiveness of the irony and overlooks the manner in which irony shapes this entire narrative, e.g., the particularity to the major decision called for in these three chapters or the significance of the 'kiss' in 1 Kgs 19.20.

45. Duke, *Irony in the Fourth Gospel*, pp. 26ff., calls this 'irony of events'.

46. See Duke, *Irony in the Fourth Gospel*, pp. 26ff., and his discussion of 'irony of self-betrayal', 'irony of imagery', and 'irony of characterization'.

47. See Alter, *The Art of Biblical Narrative* (New York: Basic Books, 1981), p. 82, who calls this 'pretemporal exposition'.

48. See 2 Kgs 3.14 and 5.16 for the Elisha material.

49. See Martin Noth, *Die israelitischen Personennamen im Rahmen der gemeinsemitischen Namengebung* (Hildesheim: Georg Olms, 1966), pp. 16ff., 70, 139ff.; Gray, *1 & 2 Kings, A Commentary*, 2nd edn (Philadelphia: Westminster, 1965), p. 402; Claude Hermann Walter Johns, *The Religious Significance of Semitic Proper Names* (Cambridge: A.P. Dixon, 1912), pp. 101ff.; Rudolf Smend, 'Der biblische und der historische Elia', *Supplements to Vetus Testamentum* 28 (1975), p. 177.

50. Elijah matches significant criteria which pertain to the prophet's message, personhood, and chronology in the list presented by James Crenshaw, *Prophetic Conflict: Its Effect upon Israelite Religion* (Berlin: Walter de Gruyter, 1971), pp. 49ff.

51. See Jean Steinmann, 'La geste d'Élie dans l'Ancien Testament', *Élie le prophète* (Les Études Carmélitaines: Desclée de Brouwer, 1956), pp. 1, 114; Fohrer, *Elia*, p. 85; and Gunkel, *Elias, Jahve, und Baal*, p. 16.

52. The RSV translation is used unless specified.

53. This observation reflects the thought of Seymour Chatman, *Story and Discourse* (Ithaca: Cornell University Press, 1978), p. 72.

54. Cf. Fohrer, *Elia*, p. 18, who claims that this trial upon Carmel is not to indicate the power of Elijah but to establish Yahweh as 'the' god for Israel.

55. This characteristic is described excellently in the classic treatment of

Axel Olrik, 'Epic Laws of Folk Narrative', *The Study of Folklore*, ed. Alan Dundes (Englewood Cliffs: Prentice-Hall, 1965), p. 138.

56. Kenneth Gros Louis, 'Elijah and Elisha', *Literary Interpretations of Biblical Narratives*, ed. Kenneth Gros Louis, James Ackerman, and Thayer Warshaw (Nashville: Abingdon Press, 1974), p. 190.

57. This statement rests on the correspondence of these scenes and the use of the verbal stem יתר (to remain).

58. Cf. Ludwig H. Köhler, *Hebrew Man*, trans. Peter Ackroyd (London: SCM, 1956), p. 123. The psychologization witnessed in Köhler commits at least two errors. First, the assessment of the Hebrew mind is drawn from a very limited number of documents or texts which exhibit literary shaping in many cases. These texts may reflect certain psychological dynamics, but their use as sources of psychological truths of Hebrew culture must be monitored closely. Second, this sort of explanation commits the same error as explanations which base their interpretation upon the identification of the author, the author's intention, or the time(s) during which the piece was composed. This is not to say that examination of the psychological dimensions of the text should not take place, but such a task should be focused within the text itself. Martin Buss, 'Understanding Communication', *Encounter With the Text: Form and History in the Hebrew Bible* (Missoula: Scholars Press, 1979), p. 28, offers an acceptable model of such a project.

59. Steinmann, 'La geste d'Élie', p. 100. He believes such defiance requires from Elijah a singular faith in Yahweh's protection. My thesis questions Elijah's sincerity and thus his faith.

60. Leah Bronner, *The Stories of Elijah and Elisha* (Leiden: E.J. Brill, 1968), p. x.

61. W. Slotki, *Kings*, Soncino Books of the Bible (London: Soncino, 1950), p. 124, advances this thesis. Cf. Fichtner, *Das erste Buch*, p. 256, maintains that Elijah could tell the widow by her dress or wardrobe. To be fair, one might claim that the storyteller paid no attention to this detail. However, one must give due regard to the haste Elijah exercised in the earlier episode compared with this one.

62. Here lies an example of the usefulness but not the necessity of knowledge retrieved from the 'lost world'. This search stands on its own in this developing story; a drought anywhere, anytime, calls for such action. Yet the story is enhanced by information concerning the size of Ahab's chariot force. For the defense of his country, Ahab needed animals unaffected by the drought. The text titled 'The Fight against the Aramean Coalition', from the reign of Shalmaneser III, grants this information. See James B. Pritchard, ed., *Ancient Near Eastern Texts*, 3rd edn with supplement (Princeton: Princeton University Press, 1969), p. 279.

63. See Steck, *Überlieferung*, pp. 5ff.; Fichtner, *Das erste Buch*, p. 273; Fohrer, *Elia*, pp. 34ff.; Albrecht Alt, 'Das Gottesurteil auf dem Karmel',

Festschrift Georg Beer zum 70. Geburtstag (Stuttgart: W. Kohlhammer, 1935), p. 135.

64. See R. Patai, 'The Control of Rain in Ancient Palestine', *Hebrew Union College Annual* 14 (1939), pp. 251ff.; Norman Snaith, *The First and Second Book of Kings*, The Interpreter's Bible (New York: Abingdon, 1954), pp. 157ff. Cf. Roland de Vaux, 'Notes on the Text', *Élie le prophète* (Les Études Carmélitaines: Desclée de Brouwer, 1956), pp. 1, 63; Steinmann, 'La Geste', p. 104; J.A. Montgomery, *Critical and Exegetical Commentary on the Book of Kings* (New York: Charles Scribner's Sons, 1951), p. 308.

65. H.H. Rowley, 'Elijah on Mount Carmel', *Bulletin of the John Rylands Library* 43 (1960), p. 210, believes that for this many people on the mountain to have no water would be more unusual than the presence of water. Childs, 'On Reading the Elijah Narratives', *Interpretation* 34 (1980), pp. 132ff., maintains this use of precious water was an act of faith.

66. Eissfeldt, *Der Gott Karmel*, p. 34. R.A. Carlson, 'Élie a l'Horeb', *VT* 19 (1969), p. 424, points out that three times four equals the number of stones.

67. See T.K. Cheyne, *The Hallowing of Criticism* (London: Hodder Stoughton, 1888), p. 76, who states that Elijah got the water from a fountain. Steinmann, 'La geste', p. 104, thinks the sea was close enough to be used as a source of water.

68. Dennis Baly, *God and History in the Old Testament* (New York: Harper & Row, 1976), p. 85.

69. My translation supports a singular rendering of the Hebrew.

70. The meaning of this phrase is by no means clear. De Vaux, 'Notes', p. 66, interprets it as an expression of mortality, of incredible fatigue. Slotki, *Kings*, similarly perceives this expression as Elijah's acceptance of a mortality like his forebears and an attempt to move up the occasion to join them. By this wish, Elijah relegates the past to a category of failure, and the future to a category of hopelessness. W. Milligan, *Elijah, His Life and Times* (New York: Anson D.F. Randolph, 1890), pp. 84ff., underscores Elijah's despondency and subsequent downgrading of the past. J. Robinson, *The First Book of Kings*, Cambridge Bible Commentary (Cambridge: Cambridge University Press, 1972), p. 218, maintains that this statement is merely a way to appeal for a quick death. Fichtner, *Das erste Buch*, p. 283, believes Elijah's plea refers probably to God's servants who were abandoned in earlier generations. Fohrer, *Elia*, p. 22, implies that this means Elijah's time of service is past. Steinmann, 'La geste', p. 107, asserts that Elijah was attempting to remake the Exodus or to go back to the wilderness/Horeb period in order to erase three and one half centuries of history. In the final analysis, Elijah could not measure up to Moses and his momentous work. J.O.A. Clark, *Elijah Vindicated* (Nashville: ME Church, South, 1893), p. 329, states that Elijah believed himself to be ineffective in comparison to

his distinguished forebears; therefore, he asks to die rather than to be translated. All these views rightfully look to the past of Elijah's reference; they neglect the irony of Elijah's predicament.

71. This certainly accords with the primary benefit of covenant faithfulness, i.e., life (Deut. 30.9, 19).

72. Shlomith Rimmon, *The Concept of Ambiguity—the Example of James* (Chicago: University of Chicago Press, 1977), p. 26. She defines ambiguity strictly; ambiguity never allows for a resolution, but forever provides different alternatives.

73. My translation. See Ronald Williams, *Hebrew Syntax: An Outline*, 2nd edn (Toronto: University of Toronto Press, 1976), p. 23, who details the anaphoric use of הוא.

74. See Robinson, *The First Book of Kings*, p. 217. He agrees that אלהים should be translated in the singular.

75. Thomas Berger, *Little Big Man* (New York: Dial, 1964), pp. 436ff. In the book, *Old Lodge Skins*, a delightful and discerning Human Being, aged and tired of fighting the white man who proves so destructive, lies down and actually dies. In the film, he gets back up when the rain begins to fall on his closed eyes.

76. Gray, *1 & 2 Kings*, p. 396, states that Elijah deals with the assembled Israelites, the religious community. I do not disagree for that usage is common, especially in the Deuteronomistic History, but I do sense the irony and ambiguity in the phrase.

77. My translation. The RSV translates 'in a cave' even though the preposition ב carries the marking of a definite article. See Gray, *1 & 2 Kings*, p. 386, for his discussion of this point and his suggestion for translation of this troublesome phrase: 'Obadiah had taken . . . and hidden them by fives in the caves'. Or, Montgomery, *A Critical Commentary*, p. 298.

78. Many commentators draw a parallel between this cave and the cleft that Moses stood within while Yahweh passed by. See Baly, *God and History*, p. 87; de Vaux, 'Notes', p. 67; Fohrer, *Elia*, pp. 55ff.; Gray, *1 & 2 Kings*, p. 409; Gunkel, *Elias, Jahve, und Baal*, p. 23; Robinson, *The First Book of Kings*, p. 218; Slotki, *Kings*, p. 138; Snaith, *The First and Second Books of Kings*, p. 162; Childs, 'On Reading', pp. 135ff.; Seybold, 'Elia am Gottesberg', p. 10. Fichtner, *Das erste Buch*, p. 284, considers this speculation an idle endeavor; he notes that different words are used.

79. Gunkel, *Elias, Jahve, und Baal*, p. 17.

80. The related root תלל means 'to mock, deceive, trifle with'. See Francis Brown, S.R. Driver, and Charles Briggs, *A Hebrew and English Lexicon of the Old Testament* (Oxford: Clarendon, 1968), p. 1068.

81. My translation. Cf. Leo Hayman, 'A Note on 1 Kings 18.27', *JNES* 10 (1951), pp. 57ff., and Hans-Peter Müller, 'Die Hebräische Wurzel שיח', *VT* 19 (1969), pp. 361ff., for two novel interpretations of this verse. For the standard perspective, see Gray, *1 & 2 Kings*, p. 397.

82. See Childs, 'On Reading', p. 131, and George Saint-Laurent, 'Light from Ras Shamra on Elijah's Ordeal upon Mount Carmel', *Scripture in Context: Essays on the Comparative Method*, ed. Carl Evans, William Holow, and John White; Pittsburgh Theological Monograph Series 34 (Pittsburgh: Pickwick, 1980), pp. 130ff.

83. See David Jobling, *The Sense of Biblical Narrative* (Sheffield: JSOT, 1978), pp. 71ff. He offers a fascinating study of 1 Kings 17–18 and underscores the advantage that Elijah had at the very beginning. The victory of Yahweh was previewed in verse 24 when the people accepted Elijah's offer according to Jobling.

84. Gressmann, *Die älteste Geschichtsschreibung*, p. 267, maintains that chapter 19 is not a further development of chapter 18, but the antithesis of that which is reported in the earlier chapter. In his opinion, these chapters are better understood as parallel. Cf. Childs, 'On Reading', pp. 135ff. Von Rad, *Biblical Interpretations in Preaching*, trans. John Steasdy (Nashville: Abingdon, 1977), p. 34, says they both treat the same theme: Yahweh's self-disclosure in a situation of utter hopelessness. Furthermore, in Gerhard von Rad, *Old Testament Theology*, trans. D.M.G. Stalker (New York: Harper & Row, 1965), II, p. 19, he lists three other affinities: the same starting point (the desperate plight of Yahweh which is the original reason for Elijah's despair in chapter 19); same mention of a manifestation of Yahweh; and the same conclusion (a pronouncement of penalty, although in 19 it is not carried out). Eissfeldt, *Der Gott Karmel*, pp. 36ff., stresses the affinities and quotes Gunkel to undergird his perceptions. One difference he notes is the participation of Elijah in chapter 18 in the demise of the prophets of Baal over against Elijah's non-participation in chapter 19. This project finds that difference easy enough to explain; Elijah's time was up.

85. This author's opinion is not to be confused with the claim of Andre Neher, 'A Reflection on the Silence of God', *Judaism* 16 (1967), p. 434, who states that chapter 19 is an ironic reply to chapter 18. He asserts that one finds in chapter 18 a god, Baal, who is powerless to speak, to answer, or to regard the pleas of his prophets. In chapter 19, one finds a god, Yahweh, who in the silence of Yahweh's presence is revealed more than by Yahweh's word. There certainly is some contrast here between the impotent silence of Baal and the powerful (modified) silence of Yahweh, but the author finds that the significance of that muted voice of Yahweh and the shift from דבר to קול resides in a somewhat different perception of the relations in the story.

86. R.A. Carlson, 'Élie à l'Horeb', *VT* (1969), p. 433, underscores Elijah's neglect of his overlord's wishes.

87. Gunkel, *Elias, Jahve und Baal*, pp. 13ff.

88. Gressmann, *Die älteste Geschichtsschreibung*, p. 261.

89. Robert Coote, 'Yahweh Recalls Elijah', *Traditions in Transformation*, ed. Baruch Halpern and Jon Levenson (Winona Lake, In.: Eisenbrauns, 1981), pp. 118ff., identifies this combination of seemingly contradictory

words as an oxymoron. See Macholz, 'Psalm 29 und 1. Könige 19', *Werden und Wirken des Alten Testaments* (Göttingen: Vandenhoeck & Ruprecht, 1980), p. 332.

90. See Coote, 'Yahweh Recalls Elijah', pp. 118ff.; Silberman, 'Between God and Man: The Meaning of Revelation for the Contemporary Jew', *Tradition and Contemporary Experience* (New York: Schocken Books, 1970), p. 93.

91. Cf. 2 Kgs 7.7-15; 9.1-13; 10.18-33.

92. See Ps. 44.24 which calls Yahweh to awaken from slumber (but cf. 78.65; 121.4).

93. See Erich Zenger, 'Review of Überlieferung and Zeitgeschichte in den Elia-Erzählungen', *Bib* 51 (1970), p. 143; J.J. Stamm, 'Elia am Horeb', *Studia Biblica et Semitica*, ed. W.S. van Unnik and A.S. van der Woude (Wageningen: H. Veenman & Zonen, 1966), p. 355. Cf. Ernst Würthwein, 'Elijah at Horeb: Reflections on 1 Kgs 19.9-18', *Proclamation and Presence*, ed. John Durham and J.R. Porter (Richmond: John Knox Press, 1970), pp. 156ff.

94. The number 7000 is not historical, but symbolic.

95. See Coote, 'Yahweh Recalls Elijah', p. 200.

96. 1 Kgs 19.10, 14.

97. Gerhard von Rad, *Old Testament Theology*, trans. D.M.G. Stalker (New York: Harper & Row, 1962), pp. 1, 121ff.

98. See Bar-Efrat, 'Some Observations on the Analysis of Structure in Biblical Narrative', *VT* 30 (1980), pp. 160ff., and Levenson, '1 Samuel—as Literature and History', *CBQ* 40 (1978), p. 22.

99. Cf. Steck, *Überlieferung*, pp. 25, 29ff., 132ff. However, what if Elijah's charge be true? What if the people, striving to save their own lives in the face of Jezebel's rage and consistent purpose, do forsake, kill, and seek him as instruments of the monarchy as they were instruments of Elijah at Carmel? What if this information has been held until now to be revealed so that the circle is ever-widening, at least in the narrative's perspective—from the explicit implication of Jezebel and Ahab, to the whole people? See Robert Wilson, *Prophecy and Society in Ancient Israel* (Philadelphia: Fortress, 1980), p. 199, who maintains that Elijah acted on Carmel without having or winning broad enough social support for his movement. I support his observation in its narrative implications but reserve judgment on the historical accuracy.

Notes to Chapter 2

1. This author disagrees with David J.A. Clines, 'Theme in Genesis 1–11', *CBQ* 38 (1976), pp. 485ff., who claims that there cannot be more than one theme in a literary work. He believes that the emergence of different,

divergent, or contradictory themes necessitates the adaptation by the critic of a broader thematic statement. He does acknowledge different levels on which theme is sought, identified, and articulated, but he remains committed to the 'one story (unity)/one theme' rule. It seems to this author that there may be an overriding theme that is supplemented by other themes and motifs.

2. Carlson, 'Élie à l'Horeb', p. 430.

3. In the choice of this theme, Carlson stands firmly in customary interpretation. See W.F. Albright, *Yahweh and the Gods of Canaan* (London: Athlone, 1968), pp. 179, 181ff.; John Gray, *The Legacy of Canaan*, 2nd edn, Supplements to Vetus Testamentum 5 (Leiden: E.J. Brill, 1965), pp. 183, 203; Bronner, *The Stories of Elijah and Elisha*, pp. 49, 139ff.; Frank E. Eakin, Jr, 'Yahwism and Baalism before the Exile', *JBL* 84 (1965), pp. 413ff.; Arvid S. Kapelrud, *The Ras Shamra Discoveries and the Old Testament* (Norman: University of Oklahoma Press, 1963), p. 33; F.C. Fensham, 'A Few Observations on the Polarisation between Yahweh and Baal in 1 Kings 17–19', *ZAW* 92 (1980), pp. 232, 235ff.; Norman Habel, *Yahweh Versus Baal: A Conflict of Religious Cultures* (New York: Bookman Associates, 1965), pp. 31, 103; Flemming Friis Hvidberg, *Weeping and Laughter in the Old Testament* (Leiden: E.J. Brill, 1962), p. 136; Gunnar Ostborn, *Yahweh and Baal* (Lund: C.W.K. Gleerup, 1956), p. 56.

4. Carlson, 'Élie à l'Horeb', pp. 429ff.

5. Some critics suggest that Elijah was connected to the Rechabites and this link accounted for much of his zeal. There seems to be no evidence that irrefutably supports this supposition. However, the explicit connection of Elijah to Gilead in 1 Kgs 17.1 does provide a clue to Elijah's character, even if that clue harkens more to the imagination than to the intellect. Von Rad, *Biblical Interpretations*, p. 13, comments: 'When a geographical name appears, it must not remain a mere sound. Surprising perspectives will often open up through the use of such names'. Von Rad, *Old Testament Theology*, pp. 2, 15, recalls the distance of Gilead from Canaan and suggests the possibility that this place was a fertile base for the continuing partriarchal Yahwism. See Robinson, *The First Book of Kings*, p. 199; Milligan, *Elijah: His Life and Times*, pp. 2ff.; Bronner, *The Stories of Elijah and Elisha*, p. 20; Gunkel, *Elias, Jahve und Baal*, p. 58.

6. Von Rad, *Old Testament Theology*, II, pp. 17ff., notes possible similarities and differences to the covenant renewal ceremony depicted in Joshua 24. There the people answered, here in 1 Kings 18, God answers before the people actually choose, or at least before they express their decision.

7. David Jobling, *The Sense of Biblical Narrative*, pp. 63ff., treats 1 Kgs 17–18. His article contains two suggestive aids to the study of this material in the present study. First, by employing A.J. Greimas's scheme, he analyzes the drought sequence and the combat sequence. His conclusion concerning

the Carmel material or the combat story proves especially interesting. He notes the three stages of the story reflected in the people's role and the three perspectives that correspond to these stages. He presents his finding in a chart (p. 77):

Vv.	Role of the people	Choice	Symmetry	Knowledge
21a	—	—	Symmetry	None
21b	Villain	Unwillingness to choose	—	—
22-24a	—	—	—	—
24b	Helper	Willingess to choose	Broken symmetry	Implicit
24-37	—	—	Symmetry abandoned	—
38-40	Hero	—	Choice	Explicit

Second, Jobling suggests that the drought narrative and the combat narrative to be compared. That comparison juxtaposes the responses of Ahab and the people to Elijah and, thereby, to Yahweh. He offers the essentials of the comparison in a table (p. 80):

	The drought (Elijah and Ahab)	The combat (Elijah and the people)
First approach of Elijah	17.1	18.21a
Its failure	Implicit	18.21b
	The drought (Elijah and Ahab)	The combat (Elijah and the people)
Second approach of Elijah	18.17-19	18.22-24a
Provides knowledge	Explicit (epistemological turning-point)	Implicit
Demands domination Baal prophets	18.19	18.23-24a
Its success	18.20 (volitional turning-point)	18.24b (volitional turning-point)
Various minor contracts	18.41-42	18.30
accepted	18.44-45	18.34 Explicit knowledge 18.38 (epistemological turning-point) Fulfillment of initial contract 18.39-40

Although his analysis is stimulating and highlights the theme of choice, I remain somewhat wary on two counts: his use of Propp and Greimas at times gives the impression that he has pressed outside criteria upon the literature before its whole story is heard; and his division of these two chapters closely resembles the old boundaries of historical criticism. The whole story begs to be heard and analyzed, not stretched or pressed. In terms of this present analysis, his scheme should be tested more widely in the three chapter expanse.

8. See Nicholas J. Tromp, 'Water and Fire on Mount Carmel', *Bib* (1975), p. 493.

9. This expression 'limping (dancing) between two boughs', always a moot point, includes both those who jump from one to the other or those who walk on both at the same time. The latter may point to a composite ceremony which reveals a mosaic of cultic practice. In any case, the message calls for an end to indecision and if one is to be faithful to Yahweh, one must cease the apostasy of indecision. See de Vaux, 'Notes', p. 59, who notes the appropriateness of Carmel which looks out over the sea claimed by Baal and over the land claimed by Yahweh. Also, J. Alberto Soggin, *Introduction to the Old Testament*, trans. John Bowden; The Old Testament Library (Philadelphia: Westminster, 1976), p. 121, who represents Carmel as a welcome sight to sailors.

10. See Fichtner, *Das erste Buch*, p. 270.

11. Jobling, *Sense of Biblical Narrative*, p. 71.

12. See Snaith, 'The First and Second Books of Kings', p. 157, who claims this rite entails sympathetic magic. De Vaux, 'Notes', p. 63, counters such a suggestion and maintains that the water is used to inhibit the fire. Fohrer, *Elia*, pp. 17ff., mentions both as possibilities. Childs, 'On Reading', pp. 132ff., connects this bold act with the confidence of Elijah.

13. The text reads: 'Elijah, the prophet, *approached* and said. . . ' Twice the italicized word has been used by Elijah to direct the people. Indeed, this is the word which begins and splits this episode. As director, Elijah has been free to guide the action. Now, by use of this phrase, the composer has revealed to the audience the true director of all the events: Elijah approaches Yahweh, the god of Israel. Perhaps, in terms of the setting, Elijah moves to the border of the area he has set off; in terms of the story, Elijah approaches to instruct the deity who commissioned him.

14. See Jack Corvin, 'A Stylistic and Functional Study of the Prose Prayers in the Historical Narratives of the Old Testament' (Ph.D. dissertation, Emory University, 1972), pp. 183ff., 191ff.

15. See Edwin Staudt III, 'Prayer and the People in the Deuteronomist' (Ph.D. dissertation, Vanderbilt University, 1980), pp. 272ff.

16. This adverb, which means 'afterwards' or 'backwards', is found five times in the biblical record and clearly means 'backwards' in the other four examples (Gen. 9.23; 1 Sam. 4.18; 2 Kgs 20.10; Isa. 38.8). However, those

few instances are no basis for a narrow meaning. This author chooses to translate the word in line with the connotations of similar words and with a consistent emphasis on Elijah's management of Yahweh's acts. See Brown, Driver, and Briggs, *Hebrew and English Lexicon*, p. 30.

17. See C.F.D. Moule, *An Idiom-Book of New Testament Greek*, 2nd edn (Cambridge: Cambridge University Press, 1971), p. 48, who says: 'J.S. Stewart writes: "It was a dictum of Luther's that all religion lies in the pronouns. . . . But Deissmann, going a step further. . ., has virtually declared that religion resides in the prepositions"'.

18. Cf. *cherem*, the total dedication or devotion in Holy War.

19. Elijah learns this lesson on Horeb which is called 'the mountain of the (one) God' (1 Kgs 19.8b), the God proved on Carmel.

20. The appearance of these words in 1 Kgs 17.20 (אני), 18. 6 (לבדו), 18.8 (אני), and 19.4 (אנכי) is not germane to this discussion.

21. See R.P. Carroll, 'The Elijah-Elisha Sagas: Some Remarks on Prophetic Succession in Ancient Israel', *VT* 19 (1969), p. 405.

22. See Fohrer, *Elia*, p. 24; Slotki, *Kings*, p. 141.

23. See A. von Selms, 'Motivated Interrogative Sentences in Biblical Hebrew', *Semitics* 2 (1971-72), p. 143.

24. See H.J. Blair, 'Putting One's Hand to the Plough: Luke 9.62 and 1 Kgs 19.19-21', *Expost* 79 (1968), p. 342; Elie Wiesel, *Five Biblical Portraits* (Notre Dame: University of Notre Dame Press, 1981), pp. 65ff.; Milligan, *Elijah*, pp. 116ff.; Slotki, *Kings*, p. 141; Gray, *1 & 2 Kings*, p. 414; Gressmann, *Die älteste Geschichtsschreibung*, p. 268; Coote, 'Yahweh Recalls Elijah', p. 120.

25. This recalls the situation of David and Solomon or Moses and Joshua. The first of either pair ranks as the more important and contributes uniquely to Israel's history and religion. Yet, the second finishes the task of the first in a dramatic manner. Joshua led the conquest which fulfilled the promise to Abraham, and, in a sense, completed the Exodus; Solomon built the temple which cemented the power of the Davidic dynasty and the centrality of Jerusalem.

26. See Smith, *Poetic Closure*, pp. 120, 172, 258.

27. This curse and its contents recall the day when Elijah did appear in fact before Ahab to declare the commencement of this drought (1 Kgs 17.1). In terms of the narrative, such a recollection undergirds the reliability of Elijah.

28. An exhaustive list of the decisions called for reveals two features: they call carry the force of the imperative and some are fulfilled immediately to assist the flow of the plot (A) whereas some pose a difficulty to the person asked in order to inhibit the flow of the plot (I). The decisions called for by Elijah include: bring water (1 Kgs 17.10b—A); bring bread (1 Kgs 17.11b—I); do as you say (1 Kgs 17.13-14—A); give son (1 Kgs 17.19—I/A); heal boy (1 Kgs 17.21b—A); go, tell (1 Kgs 18.8—I); cry aloud (18.27—A); come near

(1 Kgs 18.30—A); fill jars (1 Kgs 18.33-34—A); go up to see (1 Kgs 18.43—A); go up to tell (1 Kgs 18.44—command within a command—A); take my life (1 Kgs 19.4b—I); and go back (1 Kgs 19.20—A). The decisions called for by Yahweh include: go to Cherith (1 Kgs 17.2—A); go to Zarephath (1 Kgs 17.9—A); go to Ahab (1 Kgs 18.1—A); go forth (1 Kgs 19.11—I); and go, return (1 Kgs 19.15—a series—A in a proleptic sense). The decision called for by Ahab is: go check on water (1 Kgs 18.5—A). The decisions called for by the messenger are significantly similar and different: arise and eat (1 Kgs 19.5—A) and arise and eat for. . . (1 Kgs 19.7—A). The decisions which are not immediately met by some indication of an affirmative response have to be mediated. This is done by some word, deed, or experience which allows the forward flow of the plot to begin again.

29. Steinmann, 'La geste', pp. 100ff.

30. See above, p.79.

31. See above, pp.79ff.

32. The mention of the meat in the account in which the ravens serve as the hosts may be a narrative accommodation to the character of these animals; they are carrion fowl.

33. Carlson, 'Élie à l'Horeb', pp. 421, 423.

34. Rovert C. Tannehill, *The Sword of His Mouth*, Semeia Supplements, 1 (Missoula, MT: Scholars Press, 1975), pp. 40ff.

35. A diagram might be arranged as follows.

```
             tells              about
Obadiah ─────────── Elijah ──────────── death of prophets (removes threat)


             tells              about
Ahab ─────────── Jezebel ──────────── death of prophets (brings threat)


(Jezebel)                  opposition   (Obadiah)
Kill prophets (Yahwistic) ─────────── Save prophets
(Yahwistic)


                          concord
Kill prophets (Baalistic) ─────────── Save Yahwism (prophets)
(Elijah)                               (Elijah)
```

36. My translation.

37. See Vater, 'Narrative Patterns for the Story of Commmissioned Communication in the Old Testament', *JBL* 99 (1980), pp. 378ff., who claims this pattern of commissioned communication functions 'to remove the messenger from the scene completely, so as to unite dramatically and psychologically two parties, or two events'.

38. The standard treatment of this exact paralleling consists of the

excision, as Julius Wellhausen, *Die Composition des Hexateuchs und der historischen Bücher des Alten Testaments*, 4th edn, reprint of 3rd edn (Berlin: Walter de Gruyter, 1963), p. 280 n. 1, of verses 9b-11a, as a gloss. Cf. Würthwein, 'Elijah at Horeb', p. 161, who thinks the second appearance is the interpolation.

39. See Tannehill, *Sword*, p. 41.

40. This shift generally serves as part of the evidence concerning the interpolation of this material. Here, my purpose is to consider what the present text exhibits.

41. See Silberman, 'Between God and Man', pp. 92ff. Cf. Christian Macholz, 'Psalm 29 and 1. Könige 19: Jahwes und Baals Theophanie', *Werden und Wirken des Alten Testaments*, ed. Ranier Albertz, Hans-Peter Müller, Hans Walter Wolff, and Walter Zimmerli (Göttingen: Vandenhoeck & Ruprecht, 1980), p. 332.

42. This change does not necessarily signal a whole new era in the means of Yahweh's revelation. That interpretation places too much strain upon one incident among many. My interpretation leaves room for the innerbiblical exegesis that may be occurring here. To jostle an old story or image is not the same as to render the old traditions no longer theologically relevant. See Fishbane, 'Revelation and Tradition: Aspects of Innerbiblical Exegesis', *JBL* 99 (1980), pp. 343, 351.

43. Compare Deuteronomy 32.48-52.

44. See above, p. 93.

Notes to Chapter 3

1. Deuteronomy 13, especially vv. 5, 7-12, 13ff. See von Rad, *Old Testament Theology*, II, p. 18; Childs, 'On Reading', p. 133. Cf. Wiener, *Elijah*, p. 12.

2. The importance of the name in the ancient Near East is widely known; the name 'Israel' is especially important to this narrative. See below, pp. 104ff.

3. See Artur Weiser, *The Psalms*, The Old Testament Library (Philadelphia: Westminster, 1962), p. 564.

4. See Helmer Ringgren, *Religions of the Ancient Near East*, trans. John Sturdy (Philadelphia: Westminster, 1973), pp. 132ff., who notes that Baal possessed a voice so strong that the world trembled when Baal, the Most High God, spoke.

5. See Gunkel, *Elias, Jahve, und Baal*, p. 22. De Vaux, 'Notes', p. 107, shows that both scenes occur at the same place, involve the resting beneath a tree or bush, entail the mediation of an angel of God, and portray the gift of physical comfort (the well and the food, respectively).

6. My translation.

7. See Eckhard V. Nordheim, 'Ein Prophet kündigt sein Amt auf (Elia am Horeb)', *Bib* 59 (1978), p. 167. Cf. Coote, 'Yahweh Recalls Elijah', p. 116.

8. The most extensive treatment of such parallels continues to be Fohrer, *Elia*, pp. 55ff. He mentions: the sustaining care (1 Kgs 17.6); the challenge to God (1 Kgs 17.20); the contest on Carmel (1 Kgs 18.20-40); Elijah on Horeb (1 Kgs 19.8ff.); the trip of 40 days and nights (1 Kgs 19.8); hiding in the cave when Yahweh passed by (1 Kgs 19.9ff.); the theophany (1 Kgs 19.9ff.); Elijah's hiding his face (19.13); the 7000 true believers (1 Kgs 19.18); Elijah's fleeing to a foreign land (1 Kgs 17.2ff.); and the confrontation between Elijah and the people (1 Kgs 18.20ff.). See Steck, *Überlieferung und Zeitgeschichte*, pp. 109ff.; Childs, 'On Reading', pp. 135ff.; Smend, 'Der biblische', pp. 183ff.; Carroll, 'The Elijah-Elisha Sagas', pp. 411ff.; Nordheim, 'Ein Prophet', p. 162; Carlson, 'Elie à l'Horeb', p. 432; Seybold, 'Elia am Gottesberg', p. 17; Rowley, 'Elijah on Mount Carmel', p. 219; Snaith, 'The First and Second Book of Kings', p. 162; Gray, *1 & 2 Kings*, p. 409; de Vaux, 'Notes', p. 65; Montgomery, *A Critical and Exegetical Commentary*, p. 313; Yehuda Radday, 'Chiasm in Kings', *Linguistica Biblica* 31 (1974), p. 61.

9. Many scholars have noted the correspondence between Moses' covering his face on Horeb when he received his call and Elijah's covering his face when Yahweh addresses him. This comparison is correct but shallow. What lies in that correlation is an example of literary genius. The composer of the Elijah story in 1 Kings 17–19 has displaced the call narrative until later. On Horeb, Elijah receives the call; hears the address of God, raises an objection, obtains the answer to his objection, acquires a commission, and receives proof that Yahweh protects his own. There are two major differences between this call narrative (form criticism) or type scene (literary criticism) and that in the material on Moses or the prophets; his call occurs at the end of the narrative and not at the beginning. Second, the commission terminates his service and initiates his successor's tenure. This appropriation fits the character of the narrative. See Walther Zimmerli, *Ezekiel*, trans. Ronald Clements, Hermeneia (Philadelphia: Fortress, 1979), pt. 1, pp. 97ff., or Lynne Deming, 'The Prophetic Call Narrative as a Biblical Type Scene', paper presented at the Southeastern Society of Biblical Literature Meeting, March 19, 1982, pp. 3ff.

10. See Rowley, 'Elijah on Mount Carmel', p. 219.

11. See Nordheim, 'Ein Prophet', p. 162.

12. See Macholz, 'Psalm 29 and 1. Könige 19', p. 322, and Jörg Jeremias, *Theophanie: Die Geschichte einer alttestamentlichen Gattung* (Neukirchen-Vluyn: Neukirchener Verlag, 1965), pp. 107, 113ff.

13. See Carroll, 'The Elijah-Elisha Sagas', p. 410.

14. See Crenshaw, *Samson*, pp. 46ff.; Magonet, *Form and Meaning: Studies in Literrary Techniques in the Book of Jonah* (Bern: Herbert Lang,

1976), p. 102; Terence Fretheim, *The Message of Jonah* (Minneapolis: Augsburg, 1977), pp. 121ff.

15. See Trible, 'Studies', pp. 267ff.

16. Magonet, *Form and Meaning*, pp. 67ff.

BIBLIOGRAPHY

Albright, W.F., *Yahweh and the Gods of Canaan*, London: Athlone, 1968.

Alt, Albrecht, 'Das Gottesurteil auf dem Karmel', *Festschrift Georg Beer zum 70. Geburtstag*, Stuttgart: W. Kohlhammer, 1935, 1-18.

Alter, Robert, *The Art of Biblical Narrative*, New York: Basic Books, 1981.

Baly, Dennis, *God and History in the Old Testament*, New York: Harper & Row, 1976.

Bar-Efrat, Shimon, 'Some Observations on the Analysis of Structure in Biblical Narrative', in *VT* (1980), 154-73.

Barfield, Owen, *Poetic Diction*, 3rd edn, Middletown: Wesleyan University Press, 1973.

Berger, Thomas, *Little Big Man*, New York: Dial, 1964.

Blair, H.J., 'Putting One's Hand to the Plough: Luke 9.62 and 1 Kgs 19.19-21', *ET* 79 (1968), 342-43.

Booth, Wayne, *A Rhetoric of Irony*, Chicago: University of Chicago Press, 1961.

—'The Pleasures and Pitfalls of Irony: Or, Why Don't You Say What You Mean?' *Rhetoric, Philosophy and Literature: An Exploration*, ed. Don Burks, West Lafayette: Purdue University Press, 1978, 1-13.

Bradbury, Ray, *The Illustrated Man*, New York: Doubleday, 1951.

Bronner, Leah, *The Stories of Elijah and Elisha as Polemics against Baal Worship*, Leiden: Brill, 1968.

Brown, Francis, ed., *The New Brown, Driver, and Briggs Hebrew and English Lexicon of the Old Testament*, London: Oxford, 1907.

Buss, Martin, 'Understanding Communication, Encounter with the Text: Form and History', in the *Hebrew Bible*, Semeia Supplements, Missoula, Montana: Scholars Press, 1979, 3-44.

Carlson, R.A., 'Elie à l'Horeb', *VT* 19 (1969), 416-39.

Carroll, R.P., 'The Elijah-Elisha Sagas: Some Remarks on Prophetic Succession in Ancient Israel', *VT* 19 (1969), 400-15.

Chatman, Seymore, *Story and Discourse*, Ithaca: Cornell University Press, 1978.

Cheyne, T.K., *The Hallowing of Criticism*, London: Hodder & Stoughton, 1888.

Childs, Brevard, 'On Reading the Elijah Narratives', *Int* 34 (1980), 128-137.

Clark, J.O.A., *Elijah Vindicated*, Nashville: ME Church, South, 1893.

Clines, David J.A., 'Theme in Genesis 1-11', *CBQ* 38 (9176), 483-507.

Cohn, Robert L., 'The Literary Logic of 1 Kings 17-19', *JBL* 101 (1982), 333-50.

Coogan, Michael David, *Stories from Ancient Canaan*, Philadelphia: Westminster, 1978.

Coote, Robert E., 'Yahweh Recalls Elijah', in *Traditions in Transformation: Turning Points in Biblical Faith*, ed. Baruch Halpern and Jon D. Levenson, Winona Lake, Indiana: Eisenbrauns, 1981, 115-20.

Corvin, Jack, 'A Stylistic and Functional Study of the Prose Prayers in the Historical Narratives of the Old Testament', Ph.D. dissertation, Emory University, 1972.

Crenshaw, James, *Prophetic Conflict: Its Effect upon Israelite Religion*, Berlin: Walter de Gruyter, 1971.

—*Samson: A Secret Betrayed, A Vow Ignored*, Atlanta: John Knox Press, 1978.

Deming, Lynne, 'The Prophetic Call Narrative as a Biblical Type Scene', paper presented at the Southeastern Society of Biblical Literature Meeting, March 19, 1982.

Duke, Paul, *Irony in the Forth Gospel*, Atlanta: John Knox, 1985.

Eakin, Frank E., Jr., 'Yahwism and Baalism before the Exile', *JBL* 84 (1965), 407-14.

Eissfeldt, Otto, *The Old Testament: An Introduction*, trans. Peter R. Ackroyd, New York: Harper & Row, 1965.

—*Der Gott Karmel*, Berlin: Akademie-Verlag, 1954.

—'Die Komposition von 1 Reg 16.29-2 Reg 13-25', in *Festschrift L. Rost*, BZAW 105, 49-58.

Fensham, F.C., 'A Few Observations on the Polarisation between Yahweh and Baal in 1 Kings 17-19', *ZAW* 92 (1980), 227-36.

Fichtner, Johannes, *Das erste Buch von den Königen*, Die Botschaft des Alten Testaments 12, Part I, Stuttgart: Calwer, 1964.

Fishbane, Michael, 'Revelation and Tradition: Aspects of Inner-Biblical Exegesis', *JBL* 99 (1980), 343-61.

Fohrer, Georg, *Introduction to the Old Testament*, trans. David E. Green, Nashville: Abingdon Press, 1965.

—*Elia*, Zürich: Zwingli-Verlag, 1957, 1968.

Fokkelman, J.P., *Narrative Art in Genesis*, Amsterdam: van Gorcum, Assen, 1975.

Fretheim, Terence, *The Message of Jonah*, Minneapolis: Augsburg, 1977.

Good, Edwin, *Irony in the Old Testament*, Philadelphia: Westminster, 1965.

Gray, John, *1 & 2 Kings: A Commentary*, 2nd edn, The Old Testament Library, Philadelphia: Westminster 1970.

—*The Legacy of Canaan*, 2nd edn, Supplements to *VT* 5, Leiden: E.J. Brill, 1965.

Gressmann, Hugo, *Die älteste Geschichtsschreibung und Prophetie Israels*, Die Schriften des Alten Testaments von Gressmann, Gunkel, Haller, Schmidt, Stark, und Volz, vol. 2, Göttingen: Vandenhoeck & Ruprecht, 1910.

Gros-Louis, Kenneth, 'Elijah and Elisha', *Literary Interpretations of Biblical Narratives*, eds. Kenneth Gros-Louis, James Ackerman, and Thayer Warshaw, Nashville: Abingdon Press, 1974, 177-90.

Gunkel, H., *Elias Jahve und Baal*, Religionsgeschichtliche Volksbücher für die Deutsche Christliche Gegenwart II/8, Tübingen: Mohr, 1906.

Habel, Norman, *Yahweh Versus Baal: A Conflict of Religious Cultures*, New York: Bookman Associates, 1965.

Hauser, Alan J., 'Jonah: In Pursuit of the Dove', *JBL* 104 (1985), 21-37.

Hayman, Leo, 'A Note on 1 Kings 18.27', *JNES* 10 (1951), 57-58.

Hvidberg, Flemming Friis, *Weeping and Laughter in the Old Testament*, Leiden: E.J. Brill, 1962.

Jepsen, A., 'Librum Regum', *Biblia Hebraica Stuttgartensia*, Stuttgart: Deutsche Bibelgesellschaft, 1967.

Jeremias, Jörg, *Theophanie: Die Geschichte einer altestamentlichen Gattung*, Neukirchen-Vluyn: Neukirchener Verlag, 1965.

Jobling, David, *The Sense of Biblical Narrative*, Sheffield: JSOT, 1978.

Johns, Claude Hermann Walter, *The Religious Significance of Semitic Proper Names*, Cambridge: A.P. Dixon, 1912.

Kapelrud, Arvid S., *The Ras Shamra Discoveries and the Old Testament*, Norman: University of Oklahoma Press, 1963.

Kermode, John Frank, *The Genesis of Secrecy: On the Interpretation of Narrative*, Cambridge, Massachusetts: Harvard University Press, 1979.

Koehler, Ludwig and Walter Baumartner, eds., *Lexicon in Veteris Testamenti Libros*, Leiden: Brill, 1958.

Kort, Wesley, *Narrative Elements and Religious Meanings*, Philadelphia: Fortress, 1975.

Levenson, Jon, '1 Samuel—As Literature in History', *CBQ* 40 (1978), 11-28.

Licht, Jacob, *Story Telling in the Bible*, Jerusalem: Magnes Press, 1978.

Long, Burke, '2 Kings 3 and Genres of Prophetic Narrative', *VT* 23 (1973), 337-48.

Macholz, Christian, 'Psalm 29 and 1. Könige 19: Jahwes und Baals Theophanie', *Werden und Wirken des Alten Testaments*, ed. Ranier Albertz, Hans-Peter Müller, Hans Walter Wolff, and Walther Zimmerli, Göttingen: Vandenhoeck & Ruprecht, 1980, 325-333.

Magonet, Jonathan, *Form and Meaning: Studies in Literary Techniques in the Book of Jonah*, Bern: Herbert Lang Publisher, 1976.

Milligan, W. *Elijah, His Life and Times*, New York: Anson D.F. Randolph, 1890.

Montgomery, James A., and Genham, Henry S., *A Critical and Exegetical Commentary on the Books of the Kings*, ICC, Edinburgh: T&T Clark, 1951.

Moule, C.F.D., *An Idom-Book of New Testament Greek*, 2nd edn, Cambridge: Cambridge University Press, 1971.

Muecke, D.C., *Irony*, Norfolk: Methuen, 1970.

Müller, Hans-Peter, 'Die hebräische Wurzel שוב' *VT* 19 (1969), 361-71.

Neher, André, 'A Reflection on the Silence of God', *Jud* 16 (1967), 42.

Nordheim, Eckhard V., 'Ein Prophet kündigt sein Amt auf (Elia am Horeb)', *Bib* 59 (1978), 153-73.

Noth, Martin, *Die israelitischen Personennamen im Rahmen der gemeinsemitischen Namengebung*, Hildesheim: Georg Olms, 1966.

Olrik, Axel, 'Epic Laws of Folk Narrative', *The Study of Folklore*, ed. Alan Dundes, Englewood Cliffs: Prentice-Hall, 1965, 129-141.

Ostborn, Gunnar, *Yahweh and Baal*, Lund: C.W.K. Gleerup, 1956.

Patai, R., 'The Control of Rain in Ancient Palestine', *HUCA* 14 (1939), 251-86.

Pritchard, James B., *The Ancient Near East in Pictures Relating to the Old Testament*, 2nd edn, Princeton: Princeton University Press, 1969.

—*Ancient Near Eastern Texts*, 3rd edn with supplement, Princeton: Princeton University Press, 1969.

Rad, G. von, *Old Testament Theology*, trans. D.M.G. Stalker, New York: Harper & Row, 1965.

Radday, Yehuda, 'Chiasm in Kings', *LB* 31 (1974), 52-67.

Ringgren, Helmer, *Religions of the Ancient Near East*, trans. John Sturdy, Philadelphia: Westminster, 1973.

Rimmon, Shlomith, *The Concept of Ambiguity—the Example of James*, Chicago: University of Chicago Press, 1977.

Robinson, J., *The First Book of Kings*, The Cambridge Bible Commentary, Cambridge: Cambridge University Press, 1972.

Rofé, Alexander, 'Classes in the Prophetical Stories: Didactic Legenda and Parable', *Supplements to VT*, 26, Leiden: E.J. Brill, 1974, 143-64.

—'Classification of the Prophetical Stories', *JBL* 89 (1970), 427-40.

Rowley, H.H., 'Elijah on Mount Carmel', *BJRL* 43 (1960), 190-219.

Saint-Laurent, George, 'Light from Ras Shamra on Elijah's Ordeal upon Mount Carmel', *Scripture in Context: Essays on the Comparative Method*, ed. Carl

Evans, William Holow, and John White, Pittsburgh Theological Monograph Series 34, Pittsburgh: Pickwick, 1980, 123-139.

Schnitt, Armin, 'Die Totenerweckung in 1 Kön XVII: 17-24: Eine form- und gattungskritische Untersuchung', *VT* 27 (1977), 454-474.

Schökel, Alonso, *Narrative Structures in the Book of Judith*, from Protocol Series of the Colloquies of the Center for Hermeneutical Studies in Hellenistic and Modern Culture, 11, Berkeley: Graduate Theological Union and University of California, 1974.

Selms, A. van, 'Motivated Interrogative Sentences in Biblical Hebrew', *Sem* 2 (1971-72), 143-49.

Seybold, Klaus, 'Elia am Gottesberg: Vorstellungen prophetischen Wirkens nach 1. König 19', *ET* 33 (January-February 1973), 3-18.

Silberman, Lou, 'Between God and Man: The Meaning of Revelation for the Contemporary Jew', *Comtemporary Experience*, Hillel Library Series, ed. Alfred Jospe, New York: Schocken Books, 1970, 91-111.

Slotki, I.W., *Kings: Hebrew Text and English Translation with an Introduction and Commentary*, London: Soncino Press, 1950.

Smend, Rudolph, 'Das Wort Jahwes an Elia: Erwägungen zur Komposition von 1 Reg. xvii—xix', *VT* 25 (1975), 525-43.

—'Der biblische und der historische Elia', *Supplements to VT* 28, Leiden: E.J. Brill, 1975, 167-84.

Smith, Barbara, *Poetic Closure*, Chicago: University of Chicago Press, 1968.

Snaith, Norman, 'The First and Second Book of Kings', *Interpreter's Bible*, ed. George A. Buttrick, 3, New York: Abingdon Press, 1954, 3-338.

Soggin, J. Alberto, *Introduction to the Old Testament*, trans. John Bowden, The Old Testament Library, Philadelphia: Westminster, 1976.

Stamm, J.J., 'Elia am Horeb', *Studia Biblica et Semitica*, ed. W.C. van Unnik and A.S. van der Woude, Wageningen: H. Veenman & Zonen, 1966, 327-334.

Staudt, Edwin, III, 'Prayer and the People in the Deuteronomist', Ph.D. dissertation, Vanderbilt University, 1980.

Steck, Odil Hannes, *Überlieferung und Zeitgeschichte in den Elia-Erzählungen*. Wissenschaftliche Monographien zum Alten und Neuen Testament 26, Neukirchen-Vluyn: Neukirchener Verlag, 1968.

Steinmann, Jean, 'La geste d'Elia dans l'Ancien Testament', in *Elia le Prophète*, Les Etudes Carmelitaines: Desclée de Brouwer, 1965, 93-115.

Tannehill, Robert C., *The Sword of His Mouth*, Semeia Supplements 1, Missoula, MT: Scholars Press, 1975.

Trible, Phyllis, 'Studies in the Book of Jonah', Ph.D. dissertation, Columbia University, 1963.

Tromp, Nicholas J., 'Water and Fire on Mount Carmel', *Bib* 56 (1975), 480-502.

Vater, Ann, 'Narrative Patterns for the Story of Commissioned Communication in the Old Testament', *JBL* 99 (1980), 365-82.

Vaux, R. de, 'Notes on the Text', *Elie le prophète*, Les Etudes Carmelitaines, Desclée de Brouwer, 1956, 53-83.

—*Ancient Israel*, 1, New York: McGraw-Hill, 1965.

Weisel, Elie, *Five Biblical Portraits*, Notre Dame: University of Notre Dame Press, 1981.

Weiser, Artur, *The Psalms*, The Old Testament Library, Philadelphia: Westminster, 1962.

Wellhausen, Julius, *Die Composition des Hexateuchs und der historischen Bücher des Alten Testaments*, 4th edn, Berlin: Walter de Gruyter, 1963.

Wiener, aharon, *The Prophetic Elijah in the Development of Judaism*, Boston: Routledge & Kegan Paul, 1978.

Williams, James G., 'Irony and Lament: Clues to Prophetic Consciousness', *Semeia* 8 (1977), 51-69.

Williams, Ronald, *Hebrew Syntax: An Outline*, 2nd edn, Toronto: University of Toronto Press, 1976.

Wilson, Robert, *Prophecy and Society in Ancient Israel*, Philadelphia: Fortress, 1980.

Wimsatt, W.K., Jr, and M.C. Beardsley, 'The Intentional Fallacy', *SR* 54 (1946), 468-87.

Würthwein, Ernst, 'Elijah at Horeb: Reflections on 1 Kings 19.9-18', in *Proclamation and Presence: Old Testament Essays in Honor of Gwynne Henton Davies*, ed. John I. Durham and J.R. Porter, Richmond, Virginia: John Knox Press, 1970, 152-66.

Zenger, Erich, 'Review of *Überlieferung and Zeitgeschichte in den Elia-Erzählungen*', *Bib* 51 (1970), 138-44.

Zimmerli, Walther, *Ezekiel*, trans. Ronald Clements, Hermeneia, Philadelphia: Fortress, 1979.

INDEXES

INDEX OF BIBLICAL REFERENCES

INDEX OF AUTHORS